Praise for T

"Like any great performer, Charity [...] audience's heart right from the beginning. Her jou[...] improbable course from the majesty of the great Rocky Mountains, to the glittering concert halls of Europe, to the quiet rooms of grief and death. But she doesn't end there. This intimate view into a courageous woman's long, dark night will remind you of the stars that light your bleakest hours, and make you grateful for every sunrise."

—Jill Biden

"This is a story about sheer will and the love of many [including her family] that enabled her to recover and become a world-class opera singer. In dark times, we need to be reminded of miracles."

—Amy Tan

"An amazing story of the human spirit."

—Kathie Lee Gifford

"*The Encore* is inspiring, memorable, and life-transforming. For me, it was a riveting read."

—Deepak Chopra

"Is opera meaningful to society today? *The Encore* is a categorical answer: Yes. Each scene breathes new purpose into some of the greatest scores in history. The music of Charity Tillemann-Dick's prose carries this impossible journey to an inspirational point of majesty and sacred beauty."

—Denyce Graves-Montgomery, international opera singer, professor of voice at Peabody Conservatory

"This is the story of a genuine medical miracle, facilitated by the best of modern medicine. *The Encore* reminds us that art and science belong together, creating synergies that promote the deepest kind of healing."

—Dr. Toby Cosgrove, president & CEO, Cleveland Clinic

"Inspiring . . . a moving memoir."

—*Publishers Weekly*

"One of the best books I've ever read about the effects of chronic illness on the human spirit."

—Terry Teachout, *The Wall Street Journal*

"As a testament to the power of faith, love, prayer, and music, this self-portrait of courage and grace under extreme pressure will engage and inspire."

—*Booklist*

"A heartwarming tale of courage and determination."

—*The Denver Post*

THE
Encore

a memoir in three acts

CHARITY
TILLEMANN-DICK

ATRIA PAPERBACK

NEW YORK   LONDON   TORONTO   SYDNEY   NEW DELHI

ATRIA
PAPERBACK

An Imprint of Simon & Schuster, Inc.
1230 Avenue of the Americas
New York, NY 10020

First Atria Paperback edition October 2018

ATRIA PAPERBACK and colophon are trademarks of Simon & Schuster, Inc.

For information about special discounts for bulk purchases, please contact Simon & Schuster Special Sales at 1-866-506-1949 or business@simonandschuster.com.

The Simon & Schuster Speakers Bureau can bring authors to your live event. For more information, or to book an event, contact the Simon & Schuster Speakers Bureau at 1-866-248-3049 or visit our website at www.simonspeakers.com.

Interior design by Kyoko Watanabe

Manufactured in the United States of America

10 9 8 7 6 5 4 3 2 1

Library of Congress Cataloging-in-Publication Data

Names: Tillemann-Dick, Charity.
Title: The encore : a memoir in three acts / Charity Tillemann-Dick.
Description: First Atria Books hardcover edition. | New York : Atria Books, 2017.
Identifiers: LCCN 2016048799 (print) | LCCN 2016049292 (ebook) | ISBN 9781501102318 (hardcover) | ISBN 9781501102325 (trade pbk.) | ISBN 9781501102332 (ebook)
Subjects: LCSH: Tillemann-Dick, Charity. | Sopranos (Singers)—United States—Biography. | Lungs—Transplantation—Patients—United States—Biography. | LCGFT: Autobiographies.
Classification: LCC ML420.T529 A3 2017 (print) | LCC ML420.T529 (ebook) | DDC 782.1092 [B]—dc23
LC record available at https://lccn.loc.gov/2016048799

ISBN 978-1-5011-0231-8
ISBN 978-1-5011-0232-5 (pbk)
ISBN 978-1-5011-0233-2 (ebook)

For Annette Marie,
The mother who gave me life

And for Flora,
The mother who gave me breath

Cast

The Diva	Charity Sunshine / coloratura soprano
The Mother	Annette / mezzo-soprano
The Romantic Foil	Yonatan Doron / baritone
The Siblings	Tomicah Sterling / bass
	Kimber Rainbow / soprano
	Levi Mills / bass
	Dulcia Luz / mezzo-soprano
	Corban Israel / tenor
	Liberty Belle / soprano
	Lincoln Justice / supernumerary
	Shiloh Benson / basso profundo
	Mercina Grace / soprano
	Glorianna Willow / mezzo-soprano
	Zenith Wisdom / tenor
The Father	Timber / basso profundo
The Grandfather	Tom Lantos / baritone
The Grandmothers	Annette Tillemann Lantos / contralto
	Nancy Dick / alto
The Teachers	Éva Márton / soprano
	Éva Ándor / mezzo-soprano
	Joan Dornemann / mezzo-soprano
The Doctors	Chris Lang / baritone

Robyn Barst / mezzo-soprano

Reda Girgis / baritone

Marie Budev / mezzo-soprano

Robin Avery / soprano

The Surgeon Kenneth McCurry / tenor

The Angels Margot Dick / soprano

Joela Jones / mezzo-soprano

Esperanza Tufani / mezzo-soprano

Danielle Groppi / soprano

Jeanne Murphy / mezzo-soprano

Mike Bates / tenor

The Family / coro

The Nurses / coro

The Friends / coro

Contents

Act I

Act II

$\mathcal{A}$ct III

THE
Encore

*S*YNOPSIS OF *S*CENES

Tosca, Gilda, Violetta, Mimi—tragic heroines are never in short supply at the opera. Even the comic ones don't have much fun. Librettos are rife with lecherous older men, betrayed wives, and scorned lovers. In opera, tragedy is constituent of female greatness—pain, sacrifice, and disappointment are prerequisites to meaningful artistic achievement. Life is full of death. Music, full of sorrow. Great artists have always amplified both. And, more than anything, I want to be Great.

OVERTURE

A pencil rolls to the floor, a shoe squeaks, a lone cough fills the void—silence is nothing but potential sound. The click clack of my five-inch heels transforms the soundscape as I teeter in from stage left. My white gown's silk tulle trails behind, rustling against the dusty floor. Cold darkness covers my arms in goose bumps, but a few steps away, klieg lights set four thousand eyes aglow.

The heat of the spotlight washes over me. Everything disappears: no microphone; no distractions; alone with the maestro, I hear the strings' tremolo. I inhale deep and wide, preparing to convert two decades of dreams and work into pure sound. It is September 21, 2011—my Lincoln Center debut.

With a flick of the conductor's baton, I begin to sing.

Breathing life into *La Traviata*'s heroine, Violetta, my voice floods the theater with Verdi's immortal aria "Sempre libera." I inhale and my lungs fill with air. When I sing, it is a joyous communion with God. More powerful than any narcotic, to me, singing is a sanctified addiction; it is the stuff of transcendence. I spin out a high C and the audience erupts in spontaneous applause.

The words of the aria read like a classic power anthem: *Sempre libera*, always free, is its constant refrain. But the music tells another story. Violetta insists she is satisfied, but as my voice accelerates up and down the scale, her truth can't hide from the melody. Biographically, Violetta's life and mine could hardly be more different. I'm a twenty-eight-year-old virgin from Denver. Violetta is a nineteenth-century Parisian prostitute. She has spent her life and career making men feel valued and loved— emotions for which she's always deeply longed but fears she may never herself experience. I've never lacked for love, but I fear my voice—trained, groomed, and nurtured over my entire life—will never reach its potential or be truly appreciated. Despite our biographical differences, angst that we may fail to accomplish those things we most desperately desire knits Violetta's emotions to my own, granting me the most powerful tool of vocal performance— empathy. As the aria forges on, though, a subtext of fear recedes as forgotten confidence emerges. Violetta doesn't know how her story will end, but she realizes that, whatever she chooses, true love awaits.

Proper singing must be felt. Approaching the final vocal lap, my chest vibrates as sound resonates in my skull and through my hips. The aria's fiendishly difficult conclusion is yet to come, but energy transfers from thousands of unseen onlookers to my singing. Transfigured by sound, any remaining barriers between Violetta and me are shattered by the resonance of my voice. Here, music carries the ultimate truth. I have never felt more alive.

Breathing into my belly and back, I step forward and steady myself as the orchestra charges toward the finale. Leaping to the vocal stratosphere, I give my all to the last high note. Suspended, naked, and shameless, it rings out into the dark. It is perfect. I sing the high E flat and I am free.

The note resolves and the auditorium explodes in thunderous applause. I stand triumphant, then bow in gratitude. I bow over and over again—to the audience, to the producers, to my conductor and directors. To my mother and my family. The ovation continues, punctuated by "Bravas!" and "Encores!" What those clapping don't know is that, in many ways, this *was* my encore.

Applause follows me as I step behind the curtain and collapse into a wheelchair. To the artist, a major debut always feels like a culmination—even a miracle. As my brother gently puts down my footrests and my sister secures an oxygen cannula around my nose, it becomes clear that *this* debut was particularly miraculous. Folding down my shawl to uncover the IV PICC line in my left arm, my siblings work together to administer the intravenous steroids and antibiotics that keep me alive.

My lungs—my instruments—*are failing. I am dying.* As we round the corner to my dressing room, tears stream down my cheeks. My dream is no longer a future hope—some distant possibility. It's real. Even if my voice is silenced forever, I've just shared the greatest performance of my life in the greatest concert hall in the world.

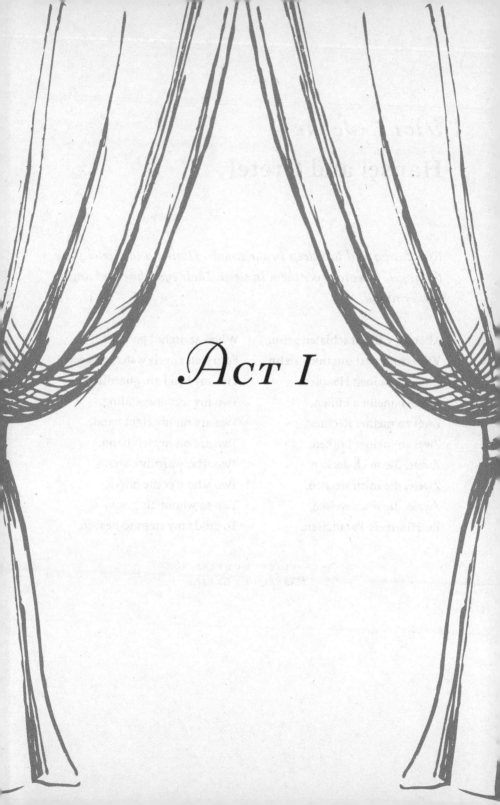

Act I

$\mathcal{A}$CT I, $\mathcal{S}$CENE 1:
Hansel and Gretel

Eyes heavy and lost deep in the woods, Hansel and Gretel pray for angels to watch over them in sleep. Their eyes close and angels gather round.

Abends, will ich schlafen gehn,	When at night I go to sleep,
Vierzehn Engel um mich stehn;	Fourteen angels watch do keep:
Zwei zu meinen Häupten,	Two my head are guarding,
Zwei zu meinen Füßen,	Two my feet are guiding,
Zwei zu meiner Rechten,	Two are on my right hand,
Zwei zu meiner Linken,	Two are on my left hand,
Zweie, die mich decken,	Two who warmly cover,
Zweie, die mich wecken,	Two who o'er me hover,
Zweie, die mich weisen,	Two to whom 'tis given,
Zu Himmels-Paradeisen.	To guide my steps to heaven.

—ENGELBERT HUMPERDINCK,
HÄNSEL UND GRETEL

I catch my breath. Floating down the balmy Danube, chandeliers twinkle, women's jewelry glistens, and Budapest's best gypsy band whips mournful melodies into feverish Hungarian dances. Even the sky is dressed in lustrous pinks and golds for the occasion. It's the perfect night for the most spectacular party I've ever attended, but something is off.

It's the summer of 2003 on the grand Europa river yacht. My grandfather is celebrating his seventy-fifth birthday with 250 of his nearest and dearest friends. Didi, the celebrant, stands by the door, his combed-back hair coordinating perfectly with his spotless cream suit and pearly-white grin. My eternally youthful mother, Annette, is on his arm. Within moments, she's deep into conversation with every person they pass; despite their slow progress, Didi can't help but beam. My dad, Timber, tall and intellectual behind wire-rimmed glasses, patiently escorts my petite grandmother, Mimo, around the ballroom. Greeting guests in the lavish setting, they are the picture of familial pride.

My ten siblings have already scattered. They're busy taking full advantage of the boat's rarefied amenities. Both in their teens, Corban and Liberty flirt with the children of other guests on the dance floor. As the sixth and seventh children, they've learned to be at ease in any situation. Mercina and Glorianna, the littlest girls in our family, twirl around each other while sipping virgin daiquiris, and Shiloh lectures Zenith on Hungarian parliamentary procedures as these two youngest brothers sample delicacies scattered on tables around the perimeter of the room. Craning my neck, I search for my four older siblings; they must be exploring the upper deck. Meanwhile, waiters wend through the assembled guests with silver platters of champagne flutes and caviar-topped eggs. I don't like caviar, but I do love food. Hungarian food, in particular. The sour cream. The butter. The paprika. What is there not to love and *why* am I not more interested in the buffet? Sitting in the midst of this fairytale opulence, my mind is inexplicably elsewhere.

As we drift by the Hungarian parliament's massive dome and towering neo-Gothic windows, a poetic justice plays out. Sixty years earlier, this country had turned its back on my family. Didi was carted away to toil in a labor camp, the rest of his family exterminated by the Nazis in Auschwitz; Mimo, the only daughter of Budapest's finest jeweler, ran when her father was taken out and shot by the Hungarian Arrow Cross along the passing banks, all to make a point: no Jew—no matter how beloved or esteemed—was safe in Hungary. Together, my grandparents fled this country's violent legacy to make a home in the United States. Yet this morning, our family gathered in the parliament's Cupola Hall as the prime minister of Hungary decorated Didi with the Cross with Star, one of the country's highest honors.

How did we ever get here? I think, smiling in disbelief. Despite the trappings of wealth surrounding us tonight, we've never been wealthy. Dad is a brilliant inventor. Issued his first patent as a freshman in college for a high-efficiency bicycle, he produced more ambitious creations with the passage of time. Baby car seats, medical devices, internal combustion engines—Dad has always approached inventing as the art of solving important problems. But his creator's soul isn't exactly brimming with business savvy, so Dad's day job as a college administrator keeps food on our very large table. Mom, a former beauty queen with a cache of advanced degrees, has spent the past twenty-five years doing the only thing that could ever fully use her boundless energy: raising kids. She started homeschooling in 1983, and since then she's welcomed a steady stream of new students into her classroom. Five feet two inches and 100 pounds of pure fire, charm, passion, strength, and will, only Mom, I'm convinced, could ever meet the demands of time, physical energy, and mental dexterity required by her particular brand of extreme childrearing. Like one of Dad's prototypes, our family started out as a bold and untested vision. Today, Mom and Dad claim my siblings and me as their greatest creative endeavor.

Though he attended college on a B'nai B'rith scholarship, Didi—Mom's dad—worked relentlessly in menial jobs so Mimo could come join him in the States. In 1950, after years of war, poverty, and separation, the childhood sweethearts married and started to rebuild their lives together. Mimo raised Mom and her sister, Katrina, while Didi worked to become a professor of economics at San Francisco State University. Didi had even greater aspirations for his American daughters than for himself, so he was not thrilled (to put it lightly) when his precious firstborn eloped with a starry-eyed tinkerer from the heart of the Rocky Mountains. Still, when Didi decided to run for office, he chose Dad to manage his campaign. My parents moved out to California, two babies in tow, and Didi won the long-shot congressional bid in 1980. In the decades since, he's grown into something of a legend: the only Holocaust survivor ever elected to the US Congress and one of the most respected statesmen in Washington, DC. Throughout their travels, Didi and Mimo have collected a great number of wealthy friends. And if anyone knows how to throw a party, they do.

I smile to myself, wondering what nineteen-year-old Didi—an orphan leaving Hungary with seven dollars and a salami in his pocket—would have to say about this welcome-home bash. But my mind is quickly beckoned back to more immediate hypotheticals. Today, nineteen years old, I am sitting on the cusp of much more than a dance floor.

After my grandfather's award ceremony that morning, I'd snuck off with my mother and our best Hungarian friend, Judit.

Judit had arranged a voice lesson for me at the Budapest Opera House. Even while I was there, the scene felt unreal. I play it over again in my mind: the cold resonance of stone floors; melodies merging in the cavernous hallway. In my head I knew this was just a first-rate field trip—before leaving for Europe, I'd accepted a music scholarship in the United States—but I couldn't help but feel I was breathing in the air of destiny in those grand old halls. After our lesson my voice teacher left the room, then reentered with a line of distinguished-looking people trailing behind her. Confused but accommodating, I sang for these newcomers. Then *I* left the room, the totally incredulous recipient of a spot at Budapest's storied Liszt Academy of Music.

This is how opera legends begin! I think to myself back in the ballroom. *I can see it now: "Young Soprano Plucked from Obscurity Goes onto Musical Greatness."* But while the story sounds like a dream come true, its reality poses some challenging logistical questions. *Am I really willing to leave everything I know behind— without a plan, preparation, or even the right language—to chase a dream so far from my home?*

A hand on my arm interrupts my musings. "Charity Sunshine! Where have you been?" demands my oldest brother, Tomicah. "We've been looking all over for you—you're late for the run-through!"

I hurry down to the lower level of the yacht. Every other year, my siblings and I put on a show for our family reunion. The process is equal parts ridiculous, entertaining, and punishing. At twenty-one and seventeen, Levi and Corban always lobby for inappropriate humor that Kimber, twenty-three, inevitably cuts. Toeing the boundary between "little kid" and "big kid," fifteen-year-old Liberty is eager to participate at the highest levels, yet thirteen-year-old Shiloh doesn't even want to dance. True to my middle-child type, I always want more solos, while Mercina and Glorianna, eleven and nine, are tired of their perfect harmonies being put center stage; six-year-old Zen will inevitably regret his willingness to tromp around stage wearing nothing but a Speedo; and Tomicah, with slightly more foresight at twenty-four, preemptively argues that the esteemed crowd will think he's too old to play the family dog. Our oldest sister, Dulcia, has opted out of the circus altogether. Disagreements over the performance range on everything from costumes to choreography, but we charge ahead—the show must go on!

Walking down the hall, I hear Kimber call out, "Again! But this time, more jazz hands!" This year, we've decided to rewrite *Fiddler on the Roof*; seated behind an electric keyboard, my sister-in-law, Sarah (wed to Tomicah earlier this year), plunks out the introduction to "Tradition" as Levi begins his monologue. He explains our loving-if-complicated family dynamic in my grandfather's hallmark Hungarian accent, confidently lecturing with equal parts insight, irreverence, and affection. It's a perfect "Levi" performance. In fact, *Fiddler* captures the quintessence of our entire family: discovering traditions, breaking traditions, adopting traditions, and creating our own. This tradition—singing and performing together—is one of my very favorites. Slowly, we make our way through the condensed show, bickering our way toward excellence. After an hour, we're dismissed until curtain.

In the ballroom, Tomicah, Kimber, Levi, Corban, Liberty, and I jostle to an opening at the front of the stage. The band seems to play more furiously as we dance, spinning and clapping in time to the fiddle and mandolin. Suddenly, the music becomes muffled and darkness seeps into my peripheral vision. It's happening again. I stagger toward a chair as the room fades to black.

I didn't know it at the time, but 1988 was a big year for me. It all started a few months after my fifth birthday. Dulcia and her best friend, a singer-slash-beauty queen, invited me to a local production of Humperdinck's opera, *Hansel and Gretel*. I had always aspired to be something of an artist, and Mom, eight months pregnant at the time, was eager to separate me from my current medium of choice: permanent marker on the dining room wall. Dressed in my best pink crepe, we headed toward the theater as the setting sun splashed gaudy saturations across the snow-capped Rockies behind us. After I'd settled into my seat, Dulcia passed me a small piece of chocolate. It melted slightly onto my fingers as I popped it into my mouth.

I loved to sing—children's songs, the hymns I learn at church, the occasional Broadway standard—but opera was an entirely different affair. Mom liked to tune into the weekend broadcasts of the Metropolitan Opera, and I found them at once very loud and very boring. Now, sitting in the dark theater, I watched as stagehands silently readied the set. Shadowy trees and candy houses twinkled dimly from the dark stage. Then the lights rose and performers plunged in from stage left, bringing the giant coloring book set to life. The orchestra and opera flooded my ears, but this time I was edified instead of annoyed.

I sat, snug and sticky in the deep red velvet chair, as rich voices washed over me. I was transfixed by a narrative that only melody could tell. I heard the difference between a dance and a lullaby, dreamy music, sad music, exciting music, and scary music. These tunes easily communicated stories lost to me amid the opera's German lyrics. I felt the weight of responsibility that Hansel and Gretel felt for each other through the musical lines that bound them together; their joy and their terror. Slowly, it dawned on me that this music was the most beautiful thing I had ever heard. I was only five, but I was a woman transformed. As I listened to Gretel's lilting high notes, I longed to be in her place, singing center stage. An unlikely dream, but, somewhere far beneath my sticky cheeks, I knew I was meant to be a great opera singer.

Within a few weeks of this epiphany, my family welcomed a new baby boy into our home. Nineteen inches long, eight pounds even, ten fingers and ten toes, Lincoln Justice was perfect. He was the first baby to whom I could be a proper big sister. Corban and Liberty were nearly as big as I was, but I could hold Lincoln all by myself. I'd watch over him kicking in his basket while Mom made dinner and the big kids did schoolwork.

Weeks after Lincoln's birth, I went to visit my grandparents in Washington, DC, for the first time. From the moment I arrived, I was smothered in love and undivided attention. Trips to the museum, introductions to staff members, and long-distance calls home made me feel particularly important. Each night at bedtime, my grandmother would kneel and pray with me.

One night, after drifting off to sleep, visions of a heavenly place filled my head. Shell-colored light draped the space in a luminous glow, softening corners and horizons into a single gracious expanse. I sat in an enormous circle with all the world's children, including my brothers and sisters. We were singing and playing a game. A familiar man appeared. Tall in white robes, he had a beard and a kind face. My eyes followed him as he walked toward my baby brother and touched his head. Lincoln had won the game! What an accomplishment—and Lincoln, just a baby! I glanced eagerly toward my siblings and they looked as happy as I felt. We were all grateful to be related to such a special little boy. As the man led Lincoln away to receive his prize, I beamed after him. I had no doubts that Lincoln was going exactly where he belonged.

When morning came, I shared the dream with Mimo (dream interpretation is a special passion of hers). Yellow pad of paper in hand, my grandmother scrawled feverishly, but offered me no elucidation. The next day, we left for Denver. *But I was supposed to stay for a whole week longer! Had I done something wrong?* I protested, but Mimo was adamant: we were leaving.

When we finally settled onto the plane, Mimo took my pudgy little hands in hers.

"Charity, we are going back to Denver because of your baby brother," she said, her dulcet Hungarian accent interrupted by nervous breaths. "He's gone back to heaven."

I cocked my head. "Like in my dream?" I asked, feeling simultaneously wise and confused.

Tears began to stream down her face. "Yes, Charity. Lincoln is in heaven."

Lincoln's enviable position did not match Mimo's sadness. Heaven was better than the best thing in the world! "Why are you crying? Heaven is a wonderful place!" I insisted, trying to comfort her.

"It *is* a wonderful place," she continued, mascara streaking her cheeks. "But Lincoln is there because he died."

A shock coursed down my spine. *Lincoln died? How could he have died?* That was something done by plants and ants and pet fish. Not baby brothers. But, looking into Mimo's grief-shot eyes, I knew she was telling the truth. I let out a piercing scream and crumpled into a pile, snot and tears raining everywhere. Maybe if I was loud enough, God would hear me. He could fix this terrible mistake. He would bring Lincoln back and we could all be together in our beautiful big circle again! But somehow, I knew He wouldn't do that.

Two nights before, Dad had put the baby to sleep in his crib. When he went in to check on him an hour later, Lincoln was already gone. Sudden infant death syndrome, or SIDS, was known for many years as crib death. Even today, its exact causes remain unclear. What was clear after Lincoln's passing was that our lives had changed. He had made death personal. My siblings and I had witnessed our healthy, happy baby brother—a little boy with our same gifts, our same potential, even our same cleft chin—snuffed out in a moment. I felt real responsibility for the first time, driven to somehow compensate for the loss of such faultless humanity.

This turmoil established the bedrock upon which I would build my personal faith. Even when five years old, in the midst of one of the most painful experiences of my life, I felt certain of one thing: I was still Lincoln's big sister. As devastating as his unexpected absence was, I knew it was only temporary. Eventually, I would again need to watch over him kicking his fat little legs in his basket. Perhaps never in this life, but rather in one to come. This central concept of eternal families braided with my own belief that, if I worked to realize the breadth of my potential, I would be worthy to rejoin not only the infinite expanse of humanity, but also my grandparents, my parents, my siblings, and, most of all, my perfect baby brother.

Ten years later, I look in the bathroom mirror, smile, and pinch my cheeks a few times for color. It's January 1998, and today is my first day of college. I had to beg my parents to let me enroll, even though it's become a bit of a family tradition by now. Back in 1993, Mom was beginning to get nervous that the whole homeschooling thing had been a big mistake. But after Tomicah, Kimber, and Levi were all accepted to college and earning perfect grades in their early teens, she stopped worrying. She and Dad say I shouldn't rush so much—they encourage me to enjoy my freedom while I have it—but I'm adamant. I want to start, and I want to start now. Alone, I walk the thirteen blocks from our house to the Registrar's Office at Regis University to sign up for classes. The semester begins a few months after my fourteenth birthday.

I may be the youngest to start school in my family, but I'm also the most eager. Money is tight, so every day I wake up at 5:00 a.m. to prep bread dough before my early-morning scripture study class. When I get home, I put it in to bake for family breakfast while I get ready for school. Every day, rain, shine, or snow, I arrive to class in formal business attire—blazers, khakis, sensible pumps. I carry my books in one of Dad's old briefcases.

Regis is the most difficult thing I've ever done, but I excel. I work hard, getting perfect grades and building strong relationships with fellow students, my professors, and advisers, racking up a record of awards and scholarships along the way. After my sophomore year, I decide I want to transfer to Yale University— just like Tomicah, Kimber, and Levi before me. One would think that the cost of attending a school like Yale would be prohibitive for a family like mine. But need-blind admissions and financial aid offices are a wonderful thing when matched with academic achievement and a family of eleven kids living on a college administrator's salary. I go out to meet the postman every day that summer, eagerly looking for a deep blue *Y* on every piece of mail he delivers. But when a letter finally does arrive for me, it's a scrawny 4 x 9" envelope—not the 9 x 11" welcome packet I had expected. I bury the rejection in the kitchen trash.

Over the last decade, the neighborhood has been changing. Dad bought the house I was born in—a little A-frame Victorian at 4320 Zenobia Street—while Mom was out of town. They moved here in the early eighties, when most of their peers had abandoned cities altogether. Northwest was one of Denver's rougher corners, but the houses had character and, more than anything, Dad appreciated strong character. He knew the neighborhood was a place he and his young family could learn; where we could grow *with* the community and give back to it. And that's exactly what we did. Dad always told us that the respect a person deserves is often inversely related to their worldly acclaim—the homeless woman living in our playroom had seen a lot more of life than most of the lawyers and lobbyists who visited our grandparents' office in Washington, DC. Through example, Dad taught us to open our hearts indiscriminately to the people around us. Mom and he soon became cornerstones of our little neighborhood.

Now eighteen, I've graduated from Regis with high honors and a degree in politics and economics. I know every major political mover and shaker in Colorado and I've already managed multiple successful legislative and political campaigns. My dad, as deeply committed to this neighborhood as anybody I know, has just won the first of two elections for Denver's City Council. There's a runoff between the top two vote getters next month and there's no way to know whether we'll win or lose. For now we're victorious and we've come out to say thank you to the community with some early-morning visibility.

Don't go near Federal Boulevard on Cinco de Mayo. Someone always dies. The old Denver adage is proven true year after year—drunk drivers, stray bullets, and large crowds are a reliably deadly combination. But on this uncharacteristically gray May 5, we're throwing conventional wisdom to the wind. Piling out of Gobo, our blue-and-silver stretch van, my siblings and I empty into the Walgreens parking lot on the corner of Speer and Federal.

This hasn't been an easy race. In fact, it's as dirty as I've ever seen. Fortunately (in some respects, if not others), all of that grime has been built up by our opponents. Steady even as his family, friends, and staff roil over the latest lie being spread by the opposition, Dad calmly explains to us that he can't claim to have integrity in his campaign literature if he gets votes by spreading rumors and exploiting fears. Sometimes I wish he wouldn't insist on teaching us valuable lessons about character during an election, but I also know his commitment to his principles is exactly why Dad needs to be in office. I'm just nervous it might keep him from ever getting there in the first place.

A pansy-filled median splits the busy thoroughfare in two. On the northeastern corner is a Steak N' Eggs attached to a pawnshop with a VFW lodge next door. Across from that is a gas station next to a payday loan center followed by a tortilla factory, then a quinceañera boutique and a liquor store. Grit meets glitter meets the fluffiest, flakiest tortillas in the history of tortillas. *That's* old-school Northwest Denver.

As I distribute campaign signs to supporters and siblings, I think about the runoff. It's a race between history, demographics, and power structures. Dad is the only candidate not backed by one of the two battling local political machines. I know he's optimistic—he always is—but the race is going to be an uphill battle. Still, win or lose, this will be my last campaign. At least, for now.

It will be a lot to leave behind. People always tell me how awful politics is, but I love it. I have to respect a trade that's honest about itself. From finance to music to consumer products and manufacturing—everything is governed by politics. It's just that other industries aren't as willing to admit it. At least that's what I've always told myself. But these campaigns—they're like drugs. Tremendous highs, brutal comedowns.

I've always known I'm going to do something big. But I only recently realized I wasn't going to do it in politics. Last fall, a senior center wouldn't let our candidate in to campaign. I made them an offer: if they listened to our stump speech, I'd throw in an aria for free. They changed their minds. After I'd finished my song, a cherubic old lady took my face in her hands—

"When you sing like an angel, why are you doing the devil's work?"

Her words struck a chord. No, I don't think politics is the devil's work, but over the past months I've realized it's not *my* work either. The longer I'm in this world, the more I worry politics are having a bigger influence on me than I'm having on them. I don't know if I'll ever become an opera singer, but I know I'll never forgive myself if I don't try.

I finish passing out signs and take one myself. Shaking signs like pompoms, our visibility team looks more like a cheer squad than your typical grimace-and-wave politicos. People honk and hurrah as they pass us. "Show Northwest Denver how much we love them!" I shout, jumping up and down to rev the crew up. I do love Northwest Denver. This town raised me. I take two signs, pumping them up and down over my head as I jog across the thoroughfare to hand one to a latecomer across the street.

The stopped cars are honking, waving, and cheering. They love Denver. They love Dad. *We're going to win!* But all of a sudden, I'm feeling short of breath . . .

I awake to the distant blare of ambulance sirens. *Did someone die?* It is Cinco de Mayo, after all. But it turns out they're headed for me. I've fainted in the middle of Federal Boulevard. Quickly back on my feet, I try to reassure the crowd that has gathered around me. *I'm sure it's just dehydration.* Stopping at Walgreens for a bottle of water, I shake off any lingering unease. The campaign is my priority right now—I have to focus. Two months from now, I'll be vacationing in Hungary and celebrating Didi's seventy-fifth birthday party. Then, I'll have time to relax.

Inhale. Exhale. Where am I? Lying on something cold. Hard. Muffled voices rise to hysterics as my eyes blink open. Flat on my back in the middle of the ballroom, I see a young doctor with a heavy Hungarian accent who stands above me, grabbing at my blouse. "Ve must take off her shirt!" he yells. "She eez too varm!"

As my consciousness coalesces I frantically clutch my cardigan closed. My father yanks the young man off me as more people push toward me, hoping to help or get a better glimpse of the spectacle. "Give her some space, people! Sheesh!" Dad shouts, spreading out his long arms as makeshift crowd control.

I insist I'm all right, but the party has already been ruined for my grandfather. He summarily puts the kibosh on any further carousing, no matter how carefully choreographed. I argue it's unfair—no, blasphemous—that one little fainting spell should spoil all of the work we've done over the past weeks. The show must go on! Even if this is just a family production, we can't dare violate that most cardinal rule of the theater. But my protests fall on deaf ears. There will be no performance tonight.

Disappointed, I go downstairs to put myself together. As I

return, Tamás Érdi, a blind Hungarian concert pianist, takes the stage. Sitting near my grandfather and my parents, the somber lilts of Beethoven's "Moonlight Sonata" capture the odd pallor my fainting spell has cast over the evening. Through octaves and broken chords, I hear Didi speaking in hushed tones to Mom and Dad.

"Nori is worried about the fainting," he whispers, referencing his childhood friend, now an esteemed physician. "There is a serious heart condition that primarily affects women around Charity's age."

This was my second fainting spell this summer. My heartbeat thuds in my ears as the pianist's ominous reaches make their way down the keyboard. I stop myself from eavesdropping on my parents' conversation any longer. *Everything is fine,* I assure myself. *Maybe I could stand to lose ten pounds—twenty even. When I do that, I'll be OK. I'm sure of it. I just need to watch what I eat and exercise more. Mom fainted when she was young. So did Dad! This isn't anything but nerves. . . .* My internal dialogue continues until it's crowded out by applause filling the ballroom. But underneath the din of clapping, I can't escape a foreboding sense of loss—of what, though?

I need some air. I get up and walk toward the stairs leading to the upper deck. Dad and Didi rush toward me, each grabbing an already steady arm. In a moment, I've gone from robust to delicate. Dad escorts me up the narrow stairway. On deck, there's a slight breeze. Clouds have muted August's typical humidity, leaving behind a whisper of autumn. Again, I try to convince Dad that we should continue with the show. "Not a chance, Cherry Bear," he answers, loving, but firm. He puts an arm around me as the boat docks. The son of one of my grandparents' friends asks if I'd like to go out dancing with him. It doesn't seem like a very prudent choice. At the moment, neither does staying in Hungary for conservatory.

———

The week's festivities proceed, and my parents, my grandparents, and I all wait for any further indication of trouble with my health. It never arrives. When our rescheduled show proceeds two days later, I'm up on stage belting tunes and high-kicking with the rest of my siblings. The performance is a smash. As our vacation winds down, my fainting spell begins to recede like a strange dream.

And anyway, there are more pressing issues to be addressed. Will I return to America or stay in Europe? I call Cathy, my voice teacher of the past three years in Denver. I can always count on her for solid technique and wise counsel.

"Charity," she mutters with a kind of excited gravity, "this is a once in a lifetime opportunity. You *have* to stay."

I've spent my life trying to keep up with my older siblings, but it's been getting harder recently. I've done my best to mime their life goals—the stellar academics, the campaign jobs, the government internships—but, if I'm being honest, following that template of accomplishment has always been harder for me than it was for them. I'd like to think I'm a one-in-a-million kind of person—a talent to be discovered and ushered into greatness. But I'm the only one who seems to realize it. That is, until last week. Last week, a panel of the best singers and voice teachers in the world validated my innermost ambitions. They told me that I belong with them. That my voice belongs with them. Deep down, I know they're right.

I kneel down to pray. When I was a child, our family car broke down. A lot. Whenever it would splutter to a stop on a highway shoulder or a gas station parking lot, I'd recommend we pray.

Unfailingly, the car started up again after "Amen." That was the beginning of a long and productive relationship with the power of meditation and prayer. As I grew older, my prayers grew less practical and more introspective. I began to use prayer as a tool with which to garner insights from God or the Universe or the wisdom that we all have the potential to collect, deep within our own souls. I trust it completely.

This time, I ask God whether I should stay in Europe, and I'm overcome with a profound sense of warmth, peace, and reassurance.

I have to stay. I want to stay. I'm going to stay.

My family leaves a few days later, but I remain in Hungary. A friend living in the States lets me stay in her Budapest apartment. My Hungarian is limited to a few folk songs, but the notoriously challenging language is in my ear and my blood. Of course I'm apprehensive about navigating a new city on my own, separated from my family, my home, and my belongings by one of the larger oceans on this planet, but mostly I'm excited. Five-year-old Charity was right. I'm going to be an opera singer.

There are many paths to success in opera, but very few are well-traveled. Danielle de Niese, an Australian-American lyric soprano, blew up after winning a TV talent show when she was nine years old; Keith Miller went from star fullback for the University of Colorado Rams to leading man at the Met; Beverly Sills took eighteen years off singing to raise her children before going on to lead the New York City Opera, the Metropolitan Opera, and Lincoln Center. These stories are the exceptions. Typically, a singer must train at one of a dozen or so prestigious conservatories or voice studios to even have a chance in the business. From there, summer programs and singing competitions offer an entrée to directors and conductors. By graduation, singers are lucky if they've nabbed an apprenticeship or young artist position that offers a small salary (generally under $30,000 a year), along with more coaching and opportunities for small roles in large productions. More likely, they move on to graduate school where they take on more debt and hope to extend their opportunities for roles and auditions within an academic setting. Each aspirant believes that if they only receive this degree or that exposure, they'll finally have the career of their dreams. In truth, the positions available to performers are extremely limited. Consequently, the stages are filled with a disproportionate number of heiresses and paupers.

A less common route for singers is to audition for a spot at a handful of European conservatories. These academic programs are significantly smaller in size and, due to state subsidies, largely affordable or free. While they typically lack the dramatic productions common in American schools, singers receive more personal attention and mentorship from faculty; the smaller European pool of conservatory graduates gives qualified singers more opportunities to audition for national and regional opera houses. The Liszt Academy is one of the premier conservatories in Europe, and Budapest, an invigorating stage. War, fascism, communism, capitalism, and corruption have taken their toll, but somehow, the city's pockmarks make its beauty pop.

At the academy, I'm slated to study with Éva, one of the most heralded singers of the twentieth century and, perhaps, the greatest Hungarian singer of all time. I've just arrived for our first lesson. Standing in the doorway of a beautiful hall with a small stage and floor-to-ceiling windows, I'm unsure of how to proceed. Before me sits Éva, shoulders squared with plum-colored scarf thrown resolutely around her neck. She's well into her sixties, but could easily be twenty-five years younger. She possesses a beauty that stems from the confidence of being truly great and deeply loved. I, on the other hand, am the youngest, least-experienced student in the entire program. While I have raw talent, I lack the musical education of my classmates—many of whom have been studying music almost exclusively for over a decade.

"Sit," beckons Éva. And so begins my musical education.

My schedule at the academy is packed tight. Éva works with me and each of her six other students two to three times a week. My other coaches and I spend time together every day. They help me with my languages—French, German, Italian, Hungarian—as well as more general repertoire. Classes in piano, music theory, German, music history, and occasional workshops in acting and movement easily fill the rest of my weekdays. My classmates are as varied as they are talented. The Liszt Academy is one of the few places in the country where ethnic Roma, Asian migrants, and Hungarian nationals study together as equals. While a connection might get someone an audition, the faculty has a reputation for brutally egalitarian honesty; the education is excellent and practically free, creating a musical meritocracy for a select group of the world's most promising talents.

Éva greets me warmly, then directs me to a music stand holding an open score. The pianist begins to play Susanna's famous aria from Mozart's *Le Nozze di Figaro*. But for the first time since I learned to read a musical staff, the page in front of me becomes nothing but a mess of black lines and dots. I miss my entrance once. Twice. Three times. My face tenses. The pianist begins to play once more. I close my eyes, relax my neck, my throat and body. Finally, I'm singing. For a moment, I feel at home as the world slows and the sun's amber rays dance with sound. Then the dancing stops.

"*Megáll!*" Éva shouts. She charges at me, pushing my lower belly and grabbing my jaw. "How you plan to sing like this?!" She pauses, wading through the thick Hungarian language to find the right English words. "Singing is sport. *Nehéz fizikai munka*," she says in the Hungarian-English hybrid that is to become the language of my musical education. "What sings?" she asks. "*Hogy énekelsz?*" she repeats in an exasperated tone.

I pause. ". . . My voice?"

"No! This sing. You sing here," she says, jabbing my lower belly. "Not here!" Éva grabs hold of my neck. "*Ismét vagy újra*—Again!" Bewildered, I repeat the phrase, hoping for an improved result.

It becomes routine: I sing my heart out and Éva forcefully explains why my heart isn't good enough. She mercilessly dissects every measure of every aria and handles my body with medical precision, tugging and pushing at my chin, cheeks, shoulders, stomach, and butt while barking out Hungarian instructions that I instinctively understand.

My insecurities motivate me. When I'm not in class, I'm Éva's shadow. I listen as she teaches other students, hoping to glean stray wisdom while I wait to start my lesson. Once she goes home for the day, I lock myself in one of the school's many practice rooms. When I'm happy with an aria, I'll open a window and begin again. As I sing, I watch people on the square below try to find the source of the music wafting down from above. The longer they search, the more confident I become. But at night, as I lie in bed listening to my heart's valves snap open and closed, I wonder what on earth I'm doing here.

Over time, I begin to recognize Éva's prods as deft technical manipulations instead of unwelcome violations of my personal space. In classical singing, natural talent can be as much of a hindrance as a help. Gifted singers become dependent on old, oftentimes bad habits in lieu of building solid vocal techniques guaranteed to produce the same sound over the course of an entire career. Ultimately, the physical act of singing primarily requires coordination. Artistry can always come later.

By now, I already have my share of habits to get over, but I'm beginning to understand a basic set of principles for good singing—the most cardinal of which must be applied before a sound ever exits my mouth.

Rule number one? Breathe.

Make no mistake, learning to breathe—really breathe—is no simple feat. First, there's proper posture: bones and their surrounding muscles from the thighs up to the forehead have to be engaged—but not tense; loose—but not sluggish; active—but not forced. As I prepare to warm up with a complicated set of arpeggios, Éva calls out a precise cue for me to expand my lungs—

"Emlékszik, bõveteni . . . most!"

A chord sounds on the piano and Éva pats my lower abdomen. As I relax the muscles at the base of my torso, my diaphragm lowers and my lungs fill with air. The inhalation expands my belly, which in turn naturally moderates the exhalation. Everything starts with breath.

The next set of exercises are octave leaps on the vowel sound *ah*. When I hear Éva shout *"Nyitva!"* I obediently open my entire singing apparatus, pushing the apples of my cheeks toward my ears and my forehead toward my scalp. By lifting my cheekbones, I open my nasal cavity and ready the amphitheater of my own skull. During the next series of exercises, sung on the *ee* vowel, Éva takes the back of my neck and chin in her hands, massaging one and rotating the other back and forth. *"Lazit,"* she croons, and I relax, allowing air to travel through my larynx and sound waves to resonate off of my sinuses, unhindered by muscle tension. As we move from warm-ups to "Caro nome" from *Rigoletto*, Éva continues to adjust me. She rolls my hips forward, elongates the back of my neck, and rotates my shoulders back and down like a high-end yoga instructor.

Increasingly, I thrive off this intensive apprenticeship. I grow to appreciate my mistakes. My voice is like the city: beautiful and flawed. But my teachers and conductors don't care for preconstructed ideals of vocal perfection. They're interested in what makes a voice different. And my voice, it turns out, is very different. As my first semester comes to an end, I have requests for concerts and performances, invitations from other great European conservatories and visiting orchestras.

But in the midst of this rapid professional progress, I'm having trouble keeping up with basic activities. In February, I faint while running to catch the streetcar a block and a half from my flat. Two weeks later, I swoon into the arms of a handsome Hungarian student during a Valentine's Day dance. In the abstract, it sounds almost romantic. In reality, it's terrifying.

That night, I kneel by my bed and offer a fervent prayer:

Dear Heavenly Father, I am so grateful. To be alive. For my family. For the amazing opportunities I've been given. But I'm afraid something's wrong with me. This is probably foolish, but if I'm all right, please, please, Dear Lord, comfort me.

I open the scriptures at random to the Book of Judges. The tale of Japheth's daughter—a sacrificial virgin—looms up at me. *Not exactly the encouragement I'm looking for right now.* I call my mother, exasperated, scared, and crying.

Mom wasn't raised religious, but she has always been a seeker. When she left home, after being admitted to the first class of women at Yale University, she dabbled in Far Eastern religions, evangelical Christianity, and Judaism. She finally found the truth she'd been seeking in the Church of Jesus Christ of Latter-Day Saints, converting to Mormonism during her freshman year of college. As my grandmother tells it, she and Didi never told Mom that she wasn't Jewish. Then again, they didn't tell her that she was, either. When Mom discovered her Hebrew roots, she moved to Israel. Then, after studying journalism at Stanford, she returned to New Haven for divinity school. That's where she met my dad—a dashing, tipsy undergrad who stumbled over her one day in Woolsey Hall. He hadn't grown up religious either, but Dad found faith when he found Mom.

It was my parents who taught me to pray and search the scriptures when I needed guidance. Still sniffling, I describe my predicament and the Bible passage I'd read to Mom over the phone—knowing she'll understand why I'm so upset by it. There's a moment of silence before she responds, likely filled by a brief, silent prayer on her end—

"Charity," Mom asks calmly, "do you want to come home now?"

"No," I reply after a pause.

"Then be careful. Go see a doctor. Don't push yourself. We'll figure things out when you get back."

A few days later, a recommendation from Judit in hand, I don full winter gear and slowly scale a small hill to catch a streetcar that runs along the city's ancient border. Rushing past Buda's snowy hills, giant pieces of ice crash down the Danube. I finally arrive at the doctor's office. In the examination room, the doctor takes my weight, temperature, vital signs. As the puffy blue pressure cuff loosens its grip on my arm, she speaks—

"You have low blood pressure," she says, her accent more con-
tinental than Hungarian.

"Is that a problem?" I ask.

"Not really," she replies, shaking her head. "Patients get a bit
more caffeine or eat more salt and it goes up again." She turns to
organize her papers before catching herself. "Now, there is a very
small chance it could be something more serious—"

"No," I interrupt her. "Low blood pressure runs in my family.
That must be it." I'm not lying—Tillemann-Dicks rarely break
100 over 60—and I don't want to hear anything about "something
more serious."

My prescription is simple and delicious: dark chocolate and
salty food. They become mainstays in my diet while taxis take up
an increasing portion of my budget. As my energy continues to
wane, I spend more and more of what remains trying to convince
myself everything will be just fine. Ambient exhaustion cuts lei-
sure activities out of my life, refocusing me onto musicianship
and musicianship alone.

It's May 2004. I'm running late.

Andrassy Street is impossibly elegant. Lined with trees and
boutiques, restaurants and theaters, it's a more weathered take
on Paris's Champs Élysées. I sit singing scales as my grimy taxi
passes the Opera House and the Hungarian National Ballet on
the way to the Thália Theatre, the venue for tonight's performance. As the driver pulls up to the curb, I spot a petite bundle
of blond hair and downy blue scarves.

"Mommy!" I rush out of the car to meet her where she stands
outside the theater. Mom has flown in from Denver—she insists
it's a special visit to witness this seminal moment in my career.

Through happy tears, I catch a glimpse of her thousand-watt grin. We walk hand in hand to the opulent theater. Judit is waiting in my dressing room with the confection of a gown I'd been fitted for earlier that day and the most exquisite bouquet of flowers I've ever seen.

Orchestra members start to arrive, suited in black and white, and whispers of a standing-room-only crowd spread through the halls. Mom and Judit leave to take their seats in the audience. I stay hidden behind the curtain, looking at the crowd settle into their seats. Then, as if by magic, silence descends.

Polite applause welcomes me onto the stage as I take my place in front of the orchestra. Anticipatory energy fills the dark theater. The orchestra strikes its first chord, then the bassoon takes over in a cantorial introduction. *Inhale. Exhale.* I breathe in the vowels for my first phrase, *"Glitter and be gay. . . ."* The strings begin and the conductor cues my entrance. I sing from a place deep within myself. My diaphragm pushes air from my lungs and I become Cunégonde from Bernstein's *Candide*; a girl who has fallen from grace—a cold, sparkly, wanton example of resilience. As the aria gets under way, each lyric exploit shines like a jewel in my vocal boudoir. The song fits my voice like a pageant queen's dress—which isn't to say it's not a bit tight in some places.

Many singers never quite settle into their higher tessitura— the upper reaches of their vocal range. A high note sung poorly can ruin a voice or end a career. At some point, every soprano needs faith: in her voice, in her training, in the composer. I brace myself for the final phrase of the aria, breathing deep and wide. My voice pierces the high E flat and the room erupts in an ovation.

For nearly five minutes, the crowd joins in synchronized applause. As it slows, I leave the stage, only to be called back as it speeds up again with renewed gusto, each reprise producing a new bouquet of flowers. When the bows finally end, I see Mom and Judit waiting backstage with Éva. I greet them, giddy with pride, relief, and gratitude. Together, we field enthusiastic theatergoers, flowers, and well wishes.

Only now do I realize the evening's biggest challenge still lies ahead: as the antique theater lacks an elevator, I must scale the front lobby's grand staircase to reach the post-performance reception. Even small flights of stairs totally exhaust me at this point, but I have no choice. Mom and the others walk ahead as I place my high-heeled foot on the first step to begin my ascent. At first, I'm fine; I follow Mom's example and talk to passersby, using each introduction as an excuse to stop and catch my breath. But as I continue, I feel my heart pumping harder. Blood drains from my face and my vision begins to tunnel. I stop, steadying myself on the ornate banister. I don't want anyone to know I'm unwell. I *don't* want tonight to end with another fainting spell. Trying to pass off sluggishness for elegance, I slowly move my foot onto the next step. Then the next. Then the next. Gradually, I lurch my way up the curved vestibule toward the upper lobby. Finally, I ascend to the reception. Mom smiles proudly as her gaze lingers on me, then her attention turns back to the milieu as she's beckoned by another guest.

After the party, I pack my dress into a garment bag and Mom and I head back to the apartment. In the car, we talk about home. About Dad and the other kids. I don't mention the staircase—how difficult it is to walk up a hill or how much I struggle to breathe. If I mention that to Mom, she might make a fuss. She might not let me ignore it any longer.

The next day, we go to my voice lesson. Éva seems as thrilled by last night's performance as I am.

"There is no doubt," she declares, looking grimly at the floor and then at me. "You are a big talent." I blush. "But you *should* be a Great."

Éva continues, "To be a Great, you need three things"— Mom whips out an old envelope from her bag and starts taking notes—"you must get very sick, you must fall in love, and you must work, work, work. Then, in ten years, you will really be something. People will want to give you many roles, but don't be fooled: They will ruin your voice before it is ready. All they care about is money, money, money. You are more than roles. *You* are going to be *a Great Artist*. Remember this."

Mom is still scribbling furiously, but it's hard for me to take Éva seriously. It's ridiculous to expect that, out of all the people wanting to make it big in opera, I could be the one to do it. Yet at the same time, I desperately hope she's right. Despite all of the misgivings I've had over these past months, I want to be Great more than almost anything else. Anyway, ten years is a very long time from now. I file Éva's advice away in the back of my mind, hoping to need it later.

The next week, I'm on a plane back home to Denver with Mom. Encouraged by both Mom and Éva, I've decided to take some time off from performing in Europe to go home and prepare to serve a full-time mission for my church.

It was missionaries who first inspired my love of singing. Before *Hansel and Gretel*, these young women were my exemplars—musical and otherwise. Their kindness, their service, their dedication, and their songs struck enduring awe into my devout little heart. I've always been certain that going on a mission is the best way to establish God as my priority; in my mind, whatever successes I do or don't have cannot happen because I've neglected my duty to Him.

Before sending in my final application for missionary service, I have to undergo a mandatory full physical. My doctor is fresh out of residency and pretty in a no-nonsense way. We chat for a few minutes and I tell her about myself: my passion for opera, my plans to serve a mission, my fainting spells, and my fatigue. She looks in my ears, throat, and eyes. She tests my reflexes and listens to my heart for a few moments longer than usual. Then she orders an EKG. The nurse places cold, studded stickers on my side, chest, ankles, and abdomen and I watch as a needle traces a jagged line onto the sheet feeding out underneath it. When the test is done, the nurse takes the sheet and leaves the door cracked behind her. I hear the doctor discussing me over the phone down the hall. Finally, she returns with my results. Sitting down, she first suggests that I not research anything she's about to discuss with me on my own. After this disclaimer, she tells me that she believes I have idiopathic pulmonary hypertension, or PH. The doctor doesn't want to give me too many details until she can confirm her diagnosis with Dr. Chris Lang, one of the region's top cardiologists. For the time being, she just tells me that she won't be able to sign my health release forms.

As soon as I get home, I sit down at our family desktop and Google "pulmonary hypertension." I click on the first result. Pulmonary hypertension is caused by a thickening of blood vessels in the lungs, which impedes oxygen absorption and increases blood pressure within the heart, making physical activity difficult. In its most advanced stages, fainting can occur with exertion. While PH is relatively common as a secondary condition of everything from pregnancy to AIDS, I've been tentatively diagnosed with the idiopathic variety of the disease, for which there's no known cause or cure. Pregnancy with PH is fatal and, without a lung transplant, nearly 70 percent of all PH patients die of heart failure within five years of diagnosis. There are fewer than seven thousand cases of the disease worldwide. *So I guess I really am one in a million*, I think wryly to myself.

I stare at the screen, feeling sick in more ways than one. *This can't be right.* I click on another search result, this one belonging to a major university hospital. It confirms all the statistics. I do the math. I'm twenty years old. Somewhere between twenty-two and twenty-five, I'll probably die. I haven't been in love yet—I've never even kissed a boy. A mission is probably off the table. Children, out of the question. I don't have ten years to become a great artist. I hurt so much that I start to laugh. Soon, tears well up and I'm left with only silent, lonely sobs.

Inhale. Exhale. Grabbing the home phone, I retreat to the basement bathroom. What do I do? The shortness of breath, the fainting, the heart palpitations; this diagnosis answers so many questions I've had for years. In a strange way, it's a relief. *It's not all in my imagination. I'm not crazy.* Something is really, really wrong. My reflexive expectation of calamity, inherited from my Jewish grandparents, has been borne out to great effect.

I decide to call Dad. He always knows how to deal with a situation. He won't panic, but he'll take this seriously. Fifteen minutes after I hang up the phone, he's left work and arrived in our driveway.

After sending the three littlest siblings downstairs to watch TV, Dad calls a family meeting. Ignoring my entreaties to hold off until we have a firmer diagnosis, he announces my condition to the family—resolute that we're going to face this trial together.

But I know this is my cross to bear. Not my brothers' or sisters'. I don't cry in front of them. I won't. I've already given everyone enough to worry about. "It could be worse!" I quip. "I still have my looks!" But the stunned, numb silence persists. I try one more time—"At least PH isn't contagious?" Nobody laughs.

Hours later, in the dead of night, Mom crawls into my bed. She holds me in the darkness and we weep together. Even without an official diagnosis, we both know that this is the beginning of a goodbye that could last a few months or a few years. Regardless of the pace of change, this disease will shape our family's future and, ultimately, end my life.

Act I, Scene 2:
Antonia

A mysterious lung disease turns life-threatening when Antonia sings. Antonia's father, Crespel, and her lover, Hoffmann, try to help her find happiness while a malevolent Doctor Miracle is intent on expediting Antonia's demise.

Viens là, comme autrefois.	Come here as before;
Ecoute, et tu verras si j'ai perdu	Listen, and you'll see if I've lost
ma voix.	my voice.
Tiens, ce doux chant d'amour	Here, the soft song of love we
que nous chantions ensemble.	sang together.
C'est une chanson d'amour.	'Tis a song of love
Qui s'envole,	That flies off,
Triste ou folle,	Sad or joyful,
Tour à tour;	Turn by turn;
C'est une chanson d'amour	'Tis a song of love
La rose nouvelle	The new rose
Sourit au printemps.	Smiles on the Spring.
Las! combien de temps	Ah! how will it be
Vivra-t-elle?	That it lives?

—JACQUES OFFENBACH,
LES CONTES D'HOFFMANN

I love meeting new people, but there's nothing fun about the onslaught of strange medical personnel who parade through my life during the next weeks. At each appointment I'm poked, prodded, and cross-examined. My weight is read off scale after scale and vial after vial of blood is extracted from my already bruised forearms. Mom is beside me through it all, but not even her titanium will can make the needles hurt less.

"Are you or have you ever been sexually active?"

Every doctor asks the same question. Every doctor gives me the same incredulous look when I answer, "No." Like a recurring nightmare, I sit red-faced and miserable between the doctor and my parents as the former questions my sexual history (or rather, complete lack of it) and the latter adamantly affirms my unblemished virginhood. One day, a doctor storms out of the room demanding that Mom and Dad leave too. Alone in a doctor's office for the first time since my initial diagnosis, I listen to their muted shouting through the thick taupe door. Eventually, a research nurse enters to conduct a second, private interview. Once I've independently confirmed my virginity, she retrieves the others, still fuming, from the hall, and we proceed with my appointment. The entire process, repeated in doctors' offices across the country, is expensive, invasive, embarrassing.

My grandfather decides to send Mom and me to New York to see Dr. Robyn Barst, a leading expert on pulmonary hypertension. Didi heard about her from her father-in-law, whom he happened to be seated beside at an event just a few weeks before my diagnosis. While he doesn't believe in God or miracles, Didi knows *beschert* (Yiddish for "destiny") when he sees it. He organizes an appointment for me immediately.

Mom and I wait in yet another dismal office as fluorescent

lights flicker nervously above us. My arms look almost gray against the yellow poplin of my blouse and my full white skirt. Dr. Barst rushes in like a vortex, her glasses perched precariously near the tip of her nose as she strides toward us, shuffling through a pile of papers. Her haircut, her figure, her gait—everything about her is powerful. After a curt introduction, she leans toward me. "I hear you're an opera singer," she clips out. "You'll definitely have to stop that immediately." My eyes widen as she continues—"I don't think you understand the severity of your disease. Those high notes are going to kill you."

She must not understand. Other doctors have told me to ease up on physical activity, to change my diet. I'm taking a battery of medications that thin my blood and give me rashes and make everything taste like tin foil. I've even been advised to stay away from Denver—my home—because of its high altitude. I can't be with my family. I can't go on my mission. I'm going to die young and childless. But if I can sing, I can face all that with a smile. According to Dr. Barst, my life must now become a series of carefully filled prescriptions. But to me, life will always be an opera. This mysterious illness is just a run-of-the-mill dramatic plot twist.

Sitting in the cold light, I feel like Antonia in *Les Contes d'Hoffmann*, my own Dr. Miracle glaring down at me. Ask me to change my diet, my school, my city, my sleep patterns, my exercise, my schedule. I'll do it. But I will never stop singing. Ever since Lincoln died, I've known that death is a part of life. But singing *is* my life. I don't know why—if it's the melodies or the stage or the physical sensations. To be honest, I don't care. I just want to live—really *live*—for however long I have left. I may never become Great, but I will be heard.

Our meeting ends and Mom takes my hand as we walk out

of the hospital. The solstice sun glows over West 165th's blond brick exteriors as a man sells cups of fresh fruit on the corner. Mom buys one and hands it to me. I hail a yellow cab and direct the driver to Grand Central. We travel in silence. Mom and I are big talkers, but nothing needs to be said right now. She already knows everything I want to tell her. Without a word, we both already know I will never enter that doctor's office again. As we share sweet pieces of mango in the back of the taxi, I notice my arms have lost their gray tinge. It's nice to be alive.

———

On top of the personal exhaustion and discomfort these appointments inflict, I fear they may also be driving my family to financial ruin. Dr. Barst didn't accept my insurance, and our meeting with her cost thousands of dollars out of pocket. The medications that manage my PH are extremely expensive, and we've been crisscrossing the country via airplane to meet different specialists. Mom wants to take me to see yet another doctor, this time in Baltimore, but I can't help but feel the cost of all these appointments is beginning to outweigh their benefit.

Through her relentless conversations about my PH with anyone who will listen, Mom has heard that Dr. Reda Girgis is a well-respected pulmonologist at Johns Hopkins. I'm sure he'll tell me the same things I've already heard from so many doctors before him: I'm very sick and I have very few, very painful options for staying alive. I call his office on the sly to cancel our appointment and his assistant asks why I won't be coming in. I disclose it's for financial reasons. After a brief hold, she explains Dr. Girgis will see me free of charge.

Maybe this is a different kind of doctor.

Tomicah lives and works in Washington, DC. Mom suggests

we all drive to Baltimore together. It will be fun! The oldest of us kids, Tomicah has been "grown up" since before I can even remember. Married, finishing his PhD, and working on the Senate Foreign Relations Committee, he's a busy guy. But he makes time for this. He drops Mom and me at the hospital and we go up to the office.

There's a weight about Dr. Girgis's presence. He's a serious man and a serious doctor. While his English sounds native, Dr. Girgis grew up in Cairo until his parents moved to Detroit. Now, he's cochair of his department at Johns Hopkins University Hospital, where he teaches and practices medicine. Eminently dry and thoughtful, he isn't an obvious match for my bubbly personality.

"Are you or do you expect to become pregnant?" he asks.

I am Diva Suprema, Goddess of Virtue, Master of My Universe. I can do anything. I can do this. "I am not sexually active," I wince out, anticipating the ensuing circus.

He looks in my eyes for an extra moment. It doesn't feel invasive. Just kind—like he wants to make sure I'm OK. In an instant, I feel like there's an understanding between us. Almost as soon as he pauses, he continues, "OK. Before you get married or if you decide to get serious with a boyfriend, make sure you speak with me or my nurse, Tracy." With that, he moves on to the next question.

This *is* a different kind of doctor.

With our appointment drawing to a close, Dr. Girgis says I can sing. He even thinks the breathing exercises I do for vocal training could be good for my lungs. To him, Denver's altitude is the real concern. He encourages me to move to sea level for good.

This is the doctor for me.

On our way back to Washington, Mom insists we stop at the Peabody Institute of Music, the oldest conservatory in North

America. This is the conservatory I was planning to attend before I diverted to Budapest. We're all exhausted and Tomicah objects to the detour, but twenty-five years have inured Mom to his protestations. Begrudgingly, we walk into Peabody's grand foyer where Mom immediately requests to see the dean. Tomicah groans, but I don't mind. It's the middle of the summer—the dean is gone anyway. Why stop her from asking?

"You're in luck," the security guard chirps. "Dean Justen happened to drop by school today!"

Mom glances back triumphantly as we follow her and the guard at a distance. Winding through the glittering foyer into a labyrinth of hallways, empty practice rooms, and elevators, we finally arrive in the anteroom of the dean's office. Late afternoon sun streaks through old blinds, illuminating a few leaves of an aloe plant, a sliver of a diploma, and a brass statue in the dark, rich room. Dean Justen greets us from underneath a crown of unruly white hair.

He is my mother's jolly Austrian counterpart. The two of them gab back and forth like old friends. He's well acquainted with Éva and the Liszt Academy and, after realizing I've already been accepted to Peabody, his face brightens. "Come back!" he beckons. "We wanted you once. After Liszt, I am certain we will only want you more!" And so, yet again, I find myself a student at one of the world's great music schools. Tomicah and I glance darkly at each other, knowing Mom will use this happy series of coincidences to justify countless impromptu field trips in the coming years, but I find myself smiling as we head back to the car. Against all of my direst expectations, this trip to Baltimore *has* been fun—just like Mom promised.

Peabody is a welcome opportunity to reintroduce a measure of structure to my crazier-than-usual life, but, like Hungary before it, Baltimore poses some logistical challenges. A forty-five-minute drive from Washington, DC, under optimal conditions, Didi, Mimo, and Tomicah won't exactly be on hand in case of a medical crisis. My parents remedy this perilous independence by demanding that my sister Liberty move across the country to live with me. They insist it will be a wonderful learning experience for her and a vital safeguard for me—disregarding the obvious facts that, as a teenage girl, Liberty is totally unfit to care for me, and, only four years older with a terminal illness, I am totally unfit to care for her. But on a sunny morning in July, I find myself retrieving her and her two small suitcases from BWI Airport.

First conservatory, then my illness have occupied most of my attention of late, and I haven't spent quality time with Liberty in a while. Over the past year, she's outgrown our family's "weird religious homeschooler" vibe much more effectively than I ever did. She listens to music by Cat Power and The Decemberists instead of Gounod and Bellini. Where her shelves house contemporary fiction, mine burst with pills and prescriptions from diuretics to Viagra (which, fun fact, was initially developed to treat PH). Liberty is sixteen going on thirty. I'm twenty going on ninety.

We settle into our strange new life together as autumn approaches. Using some contacts I've gained at my endless examinations, I'm able to help Liberty organize an internship at the American Lung Association. Meanwhile, I prepare to restart conservatory. Peabody is very different from Liszt. In Budapest, I was the star pupil in Éva's studio of seven singers. Here, each instructor manages thirty to forty voice students depending on the week, and they don't have much time to play favorites. Not wanting to label myself as damaged goods, I decide not to tell anyone at conservatory about my PH. But lately it's getting harder to pretend nothing's wrong. Hoping to avoid more invasive interventions, I've been taking an experimental oral drug since my diagnosis. Initially, I improve, but I feel myself slipping into exhaustion much more quickly in recent weeks—relying on Liberty to cook and run errands because I can't muster the energy to do so myself. Some nights, I wake up to her sitting by my bed, just watching to make sure I'm still breathing.

Every few weeks, I go to the medical school for a walk test. There are no machines. No sensors. Just an empty hallway that I pace up and down for six minutes. Afterward, my nurse, Tracy, takes my vital signs. Simple. Yet every time I come back, the hallway seems to get longer. By December of 2004, I can barely make it halfway down before needing to rest. Dr. Girgis orders a heart catheterization—a routine surgery used to measure internal pressures that most PH patients undergo once or twice a year. The surgeon and nurses make small talk with me as she snakes a catheter through a vein in my neck down to my heart; then she turns toward the monitor and goes silent. My numbers are supposed to be somewhere between 15 and 25; the monitor reads 146. I turn my head just in time to see the color drain from Tracy's face.

As far as my treatment goes, it's time to pull out the big guns. Flolan, an intravenous vasodilator, is the invasive intervention I've been avoiding. But I've run out of effective alternatives. The medication will be continuously injected directly into my veins via a pump about as large as a VHS tape, which I'll have to carry with me at all times for the rest of my life with PH. I get the device implanted just before winter break. I walk out of the hospital with a narrow tube snaking out of the bottom of my shirt and connecting me to my new pump, stored in my purse and surrounded by ice packs. My life has changed forever.

My pump and the medication it dispenses immediately become my de facto first priority. Other girls my age have boyfriends. I have Flolan. Two pieces of advice for anyone thinking of starting a relationship with Flolan: know that it's high maintenance and hope it's long term. Refrigerated, each dose of the medication lasts for one day. Once twenty-four hours have passed, it has to be immediately replaced with a new cartridge of freshly prepped medicine. Flolan is a dangerous cocktail to mix; if my prep surface isn't properly sanitized, I risk contracting a deadly infection from pathogens in my tubing. If I don't pop every bubble in the solution, air will pump into my veins and I'll suffer an aneurysm. If I'm late replacing the cartridge, the flow of medicine will be disrupted, my pulmonary veins will constrict, and I'll die. My morbid countdown clock restarts at 3:00 p.m. every day. No matter where I am or what I'm doing, I have to change my medicine by then if I want to stay alive.

Unlike me, Flolan is harshly regimented. If you mess up, there are no second chances. It's shipped to our Baltimore apartment in giant boxes—thirty doses of medication plus the needles, syringes, tubing, saline, alcohol, and ice packs required to prepare it (if there's one thing Flolan and I have in common, it's a passion for accessories). We stash kits of it across the Eastern Seaboard—at Tomicah's house; my grandparents'; Kimber's apartment in New York; the car; my purse—just in case.

One day, Liberty and I get caught in bad traffic going to visit Kimber. Once the clock hits 2:30, we exit at the first opportunity. I saturate every inch of a grimy gas station sink with rubbing alcohol and begin the delicate process of mixing my meds. Liberty stands guard at the door—I'd prefer not to have an unwitting stranger walk in on me mixing drugs in the bathroom of a roadside Sunoco. Casual passersby won't understand that, unlike other addicts, I'll literally die if I don't get my next fix.

Despite its inconveniences, Flolan is—quite literally—a life-saver. Since using it, my perpetual exhaustion has abated; I can *almost* function like a regular person. I'm very grateful for this miracle of modern pharmacology, which is a blessing, because there are only two options to stop taking it: die or get a lung transplant. I guess they're right when they say breaking up is hard to do.

With chemically renewed energy, I throw myself into my studies. Within a few weeks, my performance schedule is full. I'm singing at embassy concerts, with chamber ensembles and orchestras. There's always a party to attend, and Liberty and I take the town by storm. I start to work as the national spokesperson for the Pulmonary Hypertension Association, raising money for PH research and testifying before Congress. My fellow musicians at Peabody aren't big consumers of C-SPAN or medical news, so I tell myself that the advocacy work will go unnoticed.

I pick up a couple of unorthodox collaborators along the way—I perform in a rock concert backed up by the US ambassador to Russia on drums and the Hungarian ambassador to the United States on lead guitar. It's surreal, to say the least. Over the summer, I debut at the Kennedy Center accompanied by the current secretary of state, Condoleezza Rice. Secretary Rice and Didi had become friends while working together on foreign policy issues and she let slip that she moonlights as a concert pianist. Next thing I know, Madame Secretary and I are performing "O mio babbino caro" together for a packed house.

My career begins to coalesce around these types of unexpected opportunities. Research on an obscure Hungarian composer evolves into an invitation to debut at Cleveland's Severance Hall singing his work. A performance at one foreign embassy leads to invitations to sing at several others, until Embassy Row becomes a circuit unto itself.

Back at school, I see less success. I'm invited to sing the role of Ophelia in the world premiere of Amy Beth Kirsten's new opera, *Ophelia Forever*, but going into my second year at Peabody, I'm turned down for a number of other auditions. Eventually, I find out that a recommendation from a teacher states that I "might be the voice of a generation" before outlining, in excruciating detail, the ins and outs of my medical condition and the pump I thought I had hidden so well. Mortified, I'm grateful when a fellowship to study opera in Italy comes through. This will be a chance to start over.

Two days after I arrive in Florence, I meet a famous old conductor. He immediately takes a shine to me and casts me in a slew of roles for upcoming festivals. After my summer in Italy, a Fulbright fellowship takes me back to Budapest and, soon, I have invitations to sing everywhere from Berlin to Beijing. The coming months are a series of dreamlike scenes—late nights in the Tuscan countryside and lazy mornings at the Ritz-Carlton. Majestic soirees in Budapest concert halls and audiences with Danish royalty. I travel with a rotating cast of family characters, each one hand-delivering a new box of Flolan a week or so before my previous stash runs out. More often than not, though, we're enjoying each other's company instead of handling medical crises.

I'm no opera star—I haven't sung in any major festivals and, some nights, I only have bit parts. But when I'm cast as Queen of the Fairies or I perform as the understudy for Violetta, I feel invincible. *This is how a real career starts*, I assure myself. Gradually, my inner optimist grows even more bullish than usual, and I begin to see my ten-year path to becoming a Great Artist unfolding graciously before me. I'm so busy living that I almost forget my brief life expectancy is quickly winding down—from five years to four to three.

"What *is* that?"

I'm practicing with a new accompanist in Florence, but he seems to be having trouble focusing on our score. I ask him if everything's all right, but he waves away my question and we continue with the measure.

"There! That sound!" he interrupts again. I shake my head, incredulous, but this time he doesn't continue playing. We spend the next minute in silence as he sits at the piano bench, hunched forward in concentration.

"Again! You must have heard it that time—a mechanical little *schoowap*. Where the hell is it coming from?!"

My stomach drops. This time, I did hear the sound, and I know exactly where it's coming from. It's the action from my Flolan pump, which is currently attached to my inner thigh by an Ace bandage and a particularly snug pair of Spanx. The only person who knows about my pump out here is a costume designer I've sworn to secrecy. The European opera scene is small, talkative, and already competitive enough without directors worrying you might keel over during opening night. Up until now, no one has suspected anything.

I quickly change the subject, asking if we can just continue with the aria. I try to sing or talk over the periodic whirring of my pump, but the pianist stays on edge for the rest of our rehearsal. *I guess it's time to find a new accompanist.*

Typically gregarious, PH dictates my newfound antisociability. People have germs and germs are the enemy: if I get sick (well, sicker than I already am), I can't sing. I try to limit my interactions with others to rehearsals and voice lessons. Most of my socializing happens with dead composers and voices on the other end of a telephone. I spend a small mint on calling cards—talking to Mom and Dad every day and updating my doctors about my health. On Sundays, I go to church. Otherwise, I'm content enough to spend evenings with my piano and whatever score I'm working on at the moment.

Needless to say, I don't go on many dates. For all the passionate affairs I've acted out onstage, I lack much firsthand experience of romance. My only real relationships have been with my family, my faith, and my music (oh, and, of course, Flolan). Being wed to your craft is a little easier when the prospect of a relationship with another person is so imposing. In Mormonism, marriage is the endgame; for single members of the church, even the most casual dates are underpinned by the thought that the schlub sitting across from you could be the person with whom you spend not just the rest of your life, but your *afterlife* too.

But I guess dating is always difficult . . . Mom and Dad's courtship certainly was. Didi was already convinced that no one could ever be worthy of Mom—his beloved oldest daughter. Certainly not an Aspen ski bum with a lightly checkered past. But Dad straightened out and he and Mom eloped to the Mormon temple outside of Washington, DC, to be married for time and all eternity—all before he graduated from college. Sure, things were complicated. But they made it work because they loved each other.

Just like I love opera. I already know I'll never have kids. Even if I were to adopt, the physical limitations of PH would make raising a family nearly impossible. And eternal families—parents and children joined by a bond unbroken by death itself—are a central tenet of the church's theology. Their importance is reemphasized every single week in sermons and Sunday school, so it's pretty safe to assume that certain childlessness will be a deal breaker for most good Mormon boys. No. As far as I'm concerned, opera is my boyfriend and we have a very fulfilling romance. Like any good relationship, I make sacrifices for my art. But only because it's what I want to do.

On the other hand, I make sacrifices for my illness because it's what I *have* to do. The same isn't true of the people supporting me. Nothing forces them to upend their lives for me. It's hard to even think about all the things they do for me; it stays at the very back of my mind, like a sin left unatoned. Every time Mom flies across the country to attend a doctor's appointment with me, I know she leaves Dad and four kids at home alone—sometimes for weeks at a time if I'm undergoing a serious procedure. Liberty transferred her entire life to Baltimore on my account; when I get sick just before the holidays, fifteen-year-old Mercina and sixteen-year-old Shiloh do the same thing—leaving Denver to join me in Budapest so that I don't spend Christmas alone in a strange hospital. My family has always tried to make the best out of a bad situation, but I can't help but feel they do too much. And while I know there's genuine love and concern at the surface and at the heart of all this service, I fear somewhere in between, resentment has begun to bubble. Even worse, I'm afraid it's mutual. I never asked to be sick—maybe I need their help, but I certainly don't want it. I can't help but long for the times when *I* was the person helping all of *them*. When I was on my way to greatness *without* a dozen-and-a-half people questioning the wisdom of my every decision and the direction of my every cough.

Didi met my great-grandmother, Mary Tillemann, when he was eight years old. In 1936, he strode into the Tillemann jewelry shop announcing that he intended to purchase a birthday present for his dear mother. Mary was so charmed that she made him promise to visit again (next time with his mother) before sending the little boy home with a gift far exceeding his meager budget. By the time Didi was nine, the two mothers had colluded to betroth him to Mimo, Mary's six-year-old daughter. It would be a happy union for everyone involved. Then the Third Reich came to Hungary. By wits, luck, and his light complexion, Didi survived horrors—all while working to supply the Hungarian resistance and keeping up with his academic studies. But the war left him orphaned and separated from Mimo. Turning a B'nai B'rith scholarship at the University of Washington into a path to citizenship, Didi soon brought Mimo to join him in America. In 1950, they were married under a chuppah in a friend's backyard in Los Angeles. In the fifty-seven years since, Didi has built an academic career, a political legacy, and a massive network. He is respected, feared, and adored by untold numbers—most of all by us, his family.

In the three years since my diagnosis, my grandfather Didi has become a champion of PH. While his chairmanship of the House Foreign Affairs Committee and the Human Rights Caucus has little to do with the disease, Didi has used his platform and his seniority to make incredible strides raising awareness and furthering research efforts to find a cure for PH. Didi and I have always had a close relationship—he says I'm the only person who has never been afraid of him. But Didi has seventeen other grandchildren to attend to, so his grandfatherly attentions have often been divided. That all changed when I got PH. After my diagnosis, I quickly became the object of his laser focus. At times, it can be overwhelming to have such a powerful advocate, but I know all Didi wants is for me to live a long, fulfilling life. He knows he can't single-handedly ensure its length, but he certainly tries his darnedest. I call to speak to him and Mimo a couple of times each week, updating them on my progress with the Fulbright and the status of my health.

More and more often though, Didi isn't up to talking. It's certainly uncharacteristic, but I figure he must be busy with his responsibilities on the committee. I only really start to worry when my grandmother lets drop that his appetite has been waning—in nearly sixty years of eating Mimo's cooking, that's never happened before. Soon enough, we all know something is seriously wrong.

In December 2007, Didi is diagnosed with stage 4 esophageal cancer. Didi has faced Nazis and Communists. He's spent his career fighting corporate greed, ruthless dictators, and opposition politicians. But cancer is his most vicious opponent by far. Mom flies to DC from Denver on Christmas Day to be with him. I hear the exhaustion in her and Mimo's voices whenever I call; I know it's less from the physical demands of care than the emotional strain of witnessing their hero meet an adversary who might finally best him. The only times Didi speaks to me on the phone, an uncharacteristic waver in his still-forceful voice, is to forbid me from leaving my fellowship to see him. Disobeying Didi is never done lightly, so not wanting to upset him, I stay in Hungary. At the end of January, he finally relents and agrees to let me book a ticket back to DC. On February 11, two days before my flight leaves, Mom calls my apartment, crying.

Once again, my family gathers underneath the grand cupola of a national capitol—this time in Washington—to honor Didi, but the mood is somber instead of celebratory. Eulogies are offered by luminaries from UN Secretary General Ban Ki-moon to Elie Wiesel to Joe Biden. Bono, international rock star extraordinaire, leads the assembled mourners in a rendition of "All You Need Is Love"—sung to Mimo for Valentine's Day. But not even a personal serenade by an international superstar could distract her from her sweetheart's absence from her side.

Following the funeral, an emptiness settles into Mimo and Didi's Capitol Hill apartment. We all know someone has to be there for Mimo. I volunteer. This is my chance to be there for someone who needs me instead of vice versa. I extend my leave of absence from my fellowship and move into Mimo's guest bedroom.

When a leading man as monumental as Didi takes his final bow, it's hard to figure out how best to fill the void left on the stage of our lives. We settle on distraction. With just the two of us in the house, Mimo has become keenly aware of my singleness—a reality she either never noticed or never cared about before. All of a sudden, though, she staunchly opposes my resolved old maidenhood. After some debate—I'm no more comfortable with the idea of a romantic relationship than I've ever been—I finally relent in an attempt to maintain our battered mutual peace of mind. I start going on dates. Lots of dates. While I used to be politely disinterested, I now accept invitations from the boys I meet at church or events on Capitol Hill. After each outing, I come home and gab with Mimo about where we went, what I ate, how he dressed. I scroll through my dates' Facebook photos with her and together we cast judgment (she particularly favors high foreheads like Didi had, deeming them the conclusive mark of a *true* intellectual). It's entertaining in a sense, but hollow. I know I have no future with any of these men.

In the midst of this convoluted mourning process, I get a call from a buddy from my campaigning days. He asks if I'm free to grab lunch. I readily assent, eager to go over old war stories together. He may have been born in Israel, but Yoni Doron is a Long Island boy. Dark eyes, black hair, with an accent like fresh rye, he's excellent company. As we finish up our meal, I'm already flipping through a mental catalogue of friends, looking for a nice Jewish girl to set him up with—I just know he's going to make someone very happy one day.

A little less than two months later, at the end of March 2008, I return to Budapest. Mimo and Shiloh will spend the summer together during his internship on the Hill, so I'm free to resume my fellowship. I unlock the door of my apartment to find everything as I left it, bed unmade and sheet music strewn across the piano. It's been four years since I've been back to Denver, and this little flat has become the closest thing to home I have. I grow herbs on the balconet outside of the living room. They usually die (I have a notoriously brown thumb) but I keep trying. Feral cats congregate in the grassy court behind the apartment building; I always leave out extra food for them because it makes me feel like I have pets again. I've yet to finish mourning Didi, but I'm glad to be caring for my small corner of the world again. Opening the door to the cold night air, I water my struggling little garden then head to the bathroom to mix my medication. I attach it to my pump and fall asleep, exhausted.

The phone is ringing. Slowly, my eyes open as I wipe crusty spit from the side of my mouth. *Who on earth calls at 7:00 a.m. on a Sunday?* Partially rousing myself, I stumble toward the receiver in the living room but miss the call—voicemail picks up just before I do. I turn to go brush my teeth when the phone starts ringing again. It's my older sister, Kimber.

Three years older, Kimber is my best friend. She is effortless when I'm overworked, content when I'm restless, measured when I'm over the top; our inverse personalities balance each other perfectly. Even though she has a full life—married and working as a junior PR executive in New York with a baby on the way—we still find time to talk.

But today, her voice is *too* even.

"Are you sitting down?" she asks.

I bang my shin on an ottoman as I trip toward the couch. "Ow. Yes. OK. I'm sitting down."

"Dad's been in a car accident. No one else was hurt." If I were more awake, perhaps I'd hear the pain underscoring the calm of her voice.

"What? Is he going to be all right?" I ask, rubbing my bruised leg.

"He's seriously burned, but the doctors say he could still survive." The harshness of those words knocks any remnant of sleep from my mind, replacing it with cold terror—

". . . *Could* still survive?!"

"He has third-degree burns over eighty percent of his body, Chary. They say that's just within the threshold for possible recovery."

"I'm booking a ticket home."

"Charity . . ." she replies, her pitch softening as mine rises.

"Kimi, I'm booking a ticket!"

Kimber puts Tomicah on the line. He's slightly less mollifying—

"Charity—"

"I don't care about the stupid altitude, Tomicah!"

"I know you don't. I understand. You're scared. We're all scared. But if he's going to get through this, we need to focus on what's best for Dad. *Mom* needs to focus on what's best for Dad. If you come back to Denver right now, Chary, we all know she won't be able to do that. You'll get sick, Mom will get distracted, and Dad's care will suffer because of it."

"But—"

"I'm sorry, Chary."

I drop the receiver and slide from the couch onto the floor, sobbing. I'm furious at Tomicah for being right. In Denver, my already struggling lungs have to work harder to oxygenate my blood with thin mountain air, giving my overworked heart even less support to pump; if I go now, I'll only be in the way. I'm angry at PH for making me feel so powerless.

I call home every day. Details begin to filter in: Dad had been driving home from the mountains when the front wheel of his minivan jammed. The car rolled off the highway and down a steep embankment, bursting into flames at the bottom. Dad was able to drag himself away from the wreck, and some good Samaritans with a fire extinguisher in their trunk put out the flames and called an ambulance. But significant damage had already been done.

Dad is stable, but unresponsive. The only way to manage the pain from the burns is to place him in a medically induced coma. Mom has barely left his side since he was admitted to the hospital. The little kids have set up camp in the lobby of the burn clinic—snack wrappers and algebra books accumulating around their well-worn chairs as they wait to update the rest of us with news from Mom or the nurses.

A week after his accident, Dad is showing signs of improvement. He's fighting hard, and it's starting to look like he might win. The doctors begin to discuss his recovery. They warn that his life will be different. His mobility will be impaired. His hands won't be able to grip his tools or signature purple-ink pens like they used to. His face—the shining eyes, button nose, and handsome cleft chin—won't be recognizable. But that won't cow him. Dad has always been an ingenious fixer. To him, something being broken has always been an opportunity to improve on the original design. We all know he'll take this bushel of lemons and come up with a recipe for lemonade that no one's ever thought of before.

But almost as soon as we begin to feel hope again, Dad's situation turns. It's his lungs. They were burned worse than the doctors thought, and they're deteriorating quickly. Ten days after his car accident, Dad's lungs fail, filling with fluid. There's nothing the doctors can do. Mom and my sisters and brothers sing hymns around Dad's hospital bed as the numbers on his bedside monitor tick down to zeros.

———

I'm tired of exile. I fly back to Denver for the funeral. Over a thousand people attend, each one with their own story about how Dad served them, sat with them, counseled them. Each of the kids has prepared a memory or a scripture verse to share. As the service approaches its close, Mom takes her place behind the pulpit. She stands silent for a few moments, then begins to sing an old song by the Seekers. Unlike her children, Mom has never been a singer. Her voice is soft, husky, and cracked from grief. But I've yet to hear a more powerful performance in all my life. Beside me and behind me, tears streak down hundreds of cheeks; I've lost my father, but I, along with everybody in this room, now mourn the love of my mother's life. "I could search the whole world over / Until my life is through / But I know I'll never find another you."

As we make our way to the cemetery, her melodic elegy hangs in the air like the scent of autumn: at once, impossibly beautiful and melancholy. Just a few weeks before, as we worked together arranging Didi's funeral, Dad told me how much he appreciated the simplicity of a Jewish burial. Today, my brothers and my uncle bear him to rest in a plain pine casket. Underneath a blaze of Colorado sunshine, we say goodbye to Dad for the last time in this life.

For a week after the funeral, it's almost like we're all young again—playing dress-up, chasing the dogs around the house, going for walks around Rocky Mountain Lake. But every night at dinner the seat at the head of the table remains empty and the sunroom is filled to bursting with wilting flower arrangements. Deep down, we know home will never be the same again.

April is nearly over. I'm in no state, physically or mentally, to start rehearsals again. I cancel my European engagements and return to be with family in DC. My heart simply can't bear Colorado any longer.

Act I, Scene 3:
Violetta

Violetta, who has suffered from tuberculosis, reflects on her unexpected feelings of love toward Alfredo, the sincere and kind man who has kept her company during her illness. Convinced that she is not destined for true love, she vows to live a life focused on earthly accomplishment and freedom.

Lui che modesto e vigile	Modest and watchful, he
folleggiare di gioia in gioia . . .	visited me when I was ill
all'egre soglie ascese,	and ignited a new fever by
E nuova febbre accese	awakening my love.
Destandomi all'amor.	
. . . Follie! Follie! Delirio vano è	. . . Madness! Madness! This is
questo! . . .	vain delirium! . . .
. . . Sempre libera degg'io	. . . Always free, I must
Folleggiare di gioia en gioia . . .	flit from joy to joy . . .

—GIUSEPPE VERDI,
LA TRAVIATA

Back in DC, Yoni reaches out to me again. I invite him to Mimo's annual Fourth of July party at the national Capitol, figuring it will be the perfect place to introduce him to some of my single girlfriends. But as fireworks shimmer over the Washington Monument, Yoni takes my hand.

His timing is terrible. The very next morning, I leave for a monthlong music festival in Tel Aviv. I'm working with the grande dame of the Metropolitan Opera, Joan Dornemann, and her team of conductors, directors, and coaches. She's tough as nails, but no one knows or loves opera better than her. Every night, without fail, I come home to a phone call from Yoni. Talking with him is somehow familiar, but he's unlike anyone I've ever known before. He's confident yet humble—the type of person who boasts about being the captain of his high school football team, then in the same breath explains how he helped to maintain its title as the Losingest Team in New York State history. He's happy, kind, and unashamed. I ask him about what he wants to accomplish with his life, and he responds after a thoughtful pause—"I want a house by a lake where my wife and I can grow old together." In the midst of the desperately lofty ambitions that populate the opera world (mine included), talking to him is a much-needed release—like taking off my heels after a long day of performing. I can talk to him about singing, work, PH, my family—nothing seems to faze him. Yoni is comfortable, both with himself and with me.

As my program nears its end, Yoni asks me to visit him in New York. I tell him no. The next day, I change my mind. I've already booked a ticket to DC, but my red-eye flight has a layover at JFK. I decide to pack a change of clothes in my carry-on and jump ship in NYC. Yoni arrives at the airport just as the sun crests the city's distant skyline. I practically sleepwalk into the car and drift off as we drive along the Long Island Expressway.

I awake, disoriented. *Where am I?* A strange bedroom with bare walls. I open the curtains to reveal a winding street. To the left, a cul-de-sac, to the right, a seemingly endless row of identical split-level midcentury homes. . . . Long Island? *Ah. Yoni's house.* Slowly, my morning comes back to me. The flight from Tel Aviv. Fixing my makeup in the airport bathroom. How *late* Yoni was picking me up. Meeting his mom. His sister—and how much she already seemed to know about me. . . . *Were waffles involved?* There's a knock at the door. It's Yoni. He's made plans for the afternoon. I wash up, change my medicine, and meet him downstairs.

The list of acceptable first dates for someone with PH is notably short. My diet's extreme restrictions on salt, combined with recent tummy sensitivity due to a hike in my Flolan dosage, makes eating out uncomfortable. I generally avoid crowds and their accompanying germs, so that rules out most performances. Sports are nearly impossible. Hiking, a no-can-do. Just walking at a normal pace can be hard. A plain cup of tea is one of the few options unlikely to land me in the hospital. Maybe that's why I've turned down so many second dates—I'm always wondering if I'll outlive another outing.

Yoni and I catch a train into the city. He sits smiling next to me, but I can't help but feel trepidation. *Is this really a good idea?* We arrive in the city and Yoni charges up the subway stairs. I nervously, slowly follow behind. He looks around for three or four minutes, then turns around and charges back down into the subway. We see City Hall, Union Square, his favorite bagel shop, a random park, all in a similar fashion. It's not clear whether we're on an unconventional sightseeing trip or just plain lost. When I ask Yoni to slow down, he grabs my hand and drags me behind him. *Does he think I'm flirting?!* At the top of yet another set of stairs, my world begins to spin and tunnel. "Yoni!" I yank my hand away from his, stopping in the middle of the sidewalk. "I don't think you understand. I *really need to slow down.*"

He stops, walks back, and wraps me in his arms—holding me for a moment as people stream out of the subway around us. Then he kisses my head and something electric passes through my body. I tell myself it must be static.

"I'm sorry," he whispers. "There are just so many things I want to show you."

We stop for dinner in Little Italy. I try to navigate the menu of heavy pastas and salty pizzas, but even my plain salad leaves me feeling queasy. I end up packing most of it up in a takeaway container. My stomach settles a bit as we continue down the Bowery. We walk in silence, palms loosely pressed and fingers laced together. The August night is just cool enough that the warmth of Yoni's hand is welcome. A quiet euphoria sets in.

Every few blocks, I remind myself of all the reasons this can't be right: He's not Mormon. My health is failing. We live in different cities—soon to be different continents (I'll be returning to Europe at the start of autumn, and Yoni to Chicago). *He was late to the airport.* I've never been in a real relationship before, but this one *must* have too much going against it to ever work out. I don't know how many more chances I'll have for romance, but I'd rather never start something with Yoni in the first place than have it end badly. I decide it's best to cut it off right here and now—

"Yoni, thank you for the evening, but I think we should just be friends. I like you. I care about you, but trust me—there's no future for us. You do *not* want to date me."

"What are you talking about?" he asks, laughing.

The monologue I've been piecing together in my head since our train ride spills from my lips, "I won't have sex with you. I don't drink and, if I were dating you, I'd expect you not to drink either. My family is crazy demanding and time consuming. And on top of all that, I'm dying. You're great, but I don't want to play around anymore. I'll never have kids . . . I probably wouldn't even live until a wedding. Not that either of us are even thinking about that, of course. You're charming and handsome and young. You have everything ahead of you. You really, really don't want to date me, Yoni. I'm way too complicated."

Yoni pulls me toward him. In a panic I tuck my head into my neck like a turtle and his chin collides with my eye. Both of us laughing now, he takes a deep breath and slips two fingers beneath my chin to guide my lips to his. We kiss and I evaporate into the warm summer night along with the steam, smells, and shouts of the city around us.

Stopping, we gaze into one another's eyes for a moment before crossing the street. Then, right in the middle of the crosswalk, Yoni grabs hold of my waist and kisses me again. It's intoxicating. So much so that I realize I'm going to barf. I push him away and stumble toward the other side of the street, grabbing for the take-away bag from the restaurant. Yoni shoves it into my hands just in time for my dinner to be reunited with its leftovers. He runs to buy a bottle of water for me as a homeless woman with her cart shakes her head at me kindly.

"Already, honey bear?" she tsks, in disbelief. She thinks I'm drunk (and *not* on love).

The next morning, there's a knock on the door of the guest bedroom at Yoni's parents' home. I pull the door open just wide enough to see Yoni on the other side, smiling nervously.

"I just want to make sure you're all right," he says.

I smile, nodding my head yes. Leaning into the crack in the door, he presses his lips against mine. I look into his eyes and smile for just a moment before I shut the door, lean back against it, and slide to the ground.

Through the door, Yoni tells me he loves me.

Even though we've been friends for years, I barely know him. Other than the random occasional lunch, we haven't spent significant time together since the campaign we met on. It seems crazy—almost inconceivable—that he would say something so big so soon. But even stranger is the fact that I love him too. Despite the religion and the airport and the PH. It's complicated and early. But I've never felt this way about anyone before. *So this is what all those divas die for,* I think to myself. *I totally get it now.* This is love. Soon, Yoni and I will be back in different cities leading very different lives. Maybe I'll never see him again after this weekend. But even if it only lasts for a few days, there's no denying this is the real thing. When I see Yoni later that morning, I tell him I love him too.

When I return to Baltimore a few days later, there is another heart catheterization. The emotional trauma of 2008 has taken a serious physical toll. The right side of my heart is nearly four times too big and its function is seriously impaired. For the first time since we've met, Dr. Girgis grounds me. I can't return to Europe, and I have to cancel my performance schedule for the rest of the year.

I move back in with Mimo and Yoni leaves for Chicago to begin graduate school. I've never fallen in love with an actual person before, and I'm not sure how best to proceed. Shouldn't Yoni have a family? A *real* life? Maybe I could find someone who shares my passion for music or at least my faith or just continue not having to worry about more family than I already have. Reluctantly, Yoni agrees that we'll date other people. If neither of us find someone we want to be with more than each other, then we can try to make the long-distance thing work.

With nothing else to do, I go to receptions, parties, church, and catch up with old friends. I start dating again, more to pass the time than anything else and to keep my side of my deal. Some of the men are Mormon, some aren't. Some are people I've known for years and others I've just met. At first, it's fun. But soon enough I can't help but notice that it doesn't feel *right*. Somehow, Yoni and I are just a natural fit. In comparison, anything else feels forced. By October, going out with others brings on pangs of guilt. A month later, when Yoni and I see each other again, we decide to be exclusive.

Managing a long-distance relationship is kind of like leaving dough to rise: there's potential for something great, but if left unattended for too long, it can lead to a sticky mess. Every month, Yoni and I alternate visits, shuttling back and forth between Chicago and DC. It's maddening, exciting, and exhausting. I can't avoid the fact that Yoni is a complicating factor in an already impossibly complicated life.

By September 2009, my countdown clock has wound all the way down. Doctors almost never tell patients how long they have left, because it varies. Life expectancies are culled from averages, not scientifically laid out, patient by patient. None-theless, I'm on the tail end of the typical expectation for some-one with PH. I'm still here, as alive as I've ever been. But at twenty-six years of age, I can't help but feel that I'm living on borrowed time.

Yoni and I have been together for a year, but that's about to change. As I drive to BWI to pick him up from the airport, I wonder how we fell in love in the first place. It's not that I don't love Yoni anymore. I love him very much. But I need to focus right now more than ever. I have to make the most of every moment I have left. And that means focusing on my first love: music. When we break up, Yoni will find someone lovely. She'll do things that I can't or don't or won't. She'll be able to have his babies and make his parents happy. Yoni will be a wonderful father . . . I won't get over him easily, but I'll manage. Rounding the bend toward the Arrivals terminal, I've made my decision. I feel good. Except for my legs. There's something funny about my legs.

Yoni's waiting on the curb. He gives me a kiss and we're off to lunch. As we make small talk on the way to the café, I go over a rough draft of a speech in my head: *It's been a wonderful year, Yoni. I have truly learned so much from our time together. But at this moment in my life, I must make a choice: to love a man, or love art. I'm afraid you already know how I must answer. Yes, dearest. As much as it pains me to say it—seriously, though, what's up with my legs right now?*

I look down. My wide-legged trousers are stretched taut across my calves like leggings. Pulling over, I shimmy up a pant leg to reveal my lower extremities have morphed into those of an albino pachyderm. This is not good.

Edema, swelling in the limbs, cankles—all telltale signs of heart failure. For me, a little edema isn't unusual. But not like this.

I feel like I'm wearing three pairs of wet wool socks underneath my skin. I switch seats with Yoni and he drives me straight to the ER. I guess my speech will have to wait.

Visiting the hospital isn't abnormal for me. Between bronchitis, pneumonia, heart catheterizations, or other complications from care, I usually end up in-patient at least three or four times a year. Be it in Budapest or Baltimore, the ER is always complicated. I've waited as long as ten hours to see a doctor, all while hanging out in one of the germiest environments in existence. As we pull up to the entrance, I mention Mom's uncanny ability to cut through red tape. Yoni furrows his brow—"Why don't we call her?" He heads inside, phone glued to his ear, while I hang back in the car.

The car windows magnify the heat of the Indian summer's noonday sun. Thoughts of love and cankles swirl through my mind as my extremities expand even further in the heat. Fifteen minutes tick past on the clock, but it feels like hours. Yoni emerges from the hospital pushing a wheelchair.

"Your mom is unreal," he boasts, opening my door and helping me into the chair. He rolls me to the admissions desk, passes me the phone, and Mom's on the other end. "Charity, don't say anything. I've been talking to the nurse—"

"Thanks, Mom. Do—"

"Charity, honey, I love you, but please don't interrupt me. I'm in control. I know what I'm doing. Just give me to the nurse." I obediently hand the phone to the nurse who's just appeared, as if summoned by Mom's voice. She nods emphatically as she chats with Mom and takes my vitals. After hanging up the phone and asking the routine questions, the nurse takes my hand and stares kindly into my eyes—"Honey, we're all praying for you."

Through charm and sheer force of will, Mom has parted the

sea of medical bureaucracy and just like that, the great white doors of emergency medicine open graciously to receive me. On the other side, a pair of police officers stand outside a flimsy pastel curtain while a gin-soaked man with a scraggly blond beard leers at me from the next bed over. A nurse hands me a neatly folded paper "gown." It's not quite Versace, but it does the job. She yanks my curtain closed and I change as Yoni steps out to park the car.

Pain-fueled moans join a chorus of beeps and buzzers, all underscored by the percussive expletives of the drunkard on the other side of the curtain. It sounds like an avant-garde production of *Lucia di Lammermoor*. Peeping through my curtain to look for Yoni, I instead see my neighbor—or rather, his bare behind—wandering down the hall a few feet away from me. As if on cue, he turns, scowls at me, then vomits and poops on the floor, thus completing the grotesque mise-en-scène.

This is going to be an interesting visit.

I call Liberty. She's finishing up her senior year of college just up the street at Johns Hopkins University. Once classes are done, she promises to come see me. Both of us know there's no need to rush. Liberty has memorized all my hospital routines. She arrives, handing Yoni and me Chipotle burritos. Ravenous, I unwrap mine and pause. *Ooph. That looks like my ankles right now.* (Really, the resemblance is uncanny.) I bury my face in it anyway. On a normal day, this behavior would have been reckless. The salt in one Chipotle burrito would be enough to send me to the ER if I weren't already there. But I'll soon receive high-dosage diuretics to drain all of the excess fluid from my body and I can afford to binge. A nurse enters and inserts an IV. Flushing cold saline through my veins, she hangs a fast drip of Lasix—a common diuretic—and my deflation commences.

There's no way to tell time in the ER. No wall clock, windows, or television to mark the passing seconds. Our phones ran out of battery a while ago. Other than the occasional discharge or new admission, little changes. Time is a construct created by healthy people. I've peed buckets by now and my ankles are almost back to normal. Discharge must be imminent. We say goodbye to Liberty and plan to meet her for lunch the next afternoon.

Soon after, the nurse enters my room and informs me that the managing physician wants to formally admit me to the hospital. Around midnight, we move to an official hospital room. After a visit from a nurse, a tech, and a doctor, Yoni pulls up a couple of chairs and we settle in for the night.

———

Morning arrives and I wonder why I'm still here. My legs are back to normal. I should be able to go home. As I contemplate my situation, a small woman with a puff of grayish brown hair, big eyes, a colorful caftan, and a wide smile enters holding a large box with an inflatable mattress. It's my grandmother, Mimo.

This year without my grandfather has been hard for her. Her fifty-seven-year marriage left Mimo with the conviction that sharing the joys and sorrows and challenges of life with a partner is the most important thing someone can do. Now, she's investing herself in helping others find that same purpose. My relationship with Yoni gives her endless occupation, and she's committed herself to making sure we stay together. It's driving me a little crazy.

"Charity," she says, with her characteristic accent, "you look beautiful. Yoni should see you. Where is he?" Her eyes grow mischievously wide as she looks for him.

"He's getting some lunch for you," I say. She seems pleased at the privacy.

71

"So," Mimo asks, getting right to the point, "when are you going to marry him?"

"And what if I don't *want* to marry him, Mimo?" I respond, starting to get annoyed.

"Well, you know what they say . . ." she continues cryptically.

"Tell me." *Wait! I take it back!* But it's already too late. Darn my big mouth.

"If a man marries a woman before she is twenty-four, she's doing him a favor. If a man marries a woman after she is twenty-four, he is doing her a favor!" She's visibly pleased with this gem. *Should I laugh or scream? I am* in the hospital. Even if I don't take it too seriously, my own grandmother should! *Inhale. Exhale.*

"You do love him, don't you?" she demands.

"Of course!"

"Well, he obviously loves you," she continues. "Charity, do you think that he is a dime-a-dozen man? Sleeping on the floor of a hospital room just for the privilege of being with you? Do you think other men will be like this? You are crazy if you do. Most men will run away. They will run away as fast as they can when there is a problem! They do not want to deal with that. They want someone who is nice and easy. You are very nice, but you are not easy. This is not easy. I was married to your grandfather for almost sixty years and at the end, even I wasn't here like this, sleeping in the hospital beside him!"

Ever since I turned twenty-five, it seems everyone I know has become obsessed with marriage. It's like it's the only real life goal worth having. It doesn't matter that there is work, meaning, and opportunity beyond being a wife and mother. It's as if without a witness, a woman's life isn't worth living. It's not that I don't care about marriage, it's just not my top priority. I enjoy being in love, but I could care less about nabbing a ring. The thought of dying a virgin doesn't bother me. There are so many things I want so much more than sex. I want to sing and perform. I want to be happy. Most of all, I want to live—preferably without worrying that I'll faint, that my heart will fail, or that I'll contract an infection and die. A man is nice, but just being *alive* is a miracle. Making great music elevates that to the sublime. Mimo just can't understand.

"Mimo. I don't think *either* of us are ready to get married," I edit myself, on the edge of patience.

"Charity, he obviously is and you are not getting any younger." Mimo isn't editing anything. "He wouldn't still be here if he wasn't ready to marry you. More importantly, he's the one. I knew it with your sister and now with you. This is your match. If you let him go, you let go of your chance at happiness in this life."

Before I can respond, Yoni bursts in with sandwiches—blissfully unaware of our conversation.

"Mimo!" he says, embracing my grandmother. "Do you want turkey and cheese or egg salad?" Mimo gives me a knowing stare, then redirects her energies to lunch.

Hours later, golden glories stream through the window marking dusk's arrival. It's time for Mimo to go. She walks over and gives me a kiss, admonishing me, "Don't forget. Not a dime a dozen." With that, Yoni walks her out to the car.

A nurse enters and takes my vital signs. There's another visit from a doctor, and some unappetizing collection of food comprising dinner. The day's events blend together as Mimo's words echo in my mind.

Yoni returns from the car, smiling. "You know, being in a hospital is like being in a full-service hotel. We have a TV, the staff is nice, we don't have to clean . . . it's like a little vacation!" He has this childlike ability to see the good in everything and everyone. Later that night, as I watch Yoni snoring contentedly, the side of his face glistening with drool on Mimo's sagging air mattress, I know she was right about at least one thing: Yoni is not a dime-a-dozen kind of man.

An alarm jolts me awake just past midnight. I look at my monitors—my blood pressure has dipped to 49 over 36. A breathless resident arrives in my room. I'm fond of freshly minted MDs—they're bright and enthusiastic—but hospital mortalities spike in the first months of residencies and it's just after the start of the school year. While the attending physician is still at home, my life is in inexperienced hands.

A parade of residents promenades into my room. By now, my blood pressure's fallen even further. This is one of the rare moments that I'm grateful to know my disease so well. "Let's stop the diuretics," I suggest, knowing the medication lowers my blood pressure. A bespectacled resident with floppy hair quickly removes the drip. My numbers stop their descent.

"That's good," says his pretty colleague with a crown of black braids. "But we need to move those pressures up fast."

Within a few minutes, the team of young doctors has devised a plan. They start a new IV drip and, slowly, my blood pressure begins to tick upward. By the time the managing physician arrives around 2:00 a.m., my numbers have stabilized. The doctor and the residents disperse—except the one with the glasses. He pulls up a chair outside my room and sets in for the night.

Where is Dr. Girgis? I've been in the hospital for four days and I haven't seen him once. My water weight is practically gone and I've had just about enough of the hospital. I'm preparing my second speech of the week in my head when the door swings open.

"Charity, what have you been eating?" It's Dr. Girgis. He is not pleased.

"What do you mean?" The question catches me off guard.

"There were over twenty pounds of water on you . . ." he notices something out of the corner of his eye as his sentence trails off. Marching over to my belongings, he picks up a crackly foil bag. "Potato chips, Charity?!"

I burst into tears. Other than the strategically consumed burrito that I've conveniently forgotten, I'm maniacal about limiting my sodium intake. No bread, no processed foods, no eating out. On a typical day, I consume less salt than naturally occurs in a bunch of celery.

"Dr. Girgis!" I exclaim. "They have no salt! Look at the nutrition panel! The swelling wasn't because of salt—I promise!"

He looks at the bag, then pauses gravely—

"Charity, you are very sick. You have advanced right-heart failure. I have tried to facilitate your life, but the only way I can continue to do that is if you wait for a transplant."

I feel my heart in my throat. Transplant has always been a possibility, but to me, it sounds more like a death sentence. In medicine, lung transplant surgeries are considered some of the most complicated. Massive blood loss, permanent nerve damage, and failure of other vital organs are commonplace. With a 50 percent mortality rate at five years, the prospect for long-term survival is bleak. On top of that, I have no guarantee of a life worth living post-op. During the surgery, large breathing tubes are shoved down the larynx through the vocal cords. If that doesn't destroy my voice, the tracheotomy (where doctors cut a hole at the base of my throat to hook up a respirator) almost certainly will. So I'll be left voiceless *and* disfigured. That is, if I even survive.

I understand Dr. Girgis's point, but people have been saying I've been deathly ill for five years and I'm still here. No one in Europe could even tell I was sick! I can't believe lungs that can facilitate the kind of singing I've been doing could be in that bad of shape. I start to protest, but Dr. Girgis cuts me off—

"Five years ago when you came into my office, I believed your prognosis was better than other specialists did. It was. You've sung all over the world. You've built a career. You have a real life." He looks me squarely in the eye. "As the doctor who was confident that you could do everything you've done over the past half decade, I must tell you your situation has changed. You are going to die very soon if you do not receive a transplant. I would like to activate your listing at the Cleveland Clinic immediately. You can leave for Ohio tomorrow. Your chances for a successful surgery are higher if you wait there."

I've grown used to medical sermons, but not from Dr. Girgis. I don't want to believe he's right, but I at least owe him the respect of considering his advice.

"I'll pray about it, Dr. Girgis. If I'm supposed to go to Cleveland, it will become clear to me by tomorrow afternoon. I'll let you know my decision by then." I have faith that miracles happen. If that miracle has to be a transplant, God will let me know.

Dr. Girgis has cared for me for five years. Without him, I never would have reached my twenty-sixth birthday. He's always been focused on letting me live my life as best as I can, even with my disease. But looking into his eyes now, I realize that Dr. Reda Girgis knows I'm dying. So his response surprises me—

"That should be fine," he answers. "I'll see you tomorrow."

It's another early morning in the Nelson Building at Johns Hopkins Hospital. I'm greeted by a familiar nurse. Reddish-blond curls frame her pleasantly freckled face. Pale blue-green eyes, tired from a night of too little sleep, peek out from behind bangs. She's seen and cared for me more than a few times over the years. We're friendly and I respect her insights. She's seen thousands of patients. She knows what she's doing. When the hospital's quiet, she'll frequently linger to chat with me about family, religion, politics, or medicine. This is one of those mornings.

After getting an update on her sons, I have a question for her no one else seems willing to answer. "My doctors want me to get a transplant, but honestly, how successfully do people recover? Do you think I'll ever sing again?"

The nurse pauses, looking at me with kind concern, down to the floor, then back at me again.

"Charity, you know, I see these patients every day—the patients who need lung transplants. You're not like them. They are very, very sick. You still seem healthy." She pauses, stammering a bit before collecting herself. "A lot of people don't make it. I don't know how you'd sing. The scarring is terrible. If you live, your life will never be normal. Don't do it."

A sense of righteous vindication envelops me. "That's what I've been worried about. Thank you so much for being honest."

"I know you're going to be OK, honey," she says. "You won't need this." With that, her beeper goes off and she leaves.

"I don't like her anymore," Yoni says as she shuts the door.

"That's only because she doesn't agree with you," I counter.

"No. That was just reckless," he maintains huffily.

But as I settle in with my breakfast of applesauce, salt-free crackers, and plain oatmeal, I feel smug validation about the wisdom of my medical opinions.

I lie in bed thinking about the nurse's words, and about two young women I knew with PH who died shortly after receiving lung transplants. I'm not afraid of death. I'm afraid of not living the life I'm meant to live. Singing is more than a career or lifestyle. It's a relationship I've nurtured for decades; it's my identity. Like family and faith, it is completely integrated into who I am. Destroying my voice for a chance at a life without it seems like a grievous betrayal of everything I've worked so hard for.

If the transplant is successful, I'll no longer have PH, but at least with PH I have hope. I wake up each morning hoping that someone, somewhere, might find a cure. Once I have a transplant, that hope will evaporate. I'll live out the rest of my truncated life on borrowed time, my vocal cords destroyed by surgery. Even in the unlikely event that I can sing, I fear I'll spend the bulk of my time hiding from anything that might bring infection or rejection. Ultimately, I just don't think a transplant will do me much good.

Around noon, Kimber arrives from DC. I'm not supposed to have "juvenile visitors," but Kimber sneaks my twenty-month-old niece into the hospital, making me outrageously happy. Soon, my sister-in-law, Sarah, arrives as well. Yoni needs to get out of this hospital room almost more than I do, so he's going to a baseball game with a buddy while my sisters are here. While he's gone, we'll pray together about the transplant listing.

Sarah sits down and I explain the situation. I mention that I think Dr. Girgis almost sees himself in a paternal role—which is fine as long as he's not recommending overly conservative medical practices. I know that a transplant is a gift, I just don't think it's very well suited to me. Kimber and Sarah nod sympathetically.

Together with my sisters, I bow my head and begin to pray. I ask for reassurance that I should refuse to be listed for a transplant. Immediately, I feel a pit in my stomach.

When we finish our prayer, I open my scriptures. They read:

O ye wicked and perverse generation, how have ye forgotten the tradition of your fathers; yea, how soon ye have forgotten the commandments of God . . .

Have ye forgotten so soon how many times [The Lord] delivered our fathers out of the hands of their enemies, and preserved them from being destroyed . . .

Yea, and if it had not been for his matchless power, and his mercy, and his long-suffering . . . we should unavoidably have been cut off from the face of the earth . . .

Repent, or he will utterly destroy you from off the face of the earth.

—ALMA, 9:8–12, BOOK OF MORMON

The rebuke rings like the clarion's call, reverberating through my whole body. There's no way around it. I need to listen to my doctor's counsel. I'll die without a transplant, so I'll proceed with the listing without delay. When Dr. Girgis comes in, I concede.

"You win."

He looks up quizzically. "What do you mean?"

"I'll go to Cleveland—as soon as it's possible. I'll drive with my family."

A smile spreads across his face and his shoulders straighten, as if lightened. "You cannot drive. You'll need a nurse. There will be a special plane for your medical transportation. You'll leave tomorrow."

While I think the plane is overkill, I thank him reluctantly.

He leaves, his smile still intact. "Thank you, Charity. You're doing the right thing."

Kimber and Sarah go home to their families. Yoni's still at the game, leaving me alone for the first time in over a week. I call Mom.

We've been in a protracted debate about whether she should fly to Baltimore or stay in Denver. Now the answer is clear. At this point, the average wait for a pair of lungs is a thousand days. I know they've just implemented a new scoring system based on medical need, but I assume it will still be at least six months before they find a match for me. There's no use in Mom flying to Baltimore. She can meet us in Cleveland later in the week. I'll be there for a while anyway. I'm an adult now. I want Mom to stay at home with the little kids until my surgery is scheduled.

Since Dad's death last year, Mom's time is more precious than ever. She's the only parent for my four youngest siblings. One of the most challenging aspects of having a sick child must be having healthy children. I need a lot of attention. For every hour Mom spends with me in a doctor's office, I receive ten more— time sacrificed by my brothers and sisters.

Facing the reality of a sibling's death is hard. I know that well enough. I think back to Lincoln's death. We loved him perfectly because he *was* perfect. I am not. My siblings see me with all of my flaws. They see my pettiness, my vanity, my self-righteousness, and hypocrisy. So much love is thrown my way, but too often, my siblings are lost in the morass of disease. They're expected to show perfect love toward me, regardless of the havoc my disease wreaks on their lives.

"But, Charity, if something goes wrong, there isn't any more capable advocate for you than me," Mom argues. Her points are as valid as my own.

"I know. But I don't need an advocate yet," I insist, shifting the conversation to other important, unresolved business. "Mom, I know this seems like odd timing, but I need to break up with Yoni."

"Why would you do that?" Mom asks.

"He doesn't need this," I insist.

Mom's quiet for a moment. "Honey, I know that you have questions about Yoni. I don't know if you two will end up together. But you're his girlfriend, not his mother. He's an adult. Don't act like you're doing him a favor by breaking up with him. He can choose whom he wants to marry and whom he wants to make a life with, just like you can." She continues, "I am sure there are other people who could have been wonderful in a situation like this, but he loves you and he makes you happy. If you find someone who makes you happier, then we can have this discussion. But has that happened yet?"

"But, Mom, love is doing what's best for both people. Especially with everything that is going on, I think it's best to end this relationship now," I say emphatically.

"You do whatever you need to do," says Mom, "but I have a feeling if you decide to end this now, you'll regret it deeply."

A nurse comes in to take blood and I say goodbye to Mom. Maybe this whole medical drama is about this relationship and my unwillingness to accept romantic love as a valid life course. My declining health has all but stopped my career. Maybe, just maybe, this mess can save me from myself. I always have a life plan and God always has another plan for me. And here I am, facing the most serious decision of my life with Yoni as my hospital roommate.

Yoni returns that evening. I know he hasn't slept much, but he finally looks rested. "Honey," I say, "I'm going to Cleveland."

He wraps his arms around me and kisses my head. "I'm so proud of you." He really does seem so happy.

I, on the other hand, still have serious doubts. But maybe it won't be so bad. We have time. I like Cleveland. There's a good voice teacher in town. I have friends there from my debut at Severance Hall a few years back. I'll paint. Maybe I'll work with the symphony again. Even if it's not a thousand days, it will be a long time before we find a match. I know that much. In that time, they might even find a cure for PH!

Yoni climbs into bed and puts his arm around me. Then he opens the newspaper to a story that has nothing to do with the challenges we face. The moment is as perfect as possible. I can't believe that I'd considered ending our relationship. Hopefully, I won't need a transplant. But as I drift off to sleep, I'm pretty sure I need Yoni.

"Wake up!" Yoni nearly shouts, shaking me by the shoulder.

What's wrong this time? It's still dark outside and morning hasn't yet arrived. I suspect another problem with my blood pressure.

"Charity, you have to wake up!" Yoni repeats. "It's a miracle!"

A cure? Is my PH gone? Yoni hands me a phone.

"Charity, this is Dr. Marie Budev at the Cleveland Clinic. We have lungs!"

ENTR'ACTE

Three surgeons stand in an operating room, loose blue scrubs wrapped in an almost translucent gossamer against a backdrop of sterile white. In the foreground, Dr. Ken McCurry, a former high school football star who has matured into the star cardiothoracic surgeon at the Cleveland Clinic and, quite possibly, the best in the world. Behind him is the program's senior fellow, Dr. Chris Benjamin. Sleek and toned, he looks more like an Olympian than a doctor. In the back, the new fellow, Dr. James Yun, looks on. The youngest of the doctors, Yun is in his late thirties, a mop of precociously salt-and-pepper hair peeking out from underneath his surgical cap. The path to becoming a specialized surgeon is long and punishing. Often, training isn't completed until well into a doctor's forties. It is a calling as much as a career.

On the table before the three lies a body. Female. Twenty-six years old. Bilateral lung transplant. The doctors don't know much else about her—she'd said something about saving her voice as they were rolling her into the OR—but she is their patient, and that's enough.

"Ten milligrams propofol," orders the anesthesiologist. Administering the medication one milligram at a time, he stops as the patient's blood pressure goes into a nosedive. "What the—" Desperately he adjusts the meds and the drip, but the numbers are in free fall.

One alarm sounds. Another. Soon, a chorus of beeps, bells, sirens, and buzzes mark this great and terrible moment of mortality. The line on the heart monitor goes flat. "No blood pressure. No pulse," announces the nurse, an urgent matter-of-factness forcing her voice.

"Paddles," says Dr. McCurry, taking the handles from the nurse. "Starting ACLS protocol," he announces. Shocking the pale chest one. Two. Three times. Then again: one, two, three times. The alarms silence; one after another, beeps and bells return to their regular intervals. It's like nothing was ever wrong.

"Open her up, Benjamin," McCurry directs, stepping away.

"Iodine," calls Dr. Benjamin. The nurse places tongs clutching a piece of dripping ocher gauze into his hand. He draws slow, burnished strokes across the arc of the rib cage around to the side of the back, then up and over to the other side. "Scalpel." Entering under the left armpit, he follows the curvature underneath the patient's breasts across her chest, tracing a thin red line of entry. His hand is steady and his cuts are clean. "Oscillating saw." The nurse hands over the live power tool, the blade vibrating so quickly it's almost invisible. Sliding it between the incision, Dr. Benjamin grinds away at four rigid ribs that bar entry to the organs beneath them. "Rib spreaders." He takes a medieval-looking device with two curved metal prongs from the nurse. Placing the prongs in between his incision, he opens them wide, pulling away skin, muscle, and bone to reveal a set of lungs and a faintly pumping heart beneath.

As Dr. Benjamin attaches clamps to hold the spreaders in place, Dr. McCurry steps toward the patient for a second time. Benjamin moves aside, his bloody hands now bent up at the elbows, and McCurry begins his work.

The monitor above magnifies the inner workings of the heart

and lungs. Between the heart's right atrium and ventricle, his expert eye immediately spots a complication. Instead of opening and closing tightly, the tricuspid valve is flailing its way from open to slightly less open. The seasoned surgeon knows PH patients frequently need some kind of heart surgery, but this is extreme. Watching his patient's engorged heart struggle through every beat, McCurry knows the question is not if, but when she will crash again. He notifies the nurse, "A tricuspid valve repair is needed." With that, an impromptu open-heart surgery begins.

With extreme precision, the surgeon tightens the tired valve. An alarm sounds.

"No blood pressure. No pulse," calls the nurse again. McCurry takes the device, shocking the heart directly this time—one, two, three—until it begins to beat again. "We need ECMO," he calls.

The nurse looks toward him, startled. ECMO is the final form of life support. Playing understudy to the heart and lungs, the machine cycles a patient's blood mechanically outside the body— oxygenating it and then pumping it back into the body's labyrinth of veins. If a single infected cell finds its way into the machine, it's sent on a trip through the bloodstream, polluting everything it passes. Only used in the most desperate of situations, it is extremely expensive and exceptionally dangerous. ECMO can be a bridge to life or an express train to death.

"ECMO. Now," McCurry orders again, calm, but firm.

The nurse quickly shaves the patient's inner right thigh and douses it with iodine. Dr. Yun takes McCurry's place at the table. A shining example of good parenting and first-generation American work ethic, Dr. Yun is known for his precision, attention to detail, and ability to process disparate pieces of information quickly. "Cannula." A nurse hands him the metal trocar made for placing large tubes inside of arteries. With the gargantuan needle, he inserts a thick tube into the patient's femoral vein. The nurse places another trocar in his hand and he stabs again, pushing a second tube directly into the femoral artery. The machine whooshes on and one tube fills with dark maroon blood. In a matter of seconds, the second tube ferries the newly oxygenated blood, now candy-apple red, back into the body. After securing the cannulation with long strips of gauze, the doctors return to the transplantation.

McCurry begins carving away the fascia holding the sickly lungs in place. Hours into his work, he notices the lungs beginning to swell. "Benjamin!" he calls. "Please check the acidity in the patient's blood." McCurry continues to sort through the pleural fibers as the lungs continue to expand.

"The patient is in cardiogenic shock," declares Yun.

"Administer high-dose pressors and fluids," McCurry orders. He and the fellows step back as the anesthesiologist sets up a high-dosage drip.

Blood coagulating on Dr. McCurry's uplifted incarnadine hands, he breathes a deep sigh of concern and goes over the surgery thus far. In two hours, two vital organs have failed a total of three times. Even the best-case scenarios for this surgery involve placing the patient on nearly every form of life support available. The prophylactic antibiotics plus fluids dripping into the patient's bloodstream will likely expedite renal failure, and if the kidneys go, blood pressure will spike—leaving dialysis as the only option to stem the intense bleeding.

As if on clue, McCurry looks down and the patient's chest cavity pools with blood. "We need dialysis and setup for massive transfusion protocol immediately!" he orders, soaking hemorrhaging liquid away from the surgical site with handfuls of gauze.

In just a few hours, this surgery is edging its way to the top of a long and storied list. A scene flashes in his mind of a surgery from earlier in his career. It was the most challenging surgery he had ever performed and the outcome had not been good.

This time, he promises himself, history will not repeat itself.

In the thirteen and a half hours since I was wheeled into the OR, Mom, Yoni, and a gaggle of siblings have commandeered planes, trains, and cars to gather in Cleveland. Now, they've strewn themselves across chairs, tables, and floors in the operating suite's waiting room—snoozing as they wait for any news of the surgery's progress. Finally, Dr. McCurry enters.

"Charity Tillemann-Dick?" he questions, clearing his throat and startling the family awake. "Are you the family of Ms. Charity Tillemann-Dick?"

"Yes!" confirms Mom breathlessly as the rest of the kids shake themselves into consciousness. "How did the surgery go?! Is she awake? Can we see her?" Her hopeful inquiry is met by a pregnant pause.

"She's alive," the surgeon musters. "I'm very surprised she was approved for surgery, though. She was extremely sick."

"*She's alive?*" reiterates Mom, making certain fatigue isn't responsible for that part of the news.

"Yes," he answers tenuously.

Sensing the lack of positive messaging, Mom's political training kicks into high gear. "We're so grateful you are such a skilled surgeon! I know with your help, Charity is going to be amazing," she insists. "She'll sing and dance and run—she's going to do all the things she never could—all because of you and her donor!"

"Mrs. Tillemann-Dick—"

"You did the impossible! You're a miracle worker!" she exclaims as the rest of the family finally returns to waking.

The exhausted doctor cuts her off—"Mrs. Tillemann-Dick, during surgery, your daughter received more blood than was in her entire body in transfusions, which are ongoing. I performed an unexpected emergency heart surgery on her and she was placed on every form of life support available to us. Incorrect preliminary measurements necessitated we cut the new lungs down to fit inside of her frame. She is currently in a medically induced coma and has a very long road ahead of her—"

"But she's going to be OK," Mom manages. "She's going to be your star patient!"

Dr. McCurry stares at her blankly for a moment. "The nurses are doing their best to clean her up for you now. They'll get you when she's ready."

For the first time in recorded history, Mom is speechless.

Turning to leave, Dr. McCurry pauses to speak, softer this time. "That reminds me—her body is badly swollen and the ongoing bleeding is quite severe, so we left her chest cavity open. —Just be aware of that when you go in to see her."

As McCurry offers this detail, he heads out the door and a thud reverberates through the room. Tomicah has fainted.

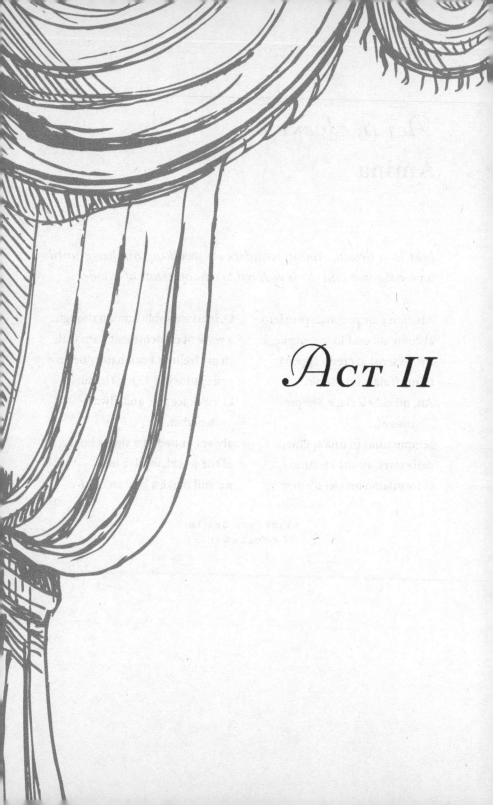

Act II

Act II, Scene 1:
Amina

Lost in a dream, Amina wanders sleepwalking aimlessly until love wakes her and she is restored to a happy state of wonder.

Ah, non giunge uman pensiero
al contento ond'io son piena:
a miei sensi io credo appena;
tu m'affida o mio tesor.
Ah, mi abbraccia, e sempre
    insieme,
sempre uniti in una speme,
della terra, in cui viviamo
ci formiamo un ciel d'amor.

O, inconceivable human thought
a wave of contentment I am full:
In my feelings I can hardly believe
you assure me, O my treasure.
O, embrace me, and always
    together,
always united in a single hope,
of the world, we live in
we will make a heaven of love.

—Vincenzo Bellini,
La Sonnambula

For five weeks, I've been lost amid a drug-induced dream of Homeric proportions. Finally, the curtains close on the oneiric epic and the lights of my subconscious dim to black. Gradually, a blank cosmic weightlessness turns to sleep. It's time for me to wake up.

Quietly, my body—back, arms, legs, hands, fingers, toes, neck, head—reenters my state of awareness. Light streams through lashes as my eyelids flicker open. *Or wait . . . am I still out?* Three backlit figures stand over me. *Are they angels? Did I die in the end—after all that?* Slowly, my eyes adjust to the room's ambient fluorescent glow and I recognize the smallest of the blurry outlines. A smile spreads from one cheek to the other—*it's Mom. She's here! Auntie Margot is right beside her. I'm awake! I'm alive.*

"Charity," Mom says, beaming, "these are the nurses who helped save your life."

Through blissful tears, I cry out, "Thank you!"

Only there is no sound.

Where is my voice?

Inha— I can't inhale. I try to take a deep drag, but no air gets past the yawn of my open mouth into my throat. Gulping down, I notice that my mouth is bone dry and I can't seem to swallow. Wide-eyed and confused, I look toward Mom.

"Everything's all right, sweetheart," Mom reassures me. "Margot and I have been here by your side, twenty-four hours a day. Everything is going to be OK now. Everything is going to be OK. Just smile and say 'thank you.'"

There are no two people I trust more to facilitate my care. Margot is my dad's older sister and one of my dearest relatives. Mom and Margot have been two of my most devoted friends and advocates since my medical ordeal began. *I'm alive.* I tell myself.

I'm alive. That's what's important right now. Using gratitude to suppress my terror, I smile wide. Then I mouth, "Thank you so much!"

A parade of ICU nurses and medical technicians drop by as Mom and Margot squeeze my hands. I feel like Rip Van Winkle after his hundred-year nap. All of these people know me, my family, my story and I have no idea what's going on.

"There are so many people who have been working to keep you alive, Chary. You've been on such an adventure!" Mom smiles with her Pollyanna optimism.

"Yoni?" I mouth, hoping he might be in the waiting room.

"He's in Chicago," Margot explains, "but he's been here almost every weekend and he'll be back soon."

Anticipating my next question, Mom adds, "Dr. Budev isn't on service, but she's been in and out to check on you."

After an afternoon of silent meet and greets, I find myself slowly drifting off. I wonder how long I'll stay asleep this time?

I jolt awake. *My pump. Where is my pump? I'll die without my pump!*

It's easy to lose track of time in the ICU. Robotic tones and bereaved sobs combine in a horrific, minimalist score. Auditory and visual patterns are on repeat. Artificial lights drone overhead 24/7, beeps and buzzers sound incessantly, and the caregivers' workdays never end—making it nearly impossible for me to know whether hours, days, or weeks have elapsed since I first woke up in this bed. Other than the dream I had during my coma, the past six weeks are a blur. I forget the call about the lungs. I forget the flight to the clinic. I forget asking Dr. McCurry to save my voice. But of all the things I don't remember, one is most pressing—I don't know I've had a lung transplant.

Shaking my head back and forth in hopes of catching someone's attention, I try to tell them what I know must be the problem—the reason I'm in the hospital.

"My pump!!!" I mouth silently toward Mom, "My pump is gone!!!"

Frantically nodding my head (I can't seem to move anything else on my body), I gesture down toward my waist where the pump should be attached, hoping someone will understand. Finally, Mom notices my flailing and sits down next to me.

"What's wrong, Chary?"

"My pump is gone!! It's why I'm sick!!" I mouth desperately.

"Slowly," Mom instructs.

"MY—"

"My," she repeats.

"PUMP"

"Bump? . . . Pup?" she pauses, squinting. Suddenly, her eyes light up. "Your pump! No, Chary. No pump."

I adamantly nod my head. *Yes, pump!*

"You don't need Flolan anymore, sweetheart. You've had a lung transplant."

". . .What?" I mouth, at a loss.

"A lung transplant, Chary. It was a very hard surgery and you were in a coma for five weeks." She takes my hand in hers. "You were so sick, Chary. Too sick, really." With that, Mom recounts the highlight reel of my surgery: the valve tightening, the transfusions, the flatlines. With every detail, my eyes grow wider. Then she goes into the aftermath—

"They kept your chest open for two weeks because you were so skinny that the lungs didn't fit inside of you! Then, once they closed you up, your kidneys stopped working and all we could do was pray to see pee in your catheter's tube. . . . Oh! And there are those awful sores we found—when I first saw them I thought they were big black roaches crawling all over your back. That's why the hospital got you this special bed. It blows silicon around inside to improve your circulation. They told me you might feel like you're lying on hot sand, which could be uncomfortable. But you haven't had a single new sore since they brought it in, so just try to pretend you're at the beach. OK, sweetheart?"

I look around me. I'm not sure even *my* imagination is up to that task. Gray curtains separate my 8 x 10 corner of the loud, crowded ICU from my neighbors'. My bed is pushed against the wall, with two overburdened IV poles flanking it like a morbid DIY headboard. On the other end lays Mom's main residence for the past five weeks—a cream-colored easy chair a nurse has wheeled in from the waiting room surrounded with a nest of papers and blankets. On the counter by the sink, there's a basket filled with something shiny. I squint—they're candies for every doctor, nurse, and technician who comes by my room (perhaps provided in hopes that they'll come by my room more often).

Besides Mom, there are the machines and monitors. I follow their snaking cords back to my own body. Beneath my thin cotton gown, four blue tubes are still draining excess fluids from my chest; a central line in my neck connects to a half-dozen IVs, all of which administer medications continuously; an arterial line in my wrist is used to draw regular blood samples; a large tube in my neck connects to a respirator a few feet away; a feeding tube hangs like a bullring from my nose. Are there two more tubes by my legs? I can't be sure. *Actually, I'm glad this isn't the beach,* I think to myself. *I'm not exactly in swimsuit shape right now.*

"You're doing so beautifully, Chary sweetheart," says Mom, contradicting my every instinct and observation. She beams down at me and squeezes my hand. I really *want* to believe her, but . . .

No. I'm *going* to believe her. I'm alive. I'm with Mom. *I don't have PH anymore!* As far as I'm concerned right now, that means I'm doing beautifully. I smile up at Mom as she continues to fill me in on what happened while I was away.

Only once the deluge of information begins to quell do I consider my surgery's most fraught implication. My brow furrows in apprehension. "Someone died?" I mouth to Mom.

Pausing for a moment, Mom squeezes my hand again—harder this time. "Yes," she confirms. "They aren't allowed to give us any details about your donor, but somebody did die. If they hadn't, you never would have gotten your transplant. We're all so grateful to them, Chary."

It's like the wind has been knocked out of my new lungs. Somewhere, as my family was celebrating my second chance at life, another family was aching over the loss that had given me that chance. Was I benefiting from that family's sorrow—somehow complicit in their tragedy? Mom and a nurse try to comfort me, but to no avail. My tears continue into the next shift of nurses and the one after that. Mom has finally fallen asleep in the recliner when Nick, a handsome blond nurse I met right after waking up, steps into the room.

"What's wrong?" he asks, crouching next to my bed.

"Do you know anything about my donor?" I mouth slowly, so he can understand. "Where was she from?"

"Actually, I was on the team that went to get your lungs." My eyes light up. "Your donor was from Texas," he says.

I know he's breaking protocol, but I have to know more.

"How old was she?"

"A year older than you."

"How did she . . . ?"

"A car crash." He pauses. "I hope you can meet the family one day. They would love you."

As he speaks, my guilt transforms into something lighter. All of a sudden, I feel a kinship with this woman. (I think of her as a woman, though Nick hasn't actually shared her gender.) I appreciate that she's very much a part of me now. My new life has been born of not one, but two atonements: the first, Christ's, was divine. The second, mortal—offered by a kind stranger's final act of compassion. My donor may have had other possessions, but she's entrusted me with her lungs and, consequently, my life. In this moment, sewn together, silent, and atrophied, I make her a promise: *I'm not just going to recover, I'm going to really live.*

Why haven't I eaten yet? It's been at least a day—maybe two— since I woke up, but somehow I haven't seen a crumb, much less eaten one. My doctors had promised me that if I got a transplant, I could eat whatever I want. No more salt restrictions or nausea. Feeding tube mush wasn't exactly what I had envisioned. I'm not hungry, exactly, but I'd give an arm for a La Casita tamale. (It's not like my arms are much good for anything else right now. Might as well bargain them away for Mexican food.)

"What do you want, sweetie?" asks my mother.

"Food!" I mouth, but it's impossible for her to understand such a formless little word.

After taking a moment to consider, Mom's sapphire eyes brighten—"Blink twice for no, once for yes," she instructs. As she cycles through a list of questions I blink twice, but my eyelids move so slowly there's no way of knowing the blinks come as a pair. When she asks if I'm hungry I blink once, but this time it's followed by an involuntary second blink—making it look like "no." Mom continues, and I have to work so hard to control my blinking that I forget her original question entirely. Moving to Plan B, Mom finds a whiteboard and marker. But when she puts the marker into my hand, it slips from my atrophied fingers. Next, Mom produces laminated pages with pictures of different problems, letters, and numbers. But it's no use. I can't even point. Later, I'll learn fine motor skills are one of the last things patients with general muscular atrophy regain. For now though, I just know the aids don't help. Mom puts them away, fixes her eyes on me, and focuses her mother's intuition.

"You're hungry?" Mom's face falls. "Sweetie, you're not allowed to have food yet. You need to have a chew-and-swallow test first."

Patients on respirators are unable to cough, so they seriously risk pneumonia if they aspirate anything into their lungs. A supervised test to prove swallowing capacity might seem prudent to most people, but I haven't eaten anything in over a month and the Food Network is playing in my room nonstop. I don't want to take a test. I want to eat. I begin to panic. *What if I die before I get to take the test?! I could totally die before I get to take the test. Then I'll never eat anything ever again.* . . . I stop myself and try to remain calm. *So I can't eat. What* can *I do?*

"Drink?" I mouth hopefully.

"I'm sorry, sweetheart," she answers, kissing my forehead. "I can't give it to you."

After learning about my donor, this is the second hardest thing I've heard since waking up. Tears stream down the side of my face, filling my ears with a drip of self-made saline. I'll take the tubes, smile through the speechlessness, and even be good humored about the extreme pain. But no *food*?

"Oh, Chary. Don't cry," Mom implores. But I can't stop. I don't want to stop. I'm exhausted. My chest feels like it's about to explode. I'm hot. Uncomfortable. Frustrated. I *want* to be happy for Mom—to put on a good face for the nurses and be a model patient—but this is simply too much to bear.

Finally, Mom caves—"I can wet this sponge and I can put it in your mouth?"

Really? If I had known my future meals would be limited to a "wet sponge," I would've eaten another burrito at the hospital in Baltimore. *Still, I guess it's better than nothing.* I nod unenthusiastically. Mom moistens a sponge with hospital ice and places it in my mouth. It's a slight improvement over the taste of dry flesh and muscle. I flash Mom a faint smile of gratitude. Then, her eye glimmers.

"Chary," she says in a hushed voice, "would you like me to wet the sponge with Diet Sprite?" My eyes spread anime-wide in happy expectation—I have never wanted anything more. "Yes?" she confirms. "OK. I'll go get it."

I can barely contain myself. Somehow, the difference between a small sponge soaked with water and a small sponge soaked with Diet Sprite is everything to me right now. Waiting for Mom to come back from the vending machine feels like waiting for Santa on Christmas Eve. When she finally returns, she carefully closes the curtain and swears me to secrecy—"I'm really not supposed to do this. Don't tell *anyone.*" A task easier done than said in my current state.

As she pours Sprite into the puce-colored cup, the fizz and pop of carbonation heralds the upcoming event. She lowers the damp sponge into my mouth and an explosive sparkle of lemon and lime erupts on my tongue. My mouth feels like an ad for vintage soda—the kind girls post on summer-themed Pinterest boards. I am joy incarnate.

Over the next days, my mind is consumed by thoughts of Diet Sprite. Its taste. Its temperature. How to get more of it. To a third-party observer, my obsession with this carbonated beverage would seem a mania born of boredom or even madness. But with all the pain and discomfort of my life within the ICU, Diet Sprite has become my reminder that there's more to life than ventilators, arterial lines, and fluorescent lights. There are also nice things—things like cold lemon-lime soda. My life has always been about accessing and sharing whatever's most wondrous and, in my current condition, Diet Sprite is pure liquid wonder. All I want is more. I fill my recumbent waking hours by plotting how to increase the number of covert "meals" Mom will allow me; they're the sunrise moments of my days of late. Then a respiratory therapist comes in, interrupting my scheming.

"I'm Chelsea," she says, a few errant curls escaped from her dark brown ponytail framing her face. She looks friendly and concerned, but there's not an ounce of pity in her. "I'm here to help you breathe on your own. But first, I want you to sit in a chair."

"I want to stand up," I retort, silent and eager.

She smiles knowingly. "That's great! But first, you have to sit in a chair."

I'm always up for a challenge. After everything I've been through, sitting in a chair doesn't exactly seem to qualify. "Let's just do it now," I mouth nonchalantly. It will be nice to be off my back—whatever the method.

Within a few minutes, two muscular men in matching polos and khakis come into my room—Rodney and Raven, my lift team. Enlisting the help of Mom, my aunt Margot, Chelsea, and four other nurses, they orchestrate the treacherous transfer, untangling cords and repositioning IV trees to ensure I don't get caught on anything during the trip.

"One . . . Two . . . Three . . . Lift!"

For the first time in weeks, a cool breeze rushes past the back of my neck and my braids tumble down behind me. Momentarily weightless. Then, with great care, the team sets my fragile frame down in a red seat next to my bed. "You sit so straight!" Upon hearing Mom's praise, I square my withered shoulders just a little more.

Chelsea explains that sitting will help to rebuild my core muscles, which in turn supports my diaphragm and my new lungs as I learn to breathe on my own again. She only expects me to sit for half an hour or so today, but I know this is just an audition for real life. The sooner I succeed, the sooner I can go home.

So I sit the hardest I've ever sat. An hour passes. Then two. At first, the hustle and bustle of the ICU around me keeps me engaged, but somewhere in the third hour my bottom starts to ache. Around hour five, I'm sure my bones are about to grind through my skin at any moment. Mom places pillows underneath me and rocks the chair back and forth, but it does little to alleviate the pain. Still, I won't lie down. Sweat beads down my face. I've been sitting still in an armchair for the past seven hours, and it's the most strenuous workout I've ever done. As the evening news begins to play on the television, we finally call Rodney and Raven to move me back to bed. I fall asleep immediately, totally spent.

The next morning, I declare I'm going to stand up. Mom's eyebrows raise, but she and my nurse Nick rally the necessary troops and support staff. Short story short, it doesn't go as planned.

Afterward, Mom stands at the end of the bed, rubbing my feet like I'm a prizefighter recovering from a KO. "Next time, baby. Next time."

I snort to myself. Never before has "baby" been a more apt term of endearment. I can't speak, I can't walk, I can't eat solid food. I rely on Mom for everything. I haven't sat on a toilet in weeks and I'm pretty sure everyone in this ICU has seen my bare bottom. I thought this transplant would allow me to take my life back, but the only thing I'm taking back now are my assumptions about whether I'll ever recover from this ordeal.

It doesn't get better. One night, I lay awake as the ventilator noisily pushes air into my body through the tube in my trachea. Just as I feel like my chest incision is about to burst from the pressure of my hyper-expanding lungs, the machine sucks the air back out. It's miserable. *I can't go on like this much longer.* No sooner does the thought enter my head than I feel pressure on my chest. But this time it's different. The ventilator is still on, but I swear I'm suffocating. Shaking my head back and forth, I try to get Mom's attention.

"What's wrong, sweetie?" she asks. Stress shoots through my body as the sensation worsens. Alarms and buzzers begin to sound.

"Hello?!" Mom shouts. "We need a nurse immediately!"

An unfamiliar respiratory therapist rattles through the curtain. Ducking behind my bed, she switches something on. Suddenly, I'm all right.

"What was that?!" demands Mom.

"Well, if we can get her off the respirator here, then she doesn't need to go to the respiratory care unit," the therapist chirps back.

"Where's Chelsea? Bill? Matt or Marco?" Mom cycles through the list of my regular respiratory therapists. "She's never had an issue weaning off the vent with them. She hasn't even realized she's doing it!" My eyes widen realizing this deception.

Another man enters the room. Medium height with thinning hair, a reddened nose, and tired eyes. "Annette," he explains, "discomfort is inevitable in this process."

"Well, I think that's pretty obvious, David," she shoots back. "None of this has been 'comfortable' for Charity."

He sighs and crouches down next to my bed—"Charity, I'm David Wheeler. I'm the head of respiratory education here at the hospital. I know it feels like you're running a marathon every day—probably like you're drowning at the same time—but the longer you stay on the vent, the harder it will be to get off. You've been doing so well we decided to be a little more aggressive. I'm sorry if it was too much. Do you want a break?"

Reluctantly, I shake my head no. I'm embarrassed at how tired I am all the time. I've only been lying in bed or sitting in my chair, but there's no rest. I'm constantly exhausted. The few things I do—helping air in and out of my lungs, holding up my body—seem to expend more energy than I have to begin with. Most of the time, I feel like the dictionary definition of "pathetic". But for the first time, it seems someone else understands my complete fatigue.

Staring genuinely into my eyes, David squeezes my shoulder. "I promise that you won't drown."

It's exactly what I need to hear.

———

After the years of care I've received in both places, I can happily and confidently state that both the Cleveland Clinic and Johns Hopkins richly deserve their burnished reputations as two of the best hospitals in the world. The former represents the cutting edge of integrative medicine; the latter embraces an older style of medical apprenticeship. Regardless of their different approaches, both institutions jointly excel in one meaningful respect: saving lives that seem past saving. Lives like mine.

But even the best hospitals are unforgiving workplaces. Doctors do the work of healing—a purview formerly relegated to magicians, saints, and angels. For patients and families, it often feels like there's no room for human error, miscalculation, or even a less-than-sympathetic bedside manner. Oftentimes, there isn't. Yet, even after years of study and scores of lives saved and improved, physicians remain eminently human. And the pressure inevitably invites discord. People always expect their health-care professionals, *especially* their doctors, to know more and be better. But while wisdom and goodness are in ample supply at the clinic, no doctor is omniscient or omnipotent. They are lim-ited not only by their own subjectivity—personal histories and character flaws—but by all the untold mysteries still concealed within an infinite amount of information. The best medicine is collaborative—often minimizing risks of human error. My chal-lenge is knowing when to take center stage, highlighting possible mistakes or oversight, and when to fade into the chorus of this human drama.

After a long day of work on the respirator, Mom enters with a glass of Sprite. She closes the curtain while I enjoy my contra-band. All of a sudden, the curtain is flung open. A square-shaped man with dark hair and a shiny scalp walks toward Mom and takes the Styrofoam cup from her hands. He takes a whiff.

"What is this?" he sneers.

"It's Diet Sprite," chirps back Mom.

"You're giving this to her?" he asks.

"I'm just wetting the sponge with it, Doctor," she clarifies. "It's the one thing that Charity enjoys here."

"She's not in the hospital to enjoy it. She's on the brink of death and you are putting her at risk for aspiration. She hasn't even had the swallow test!" he hollers.

"Could I please speak to you in the hall, Doctor?" Mom calmly steers him to the other side of the curtain.

Amused that Mom thinks I won't be able to hear them, I eavesdrop on their sparring from the relative peace of my sand bed.

"A huge amount of work has been done to keep her from dying and I won't let you come in here and destroy that," the doctor hisses. "I will not let you back in that room if you do not promise me that you will not give the patient ice or Diet Sprite again."

How dare he. I've never seen this doctor before. My mother, on the other hand, has been at my side, twenty-four hours a day, seven days a week. Mom knows my charts, my condition, my medications, my bedsores, my wounds, my tubes, my preferences, my strengths and weaknesses. Better than anyone in the entire hospital. Better than anyone in the world. How dare this brute threaten her! I don't care that aspiration is, *technically speaking*, a medically valid concern. That's not important to me. But ice, Diet Sprite, and Mom are everything I have right now. *So why does this doctor seem so intent on taking them all away?* I have to stop him. As the conversation continues to escalate outside, I ask the nurse next to me to please open the curtain. She obliges and I wave down the doctor.

"Doctor," I mouth, "can I just have a swallow test?"

"What?" he snaps.

The nurse translates: "She wants the swallow test here."

"In the ICU?" asks the doctor.

"Yes," replies my nurse. "We've been trying to get her up to a real unit for a few days with no luck."

"I know I could pass a swallow test," I mouth hopefully.

"What is she saying?" asks the doctor.

"That she's ready for the test."

He walks over near the foot of my bed. "I promise that after we get you up to a real room, we'll give you a swallow test," he says with an air of condescension.

"No, thank you," I mouth. "Now, please."

"I can't deal with this." He throws up his hands and walks away. "Nurse, make sure she doesn't get any more Sprite." I glower at his back as he leaves. All I want is a break for Mom . . . and maybe some Diet Sprite.

Why haven't I seen Yoni yet? My comatose dream was crazy, but at times instructional. For example, when I woke up, I knew beyond doubt that Yoni was the love of my life. But each time I ask Mom about him, she says the same thing: "He'll be here soon." She's been saying that for nearly a week now.

Yoni is in his final year of grad school at the University of Chicago. I know he has work and school and that he lives 500 miles away, but all I want is to see him. To hold his hand. To hear him say he loves me. Initially, I take each of Mom's reassurances literally. I stay up late into the night, sure that Yoni has just caught a late flight into Ohio. When he arrives, it will be magical: I'll tell him how sorry I am for wanting to break up with him—how much I love him and how I want to be with him forever.

One night, as I'm staging our overwrought reunion scene in my head, I see him. He's standing in the distance, his distinctive plume of black hair parted on the side with a natural mini-Elvis curl in front. Some combination of joy, desire, and love fills my body and beams out through a smile I've been saving just for him. Even without my glasses, I can tell he's smiling too. *He's lost weight*, I think to myself as he nears. Finally, he speaks: "What a pleasure to meet you, Miss Tillemann-Dick! I'll be filling in for Paula tonight."

It's not Yoni. As the new tech takes my vitals, I try to mask my disappointment. But the tears flow despite my efforts.

"Annette," the doppelgänger calls to my mother. "Something is wrong."

"Honey! What's the matter?"

"Yoni!" I mouth in anguish.

"He's not here, honey," replies Mom.

"I know! Why not?!" I demand.

"Slow down, sweetie. I can't understand you."

I try to collect myself, pausing between every word—

"Why . . ."

"Why . . ." Mom repeats.

"Won't."

"Won't."

"Yoni."

"Yoni."

"Come?"

"Oh, Chary." Mom smiles and shakes her head. "You wanted to break up with him before the transplant!"

"I was wrong!" I mouth through silent sobs.

"*I* told you it was a mistake," she reminds me.

I sob harder.

"Oh, honey, he'll be here soon. If you just—"

"No, Mommy! Not soon. *When?!*" I demand, halfway certain she's just trying to hide the fact that Yoni finally followed my advice and found somebody else. Someone less complicated.

"The day after tomorrow," she clarifies to my happy surprise. I stop crying. "He's coming Thursday night. After school."

"Promise?" I ask, unable to wipe the tears from my sodden face.

Mom finally understands. "Charity, that boy loves you. If you ever want to get rid of him, it's not going to be that easy." She leans down to kiss me on the forehead, drying my face with her sleeve. "And I love you too."

I start to cry again. While I've been preoccupied by thoughts of myself and Yoni and Sprite for the past two weeks, I've all but disregarded the person sleeping at the other end of my bed every single night. No one could ever understand what Mom has done for me. Probably not even me. She's been my protector. My friend. My cheerleader. She's made the entire hospital ward believe that if they do their job—if they go above and beyond what's expected of them—I'll survive. I'll thrive. Against all odds, I'll sing again. Despite my hopeless situation, she really believes it. She's made all of us believe it, too.

"I love you too, Mommy." If I could speak, I'd say it in a whisper. She smiles, resting her hand atop mine as I drift toward sleep.

———

Music schools and summer programs often stage operatic potpourris: productions made up of disjointed scenes from different operas combined into one show. Disparate characters make cameos to allow inexperienced singers coveted minutes of stage time. The ICU—where I'll ultimately spend nearly seven weeks—is strangely evocative of these patchwork operatic productions. A constantly shifting cast of nurses, doctors, neighbors, family members, and friends enter from stage right or stage left for discreet moments of tragedy or commotion, comedy or intrigue—all uncomfortably strung together by the brief intermissions of my semi-waking naps.

One day, I awake to a man with a broad smile, shaved head, and tightly packed physique flexing my foot back and forth. It's Dean, my physical therapist.

"Annette," he says with a kind, raspy voice, "I'm just so impressed at how you've been working with her. This passive motion does wonders for regaining muscle strength." He looks up at me with a grin. "So whaddya say, Charity? You want to walk?"

Finally!

After giving me and Mom a long list of exercises, Dean exits. I make my own goal: by the end of today, I'm going to move my arms. All afternoon, I silently shift my shoulders from side to side, heaving my spindly arms onto my chest. Once that's done, I work to bend my elbows and rest them on my bed rails. By the time the evening shift arrives, I've finally done it: my hands are resting on my torso, fingers interlaced just above my diaphragm. My progress is so slow that no one even notices what I feel is a major achievement. I'm too embarrassed to call any attention to it myself (or how much it exhausted me). Soon, I just fall asleep.

When I wake, my fingers are locked in the same position. I try pulling them apart, but to no avail. I've pinched a nerve. Now, my hands are stuck in a clawlike position and my left arm won't straighten. For every step forward I take, I go two or three back. Clutching my newly lame arm, I feel hopeless.

Later that evening, Mom stops reading to me to go talk to a man in a long black overcoat at the end of the hall. Through a crack in the curtain, I see him nod his head as Mom speaks, glancing back toward me occasionally. As their conversation continues, I wonder if he's a doctor or a nurse. I've met Dr. Yun and Dr. Benjamin—the surgical fellows who assisted in my transplant. Could this be the legendary Dr. McCurry? He turns so I can see his face.

It's Yoni?

It's Yoni!

"Look who's awake!" he says, opening the curtain and coming to kiss my forehead.

"I was beginning to think you'd never visit!" I whine.

"Huh?" Yoni is clueless.

I mouth it two more times.

"Hon," he finally says, "I love you so much, but I have no idea what you're trying to say." He takes my hand and kisses it instead.

Mom walks over—"Chary, Yoni's going to stay with you for a while."

She leaves the ICU, and Yoni smiles at me. "I missed you." He hasn't quite figured out how to read my lips, so he talks instead. He tells me for his birthday he asked all of his friends for extra airline miles so he could visit me every other weekend. In Chicago he's working three jobs on top of school—it's a lot for anyone to handle, and I start to fear that adding a girlfriend in critical condition is a recipe for failure. But it's like he's read my mind— "You know, I was worried that with everything this semester, my grades would take a beating. But you know? They've been the best grades of my academic career!" I smile, grateful. Relieved. Two of his professors want him to pursue a PhD. He's received a fellowship to travel to Israel next spring and he has a job offer from a major foundation. I'm so proud of him.

"Yoni," I say with my sweetest face.

"Yes, Chary?" he says, smiling back.

Batting my lashes, I mouth, "I want Sprite."

"Huh?"

"*Sprite.*"

A stern expression quickly replaces his doe eyes.

"Sprite? No! You aren't supposed to have that, Chary!"

"Mom gives it to me!"

"Well, you should know I'm not your mother," he shoots back.

I protest, but he's immovable. Salty tears of betrayal begin streaming down my face. Ever since I woke up, all I wanted was to see Yoni. But now that he's here, he's forcing me to choose between the two things that are most important to me: Yoni and Diet Sprite. He should have just stayed in Chicago. . . . *No. Stop being spiteful, Charity.* But it's too late. The gossamer is gone. Yoni is no longer a fantasy I can conjure to entertain myself during dreary days in the ICU. He's real. He's here. And he's as maddening as he was when I first fell in love with him.

The curtains open and Mom's head pops in. "Yoni," she chirps, "why is Charity crying?"

"She wants soda or something, but the doctor told me she can't drink anything," he explains.

"Oh. That is what they say. But she actually swallows quite well!" Mom says encouragingly.

"Annette," replies Yoni, dead serious, "I'm not going to just sit by and watch while you threaten Charity's life!"

Mom and I roll our eyes at each other.

"Well, then why don't you go get dinner? I'll stay with Charity and when you get back, I'll go and rest again. How's that?"

"I haven't eaten since this morning . . ." Yoni reflects, his stomach easily distracting him from his crusade. "That would be great. I'll be right back."

"Take your time!" Mom calls after him.

After Yoni's had his dinner and I've had my Sprite, Mom goes back to her underutilized hotel room to sleep in an actual bed. Yoni and I settle into our old hospital routine. He takes out two books from his carry-on and pulls up some interesting articles on his phone. The first one he starts reading is about suicide bombings in Baghdad. As he relates the brutality of humankind, the comfort of our old habit is replaced by anguish. I'm so tired of pain—both my own and others'. I begin to cry yet again. Yoni looks over and stops, mortified. "Chary, honey, are you OK? Does something hurt?"

"Please stop," I mouth. "Too sad."

"Oh . . . Oh, Chary, I'm so sorry. What would you like to read?"

I point to my scriptures, left open to the Sermon on the Mount, and he begins anew:

"Blessed are the sick, are the poor, are the meek, for they shall inherit the kingdom of God . . ."

I drift off to the sound of Yoni's voice.

Act II, Scene 2:

Norma

The high priestess Norma offers a prayer and a plea for things to return to the way they once were, promising protection and fidelity.

Ah! bello a me ritorna	Ah! Return to me beautiful
Del fido amor primiero;	In your first true love;
E contro il mondo intiero . . .	I'll protect you
Difesa a te sarò.	Against the entire world.
Ah! bello a me ritorna	Ah! Return to me beautiful
Del raggio tuo sereno;	With your serene ray;
E vita nel tuo seno,	I'll have life, sky
E patria e cielo avrò.	And homeland in your heart.
Ah, riedi ancora qual eri allora,	Ah, return again as you were then,
Quando il cor ti diedi allora,	When I gave you my heart then,
Ah, riedi a me.	Ah, come back to me.

—VINCENZO BELLINI,
NORMA

*D*ear Heavenly Father. I love You very much. I really do. I know You've already saved me from death a few times for which I am very grateful. While I'm sure there are serious miracles going down, this is not easy. And let's be honest—my name is Charity—not Patience. If I wasn't such a big Jesus fan girl, there's no chance I'd be such a good sport. But really, Heavenly Father, can You please do something? Mom and the kids have been through enough of this. Not to mention me. By the way, I still don't have a real hospital room. In Jesus' name, amen.

For days, my nurses, doctors, and techs have told me a room in the respiratory unit will open up any hour. From where I'm lying, ReSCU looks dreamy, and I'm eager to escape to this mystical unit. Practically everyone on my medical team in the ICU has been amazing: attentive, kind, responsive. But I'm lonely. Even in one of the best hospitals in the world, there's no avoiding the pain and confinement intrinsic to illness. Sometimes, I feel all but invisible. I get it. My friends and family are busy people. Time is scarce. But understanding that doesn't make it easier. Especially when no one can understand me. Does anyone other than Mom even care that I'm here? When my mind is left idle, the questions gnaw at me. I've had serious medical issues before, but I've never felt imprisoned by my body like this.

Late one evening, Rodney and Raven come into my room. I grin expectantly—whenever they turn up, things get better. Today, they don't disappoint. "Are you ready to move to a *real* room, Miss Charity?" Rodney asks.

YES! Yes! A thousand times yes! I can't actually say it, but they get the idea.

Mom gathers together her nest at the end of the bed while Nick puts a surgical mask over my nose and mouth. Then we're moving! Patient, nurse, tech, Mom, equipment; we all promenade down the hall together, a veritable microcosm of hospital life. This is the first time I've left the ICU in fifty days. My bed transforms into a magic carpet as cool air brushes past my cheeks. Without my glasses, the hospital's sleek, modern aesthetic softens into something almost whimsical. White and gray swaths flow past me like clouds, punctuated by the colorful pops of passing scrubs—indigo for nurses, viridian for techs, scarlet for phlebotomists. It's beautiful.

As we wind through the labyrinth of halls, I forget about the mask covering the lower half of my face and smile at every person we pass. Maybe it's my imagination—after all, I can't see very well—but they seem to smile back. Right now, anything feels possible.

We reach the ReSCU ward and I can't wait! I beam expectantly as Nick swings open the door to my new room. Then I stop smiling.

Simultaneously dim and fluorescent, the space is about the size of a midsized U-Haul; after we jam my bed, the respirator, two IV trees, and a chair into place, it's packed like one too. Rodney, Raven, and the team say goodbye and shut the door behind them, leaving claustrophobic silence in their place. Somehow, this room is even less comfortable—and more isolating—than the ICU.

Without a word, Mom opens a box at the foot of my bed and pulls out a handful of colorful papers. I squint—they're cards. Roll of tape in hand, Mom hangs a small print of Warhol's Campbell's soup can on the wall, "from Darrin and MaryJoy," she clarifies. Next to that she hangs a tiny Titian from our neighbor Katie in Denver. Then, a polar bear drinking cola and a photograph of a deep purple iris taken by Auntie Margot. A cartoon dog, a child's drawing. They're heartwarming, but I wonder if they might look less lonely on the windowsill. . . . *At least there's a window?* Mom turns to me and smiles. I smile back, unsuccessfully trying to ward off advancing melancholy.

Then Mom returns to the box and pulls out a second handful of cards. And they keep coming. More cards, then more boxes. There are old pictures and proverbs and *Far Side* cartoons. Glitter rainbows and baby animals. One card sings "I Will Survive" every time it flaps open. Within an hour, Mom has effectively wallpapered my room with greetings from family, friends, friends of friends, fans, well-wishers—each one, a new testament of love. Once the wall is filled, she sets out picture frames from my sisters on the windowsill and by the sink. Recently, I've felt alone—even abandoned. But the kindness pouring off every surface around me crowds out anything less than joy. This is the most beautiful hospital room I have ever seen.

There's a quick knock, then a new nurse swings open the door. "I'm here for your swallow test."

Finally! The nurse removes my respirator and places a flat cap onto the tube protruding from my trachea. "Say 'eeeeee,'" she instructs.

I wheeze air out of my throat, but no "eeeeee" follows. The blood drains from my face as, over and over again, I try to make a sound. Any sound. A minute passes, then two. But there's nothing.

"Sometimes these things just don't work out," the nurse grimaces as she pats my leg.

No. Please, God, no. I pray, *I need my voice.* Tears of desperation start down my cheeks. I shove air through my vocal cords as the nurse picks up the tube from the respirator. Just as she's about to uncap my trachea, a sound whispers through my lips; almost lost amid breath, a faint "eeeeee" wisps out. I try again, just to be sure. It's unmistakable this time. "Eeeeee." I say it again and again and again, tears streaming down my face, elated to hear my own voice after months of silence. Each time, the sound gets stronger. My vocal cords work.

Wiping a tear from her eye, the nurse puts down the respirator tube. "All right then," she says, both of us collecting ourselves. "Now for the swallow test."

The nurse pulls out a cup of bright green pudding. When I balk at the color, she elaborates—"It's so we can tell whether you've aspirated any into your lungs." She lowers a spoonful into my mouth. It's disgusting, but I gulp it down anyway. Then she uncaps my throat and feeds a suction tube into my lungs. It comes up clean.

"Looks like you're good to go!"

With that, I'm cleared for food. Well, soft food. A smorgasbord of dietary supplements is laid before me—every flavor of Ensure and Carnation Instant Breakfast. The variety is impressive, but totally unappetizing. I don't want to eat (or rather, drink) any of this.

What I really want is a salad, but that trends more "crunchy" than "soft." *What can I eat that isn't flesh-toned liquefied nutrition but also won't make me aspirate?* A bean burrito . . . Not just any bean burrito, though—Taco Bell! Shiloh, visiting for the weekend and always game for a good-food adventure, arrives later that evening with an entire bag of them. Oozy, cheesy, salty, semi-solid—this is my heaven on earth.

Now that I'm only ninety pounds, you might think I could afford to eat quite a few burritos. But my massive weight loss comes with risks; soon, my potassium soars from the beans, and I have to retreat to Carnation Instant Breakfasts. Sometimes, I feel like not dying is the only "battle" I've actually won during this recovery. I'm already facing weaning from the ventilator, regaining basic motor skills, talking, walking, recovering from the wounds on my back, front, and head. Now it doesn't even look like gaining weight is going to come easily. *If only I'd had this problem during my pageant days . . .*

Other challenges notwithstanding, my primary purpose in ReSCU is to wean off the ventilator. As the vent fills and empties my lungs, it disables me from speaking, eating comfortably, and regaining my core strength—the kind I need to breathe, walk, and live in general. Some patients are here for days, some weeks, others months. Everybody hopes my stay will be short. As for me, I'm happy with my progress in getting off the vent—it's set lower and lower every day—but then what? Doctors, nurses, techs, Mom—they do everything for me here. I miss my independence.

Russ, my respiratory therapist, has decided today's The Day. I'm going to breathe by myself, totally unassisted by the ventilator. Russ slips an oxygen cannula over my head and unhooks my ventilator. Then he presses a flat cap onto the tube at the base of my throat.

Inhale. Exhale. I'm breathing!

After a few minutes, I mouth a question—"Can I talk?" Shocked and delighted by the raspy croak that exits my mouth, the question answers itself. *I can talk!* Soon, they can't shut me up.

"Mommy," I say in a gleeful grumble, "I love you!"

Mom kisses my forehead, covering it in tears. "And I love you!"

I ask for a phone. We call Mimo. Kimber. Tomicah. I leave a message on Liberty's voicemail. My vocal fry takes center stage as we talk to grandmas, siblings, aunts, and uncles. I sound nothing like myself, but I'm so happy to be speaking that I hardly care.

After six hours, Russ reconnects the vent, finally silencing me again. I promptly fall asleep, exhausted.

I begin to breathe on my own for a few hours more each day. One morning, I hear the entire floor break out in applause. I ask my nurse what's going on.

"It's Bill—your next-door neighbor—he's walking!" she exclaims. "You won't be far behind."

"I want to be home by Thanksgiving," I declare as a new physician's assistant gives me a checkup.

Mom gasps audibly. "Charity, that's only two weeks away. Be realistic."

"If you keep up with the schedule you're on right now," interjects the PA, "I think that *is* realistic. Looking through your charts, you're making remarkably rapid progress." As he finishes up his evaluation, I'm beaming. Mom is not.

Over the past five years, Mom has done everything in her power to protect me from my disease. She's been there for every procedure. She's conducted endless negotiations with our insurance company and hospital after hospital after hospital, allowing the central conflict of *my* adult life to play out between my emerging opera career and my health—not my health and my insurance company. During the past two months, our lives have been lived in parallel. We spend the majority of our waking and sleeping moments side by side. But what Mom will never understand is that, no matter how tirelessly she supports me, I still must endure the most terrible aspects of this disease alone. I'm the one who has to be cut, stuck, and poked. I'm the one who begins each week unsure I'll live into the next. Mom thinks about—even obsesses over—my disease. But this disease is a physical part of me.

I know I wouldn't be alive without Mom on a host of different levels. But now that I can communicate, I want to start taking care of myself again. It's been so long since I've been able to communicate my needs and decide for myself—I'm desperate to start. The problem is, Mom expects to decide for me too, and, increasingly, our ideas of what my care should look like differ.

Following the past week's routine, I wake up and Russ takes me off the ventilator. But today, it feels like I'm hoisting a forty-pound weight off my chest every time I pull air into my lungs. After breathing unassisted for eleven hours yesterday, today I can barely go five hours before getting back on the vent. The following day, it's even fewer. The nurse runs to place me back on the ventilator when my oxygenation dips so much it triggers an alarm.

It gets worse.

"Charity, you need more pain medication," Mom pronounces with certainty. At this point, I can no longer speak—it takes too much energy to force sound out of my vocal cords—but I shake my head no. Pain isn't my main complaint. Still, Mom calls the nurse. "Charity is in a great deal of pain," she says. "She needs more meds. Right, Charity?"

I shake my head no again.

"She's still not totally with it," whispers Mom. (She's been unsure of my mental fitness ever since I woke up from my coma—a fact I find simultaneously offensive and amusing.) "I'd give her a bit more fentanyl."

I use whatever strength I have to, once more, shake my head no.

"Can you excuse us?" Mom asks the nurse. Increasingly uncomfortable between my mother and me, she gratefully bows out and shuts the door behind her. "How *dare* you counter me in public," Mom turns to scold me. "I have been here, day in and day out—a *slave* to your care. Do *not* contradict me."

"I don't want more medication!" I mouth. "I want less. The meds make me tired. And I don't want to get addicted to anything."

"Charity," says Mom, rolling her eyes. "People do not get addicted to pain medication recovering from surgical wounds. Pain medication exists for people like you!"

She's right. But still, I don't like the meds. They alter the way I experience the world: from the taste of food to the sound of voices to the way I process information. Life is my drug of choice—its side effects are why I love it.

The nurses have begun to find blood when they suction my lungs. While I'm sure I have pneumonia—it would explain the shortness of breath and the bleeding—my doctors and Mom insist that isn't the issue. To keep the peace, I agree to additional pain medication.

When my body absorbs the fentanyl, my world is reduced to bare sensation: heat, cold, light, darkness. Words recess into ambient noise; people flatten into two dimensions. I hate it. When it finally wears off, I'm left with a throbbing migraine and nausea—the kind meds can't fix.

The mid-November darkness settles early in the afternoon. As my window dims, a tall man with a chocolate complexion peeks through the door. "Charity"—his rich baritone voice fills my small room—"I'm one of the chaplains here. I've heard you've been having a hard time. Would you mind if I sang a song for you?"

I smile and nod my head. I'm just getting over a Fent headache and I haven't heard anyone really sing in months. I close my eyes and feel the air in the small room move as he inhales deeply. Swells of sound pulse over me as the chaplain belts the chorus of "Amazing Grace" with a rich, mature tone. His melody is a salve for my aching body. But its lyrics sting. Listening to them, I can't help but dwell on the grace I've received this year: from my donor, Mom, doctors, family, friends, and God. But no matter how hard I work, I come up short. I know grace has already saved my life; that grace will get me out of this hospital and, ultimately, lead me home. But all of this grace is frustrating.

I'm a glutton for miracles. But while other people get miracles like dream jobs, babies, debuts, and houses, my miracle is not being dead. Not dying has significant benefits. But before I got sick, my hard work was what people recognized and appreciated, not some visible or invisible hand of benevolence. Personally, I've always appreciated the human and heavenly hands at work in my life—trying to show my appreciation in the way I live and work and strive for worthy goals. And then I got sick.

Now, it's like that one Christmas when Santa obviously didn't get my letter. I have to be grateful for gifts I never asked for in the first place. Someone else has to lift my bags and hail my cabs. I need special food and perpetual hand sanitizer. I'm in a place of unending gratitude, and it can get exhausting. Some days, I'm *not* grateful that my sister carries in the groceries; I'm not grateful that my siblings are alone in Denver while Mom sleeps in my hospital room. I'm not grateful for the tubes coming out of my neck, my arms, and my chest—even though they're saving my life. I wish I had my own lungs. I wish I was back in Europe singing. I wish Mom was home in Denver sleeping in her own bed. I wish I caused less hardship and sorrow. I wish that, instead of giving me so many little miracles, God would have just given me the one miracle I most wanted. Wouldn't it have been simpler to just cure my PH? Or not give it to me in the first place! Don't get me wrong. I love miracles. And I *love* Jesus. I need grace every day. But in my life, the things other people get to claim as their own achievements turn into my miracles. It's like everything I do is accompanied by heavenly jazz hands.

As the chaplain sings the last verse, the message swirls through me in a vortex of frustrated, confused, resentful gratitude:

> *When we've been there ten thousand years,*
> *Bright shining as the sun,*
> *There's no less days to sing God's praise*
> *Than when we've first begun.*

I stifle my tears long enough to thank him before he leaves. Then I let loose. *Does God not love me enough, or does He love me too much?* Whatever it is, all of this grace is seriously messing with my head, my soul, and, most of all, my body.

Relearning how to breathe puts the body under tremendous stress. Retraining muscles, healing wounds and bones, regrowing skin—these all consume huge amounts of physical energy. Caregivers—doctors, nurses, therapists—need to push patients as far as they can go without leaving their body too weak to ward off infection. When the immune system is in perfect condition, it's a complicated dance. But when the immune system is suppressed, missteps are inevitable. Oftentimes, medicine is reactionary by necessity. With a transplant, you can only hope to be prepared for the inevitable mistakes.

Later that evening, the PA who evaluated me the week before drops back in to grab a piece of candy. He hangs back though, concerned by my drastically weakened condition.

"They're not giving her enough pain medication," Mom explains to him.

"Mmmm, I don't think so. She should be off of the ventilator by now, regardless of pain." As he's talking, a nurse comes in to suction the liquid from my lungs. He watches as thick threads of blood make their way up the tube.

"Hold on." He stops. "Blood? That wasn't there last week."

I nod in agreement, grateful that someone other than me finally notices. Mom looks at him quizzically.

"One of two things is going on," he continues. "Either, there were some large clots of blood that were jostled and a flap of tissue is growing around the trach tube in her throat, making it harder to breathe . . ."

"Or?" asks Mom.

"She has pneumonia," he concludes.

Exactly what I said! . . . well, mouthed.

Mom's not pleased. "Why hasn't anybody noticed this?!"

I noticed it, I think to myself. The PA offers another explanation—

"Think about it—how many doctors have you had?"

Mom and I look at each other. "I really don't know," she admits.

"Exactly," he continues. "Your case is already six binders thick. *No one* can make their way through all of that. So they skim. When they trim lungs in surgery like they did Charity's, there can be residual blood for months. But your lungs have already healed—I only know because I took last week's sputum samples myself. But even the best doctor would never guess that your lungs were clear just a few days ago—that's why they aren't more concerned."

"So what do we do?" asks Mom.

"Ask for a bronchoscopy—they'll put a scope down your

larynx into your lungs so they can see if there's a problem down there. It's a minimally invasive procedure, but you might have to insist on it—the doctors mean well, but they can get a bit cocky. In the end, you know your body best—they just know how to treat its symptoms."

We say goodbye and he moves on, but the validation sends adrenaline on a mad rush through my veins. I am *the* medical expert on myself. I trust Mom, my doctors, and respiratory therapists—but they aren't *me*. They don't know my body or my medical history as well as I do. They don't know what I'm feeling, when I'm hot, cold, or anxious. *This is my body.* If I ever want to get better, I have to take charge of it.

Hours later, Mom is asleep—a rare event. Richard, a new respiratory therapist, is on night duty. Tall, lanky, and older than most of the people on the floor, he doesn't say much.

Something is off. I can feel it. But I can't do anything until an alarm sounds. I'm trying to sort out my options when Richard taps on the door.

"Just wanna check in on you," he says, with a heavy Cleveland drawl. My discomfort must be evident, because he continues, "Would ya like to sit up?"

I nod and he helps me. Leaning forward, I rest my elbows on my knees and hold my forehead in my hands. My chest is heavy, my head aches. I feel like my body is fitted only loosely around my soul. It's one of the strangest sensations I've ever experienced.

"If you don't mind," says Richard, "I'd just as soon stay here. Your mom could use some sleep and, well," he pauses, "I just think you shouldn't be alone tonight. I can get a nurse if you'd rather, it's just they're usually busier than I am."

I nod, grateful for his intuition. Richard stands sentinel over me as I struggle through the night. At 3:00 a.m., I start suffocating. Within moments, a bevy of alarms sound. Richard snakes a clear tube down my throat and suctions up three giant clots of mucus and blood from my lungs, one after another. The process is extremely uncomfortable but, once he's done, I feel a bit better. Finally I fall asleep, secure with Richard as my protector.

I awake to the bleat of alarms, surrounded by nurses and respiratory therapists. I can't breathe. "On the count of three," shouts Russ, back for the morning shift. ". . . Three!" Blood spatters across me and the room as he pulls the trach out of my neck. Once he's inserted a new one, I can breathe again. A nurse pushes a shot of Fent into my IV and, in moments, I drift back to sleep.

When I awake, the new doctor on call comes into my room with Russ. "*You* are not working hard enough, Ms. Tillemann-Dick," she proclaims with a self-righteous trill, medical file in hand.

Excuse me? My eyes pop open. Even when doctors and I disagree, they've never questioned my work ethic. Mom pipes up before I can protest.

"You obviously know nothing about my daughter, Doctor. Unless it's cleaning, she never shies away from hard work."

Mom knows me so well; it warms my heart.

"I know that she was almost weaned a week ago and now she's refusing to go off the vent for more than a few hours at a time. If—" I try to interrupt her, but I can only mouth words indignantly. The doctor glares at me. "What? I can't understand her. What's she trying to say?"

"Maybe if she wasn't in so much pain . . ." interjects Mom, beginning to assert her pet theory.

Not this again. I kick my legs and wave my arms. "*Can—I—please—speak?*" Finally, Russ unhooks me from the vent and caps my trach.

"Doctor," I say, calming down immediately, "if you look at your notes, you'll see that for weeks, I made steady progress."

"Exactly. That's why I am so upset that you've suddenly lost your will to live."

I try not to roll my eyes. "I've decompensated. That's different. It indicates a bigger problem."

"The pain . . ." repeats Mom.

"No. Not the pain," I counter. "Something else is wrong."

"So *you're* the doctor now?" she asks, folding her arms in front of her.

I glare at her, steely eyed. "I want a bronchoscopy."

"I don't perform bronchs."

"Then send me to somebody who does."

"Well, I can order one if you're going to insist," she conciliates grumpily.

"Good. When's the soonest I can have it?" I ask resolutely.

"Tomorrow. You'll get it by tomorrow," she says and leaves the room. The door closes, and I finally feel my face relax.

Once the samples from the bronchoscopy are analyzed, we find out what's wrong: it's a particularly nasty case of pneumonia. But not anything the hospital can't fix. Now on full vent support, I start an intensive course of antibiotics and steroids. I'd like to feel vindicated, but I'm just too tired for that.

Back on recovery road, I'm working with Dean daily now. Simple leg lifts, reaches, and stretches leave me exhausted, but in a good way—the kind of exhaustion that means progress. I stand. I'm finally feeling human. From eating to going to the bathroom on a toilet, most normal activities are a challenge. But for the first time since waking up, I see a path home.

Thanksgiving is less than a week away and it's clear I'm still going to be here.

"Mom," I ask, "could we have Thanksgiving in the hospital?"
She looks at me skeptically. "Here? Chary, your room is tiny!"
She's right. But I keep pushing her. I know she doesn't want to disappoint me, and I take advantage. I smile as saccharinely as I can muster and bat my lashes in a performance worthy of any operetta coquette. She caves. Before anything else, we have to get RSVPs. I feel a blush of embarrassment when both Tomicah and Kimber—both of whom have small children—decline, afraid I've finally asked too much. But when Levi, Corban, Liberty, Shiloh, Mercina, Glorianna, and Zen all enthusiastically confirm, the party's back on. I'm so excited I hardly realize the bureaucratic mess I'm making for Mom. But if anyone can make this hospital dream into a reality, she can.

Of Mom's many abilities, perhaps the most formidable is her uncanny gift for making friends. In the hospital, she's compiled quite the portfolio of people. Concert pianists, congressmen, hospital staff and administrators, fellow patients and their families—all of them love her. Mom has her divinity school crowd—three chaplains from the hospital who regularly visit. There are the nurses, respiratory therapists, residents, and fellows who spend their lunch and coffee breaks visiting with us, braiding my hair and checking in just because. There's the heart transplant surgeon that Mom meets at the children's museum when my nephews are in town. She looks over my chart when we don't know the doctor on call. Then there's the tech who's taken to asking Mom for dating advice, plus everyone else who stops by to pick up a piece of chocolate or candy from her always-stocked treat jar. Then, of course, there's Jeanne.

Jeanne rose through the ranks of the Cleveland Clinic as nurse to then-famed cardiothoracic surgeon Dr. Toby Cosgrove. When Dr. Cosgrove was appointed to lead the entire hospital system as

CEO, he brought Jeanne with him. Like many nurses, her road to health care wasn't easy. But now she serves as the eyes and ears of one of the top hospital executives in the country. She is the patron saint of patients at the Cleveland Clinic.

When I wake up, Jeanne is just leaving. "Sweetheart, we're going to make sure Thanksgiving is great!" she assures me before shutting the door behind her.

"Chary! There's a conference room at the end of the hall. Jeanne's going to help us find tables from another ward so we can have Thanksgiving here!"

Mom and I finally have something to look forward to other than leaving this place. We throw ourselves into the preparations. Mom starts to collect supplies: festive paper plates and plastic cutlery, plastic glasses, napkins. I sit on my bed painting place cards for every guest. Mom and I assemble a smorgasbord of a menu. Everything is coming together perfectly.

During all this, I start walking. At first, I could only take a few steps before collapsing back into my bed, but I'm improving every day. I concoct a plan: on Thanksgiving, I'm going to walk to dinner. *How's that for a grand entrance?* Dean measures the hall for me—it's fifty steps. I train as tirelessly as an emaciated recent transplantee can, pacing back and forth endlessly across my room. So far, I'm at about thirty steps.

It's Wednesday and Thanksgiving is almost upon us. I feel excited and nervous and stressed that I'm still on the vent. I'm like an emotional Jenga tower, getting higher and less structurally sound with each passing hour.

When Mom is restless, she cleans. The problem is that each time she reorganizes our 100-square-foot room, she loses track of everything in it. "Charity," she asks, "where are the soft pink socks? I just had them . . ."

I try to gesture toward the far side of my bed, where I saw her put them down that morning.

"Oh . . . and where's the rest of the chocolate for the nurses? It was just here . . ."

Every surface in this room is filled to capacity. The wall has so many cards, we've begun to pile them one atop another. We've managed to obscure our one window with a three-foot-high stack of books, pictures, medical equipment, snacks, blankets—anything you could think to have in a hospital room and more. Boxes are shoved in the storage cabinet and under the bed, leaving about thirty square feet of floor space free from the clutter collected during our extended hospital stay.

I turn to grab my whiteboard. Now that I can use it, it's become vital for communicating words that Mom and my nurses can't lip-read. It's nice to be understood again. But my whiteboard's not where it should be. I look to my right. Then to my left. Then on my table and under my covers.

"Where's my whiteboard?" I ask.

"Chary, I can't understand you," says Mom.

"*Mom*," I mouth slowly, "*where—is—my—white—board?*"

"Oh . . . I just had it. I was putting it away somewhere . . ."

This room is making me crazy. Mom is making me crazy.

"Mom," I mouth, frustrated, "this is the only thing in this mess of stuff that I actually use. *Please* don't move it."

"Chary, I can't understand you," she repeats, as if that would be possible while she has her back turned to me.

"That's because you aren't trying, Mom! You aren't even *looking* at me!" I silently retort, to no effect. I start clicking my tongue incessantly to get her attention.

"Do you need something?" she says, her back still toward me.

I'm about to explode. This miniature whiteboard is the closest thing I have to self-sufficiency, and losing it in the morass of Mom's "organizing" is more than I can handle.

I'm still clicking my tongue furiously when Mom whips around.

"What, Charity?! I'm cleaning!" she snaps as she passes me my whiteboard.

"STOP!" I scribble in all caps, "JUST STOP." I flap the board at her until she stops to read it. She taps her foot impatiently as I erase that and write more: "Stop cleaning. Stop puttering. Sit down. Read a book. Call the kids. *This isn't helping . . .*" I turn the sign around to show Mom.

"Oh. You want me to read a book? I'd love to read a book! That's all Yoni seems to do when he's here! I wish he would clean more . . ." she mutters.

I begin a new note. "*Mom,* there is NO space to clean up. There is no space to do *anything. You are driving me nuts!*"

"STOP SCREAMING AT ME!" yells Mom.

"*Stop screaming at you!?*" I scribble. "I can't even *talk!*"

"I know you well enough to know when you're screaming at me, Charity Sunshine!!!"

We're staring daggers at each other when we hear a knock at the door. It's Michelle, one of my favorite nurses.

"Hey guuuuys!" she twitters into the room.

Mom and I smile uncomfortably at her, both of us still red in the face.

"You know? There is always *such* a wonderful spirit in here. I just feel so peaceful and happy with you guys." We stare, agape, as she continues, "It's so different from any of the other rooms in this wing."

Mom and I aren't sure whether to burst out laughing or continue our argument. Is Michelle joking? Did she hear us from the hall and come to break up our argument? Mom and I *have* become sort of like the alternate nurses' lounge—we're probably giving out two to three bags of candy to hospital staff every week . . . maybe she just wants some chocolate? Whatever her reason for coming by, we're both grateful.

"Oh! That's it!" she exclaims. "I brought you matzo ball soup from that deli I was telling you about! You're going to love it."

She scurries out of the room and is back within minutes with a brown paper bag. "I hope you like it," she says, opening the steaming carry-out container. "It's my favorite thing to eat in this city." Michelle pours some of the broth into the bowl on my desk table and a matzo ball the size of a softball splashes in. "Try it!" she insists.

I down the entire dumpling and its accompanying broth in less than a minute. When I'm done, Michelle and Mom decide to do my hair. It needs rebraiding almost every day. The steroids and surgical trauma haven't been easy on my scalp—sometimes it feels like a part-time job just keeping my hair from turning into one giant rat's nest or disappearing altogether.

As Michelle and Mom massage a heated no-rinse shampoo cap on my head, the rest of me starts to feel warm and sudsy too. On this Thanksgiving Eve, I really am grateful. For breath, for life, for my wonderful mother, and for the kind people who keep me from killing her.

Thursday dawns gray, a dour sleet streaking the window. Considering that most of the family is driving and road conditions are poor, it's unclear how many of them will actually make it to our Thanksgiving dinner. Using my recently improved fine motor skills, I finish up their place cards—hoping that if I do, my loved ones will appear to make use of them.

As I doodle away, the door opens. I look up to see Glorianna and Mercina. At sixteen and seventeen, they already look grown up. Glorianna's wearing a new pair of glasses and mascara—something that until very recently she'd use only when forced. Mercina is as perfectly coiffed as ever. A moment later, Zen walks in. Barely thirteen, he's grown nearly half a foot since I last saw him. None of us have seen each other in months and soon, we're all crying. Everyone is nervous about germs, so they wave deliriously from the foot of my bed. As I mouth greetings and questions, it becomes clear Mercina has a gift for reading lips.

Soon, Dean knocks on the door. It's time to prepare.

"We have thirty-five minutes on this oxygen tank, maybe a little less because of the walk. Are you ready to go?" he asks.

A current runs down my spine. I've practiced. I've rehearsed. I know my steps and I'm ready.

The nurse connects my trach to a giant inflated balloon he'll use to manually fill my lungs with oxygen. Then I stand, holding onto Mom and Zen instead of my walker. *Fifty steps. Fifty steps to the room, then a few more to my chair.* I take my first step. *Two . . . three . . . four . . .* The rubber soles of my oversized tennis shoes squeak against the floor. With each step, I come closer to the door. *Eight . . . nine . . . ten . . .* When I finally pass the threshold, the entire hospital wing is waiting to cheer me on. Mom and I begin to cry. This is a debut I never anticipated, and I can't help but feel ill prepared for my performance. It's thrilling nonetheless. *Thirteen . . . fourteen . . . fifteen . . .* A nurse follows behind me with a wheelchair, just in case. *Twenty . . . twenty-one . . .* Beads of sweat began to drip off of my brow. My toes burn and tingle. *Twenty-nine . . . thirty . . .* My feet have turned into lead blocks, but I continue on. *Thirty-six . . . thirty-seven . . . thirty-eight . . .*

I wonder who will actually be there—did Liberty and Corban make it out from DC? *Forty-two . . . forty-three . . .* My legs burn, but the doorway is just steps away.

. . . Fifty. Adrenaline flushes my system as I cross the doorway, my shoulders squared, my head high, and my feet really stepping—not shuffling. I feel my knees buckle, but I take one final stride toward the table before sinking into the wheelchair behind me.

Looking around the room, I see Mom, Levi, Corban, Liberty, Shiloh, Mercina, Glorianna, and Zenith. Our friends Dennis, Elizabeth, Richard, and Joela. I might not have been able to breathe on my own today, but I walked all the way from my room! I look around the stark, windowless conference space. There's a whiteboard on one wall and a large screen on the other. Thanks to an anonymous gift, there are beautiful flowers. Otherwise, the space isn't fancy or even particularly comfortable. It's about as different from our gorgeous, warm dining room as anywhere I've been. But even if we were at home in Denver, I couldn't imagine a more wonderful holiday. Soon enough, I'll walk farther—I'll run and climb and dance and breathe. But today, I walked into Thanksgiving dinner with Zen and Mom holding me arm in arm. Today, that's more than enough cause for a celebration of thanks.

It's a quiet day in ReSCU. Mom's talking to our neighbor's wife from the doorway and I'm more alone with my thoughts than I've been for a while. I think back on people I've met, places I've sung, opportunities I've had and missed out on. A few years earlier, around my twenty-second birthday, I performed at a benefit with Marvin Hamlisch. Composer of *A Chorus Line*, Pulitzer

Prize winner, one of only twelve people in history to EGOT (win at least one Emmy, Grammy, Oscar, and Tony)—Marvin was the stuff of legend. A musical theater Great of the first degree. We worked together for two weeks leading up to our performance.

Marvin had a Midas touch for crowd-pleasing scores. He believed in giving people something familiar, but still new to them. I think back to one of our rehearsals. After dashing through "I Could Have Danced All Night," from *My Fair Lady*, Marvin asked me whether I was in school. When I confirmed his suspicions, he chided me:

"You shouldn't be in school. You need to be performing. Don't get me wrong—conservatory is great for some people. But you are a performer! You need an audience. For you, they're the only teachers who matter."

Marvin told me about his first job as a composer. He was playing piano at a party where he met the director Frank Perry. In passing, Mr. Perry mentioned they were looking for a score for his next film, *The Swimmer*. Marvin got all of the information out of Mr. Perry that was possible (including his contact information) and by the end of the weekend—it might have even been the next morning—he had delivered a score for the film. Then he returned to the topic at hand: my career.

"Let me get you onstage! That shouldn't be hard . . ." He continued: "A girl like you with a voice like yours just needs to sing one standard—any crowd will fall in love!" But I demurred. There was so much more I wanted to learn—so far to go until my voice was perfect. He shook his head at me. "People who wait around for things to be perfect just wind up missing the boat. Audiences don't want perfection. They want connection."

Marvin and I kept in touch, but I never did take him up on his offer. Just thinking about it, my face flushes red. One of youth's follies, I suppose—turning down the opportunity of a lifetime as it stares you in the face.

Marvin always encouraged me. But I'm sure he wondered why I didn't jump to perform with his blessing. Lying in bed, I do too. I don't quite regret it—who knows? Maybe if I'd gone down that road, I never would have made it back to Europe to sing opera. My disease could have progressed more quickly. I probably never would have met Yoni. I'm satisfied with my decisions. *That* said, I've learned my lesson. If I ever get out of this hospital, I'm not going to overthink things. If I ever learn to breathe again—to sing again, I'm moving forward. I'm going to reach out and snatch opportunities before they pass me by.

The pneumonia is gone and it's time to finally free myself from this vent and this hospital. But filling my lungs is so much work. I can't quite believe I did it for a quarter century without thinking about it. Sitting in the corner scribbling furiously on her notepad, Mom is entirely immersed in her phone conversation. Since I've been in the hospital, she's been my eyes, ears, arms, hands, mouth, and neck. She reads every letter, returns every phone call. I couldn't survive without her. She does too much—she always has and always will—but, in my case, too much is precisely what the doctor ordered. Mom hangs up the phone and looks at me resolutely.

"I know what your problem is. *That* was your old director, Karen. Her husband was on a ventilator." I nod tentatively in recognition, and Mom continues, "She says you're forgetting how to sing. Breathe from your glutes and stomach muscles and you'll be off the vent in no time."

I furrow my brow and look up at her. Karen's absolutely right.

I've been so preoccupied with getting out of the hospital, I'd entirely forgotten that I spent the last half decade training my body to breathe correctly. I'd be embarrassed if I wasn't so excited to move forward. No use wasting time on regret now.

While my teachers would be ashamed to hear it, all I've been thinking about up until now is filling my lungs with air. Deconstructing everything I've learned about medicine and singing, I break down breath, one body part at a time.

Lungs are like two, spongy balloons. While efficient receptacles for air and blood, lungs are passive—more song than singer. Similarly, bones are important to breath, but useless on their own. Everything depends on muscles. The intercostal muscles that link ribs together are responsible for 25 percent of inhalation. In turn, most of their activity directly results from the proper use of a host of other muscles. My diaphragm, a shark-mouth-shaped muscle located just under the lungs, *should* spontaneously contract to pull air into the lungs—pushing the stomach and everything below it out in the process. When it relaxes, carbon dioxide escapes and the lungs deflate. If the rest of my muscles hadn't atrophied after my surgery, the diaphragm would work spontaneously—automatically engaging my abdominal, posterior, and lower back muscles. It's almost as if my breathing organs are actually my belly, lower back, and butt cheeks. I begin to imagine I'm breathing from my bum and the task becomes markedly easier.

The more I think about it, the more I realize that my breathing mechanism is like an entire opera company—the lungs are two miraculous, high-maintenance diva principals. The ribs and the intercostals act as the stage crew and supporting roles. The conductor, Maestro Diaphragm, is totally useless without the director (lower back muscles), the orchestra (abs), and the chorus (glutes). Some parts receive broad critical acclaim. Others do their job without fanfare. But remove a single player and the grand opera collapses.

When Dean comes in for physical therapy, I ask him to focus on my abdominal strength. He introduces me to an entire regime of belly-strengthening exercises. With each set, breathing gets easier. Soon, instinct takes over and breathing off of the ventilator is easier than breathing on it. Within days, I'm nearly weaned off the ventilator and the hospital has transferred me to a step-down unit—my final destination before discharge.

Mom begins packing up our tight, stuffed room. I watch each card come down with a sense of melancholy. They've sustained me during my time here in ReSCU, but somehow I know that, once they're off the wall, I'll never see them again.

Mom plops down onto a chair, exhausted. "How are we going to move all of this stuff alone?" she exhales concernedly. Almost as soon as she asks it, my brother Corban pops his head into the room. It's nothing less than a little miracle.

We've always called Corban "Captain America." Since he was young, he's had a warm assurance about him—it's hard to feel like a problem won't be solved when he's around. Corban plants a kiss atop my head and does the same to Mom before methodically hoisting a stack of three boxes up and ferrying them to our new room—a ten-minute walk away. By lunchtime, the last load is safely transported. Then Rodney and Raven—my lift team—arrive to transport me to the new unit.

When we arrive, Mom and I wait in the entrance, almost reverent. Clean, modern lines, large windows, walls of white, heather gray, and dark leather—this room is the opposite of the tiny, cramped space I've lived in for the past month. A doorway separates a gracious guest lobby from my room, where a large

TV screen covers the far wall. Invisible cabinets swallow messes of tubes and cords into apparent neatness. If not for my bulky hospital bed, the room could have been confused for part of a chic bachelor pad in San Francisco.

"I think Jeanne might have pulled a few strings, sweetheart," Mom whispers beside me.

Early the next morning, Corban leaves—taking a load of cards and fuzzy socks with him and officially beginning our attenuated move out. We're finally progressing toward some sort of in-patient normalcy. I exchange my well-used hospital gown for a velour tracksuit from Jeanne. The elastic on the waistband feels strange around my waist and the hoodie's zipper bumps up against my incision site. Still—it's remarkably good to be wearing actual clothes again. For the first time in months, I dust off my makeup bag. With the help of a little mascara, some lipstick, and concealer, I look almost healthy. My aunt Katrina arrives for a weekend visit just as the doctor on call comes into my room.

"Wow," he says.

"Wow," he repeats. "You look fantastic. You'll be going home any day now."

"Any day?" asks Mom, skeptically.

"Well, look at her!" He gestures toward me. True, I no longer have a half-dozen tubes in me. But I'm still very much in recovery. I have open wounds from surgery and bedsores, I weigh only ninety-five pounds. I can't climb stairs. But I guess with makeup, my gauntness comes off as almost chic. I look like I've been institutionalized for anorexia instead of for a lung transplant.

"I would release you this weekend, but we're short-staffed," he says, apologetically. "So I guess we'll have to push it out to Monday."

"I think that's wise," my aunt scoffs, shooting a sideways glance to my mortified mother. "And how exactly should Charity fill all that dead time between now and then? Perhaps by gaining a couple dozen pounds?"

He looks down at a clipboard. "It says here she still can't climb stairs?"

"Oh yes, there *is* that," says my aunt.

"So do that! Get out. Explore the hospital. Have a good time."

"Out of the ward?" Mom asks nervously.

"Sure! Make a night of it!" He ruffles through his papers while glancing back up at me a few times. "Wow," he says, shaking his head. "You really look great. So nice to see you like this."

He steps out, and my mom and Katrina burst into laughter.

"*That*," says Katrina, "is why we need more female doctors in the world. Have a pretty girl put on a little makeup and suddenly, they're cured."

They continue to laugh at the contrast between my emaciated frame and the doctors' ambitious timeline for my return home. I don't find it so funny. And I'd prefer they stop mocking the potential end of this chapter of our lives.

"That's not even the worst part!" mom exclaims, wiping tears from her eyes. "Charity, do you *remember* him?"

"No . . ." I admit tentatively.

There's a glint in her eye as she turns toward Katrina again. "That's the doctor who tried to throw me out of the ICU for giving Charity Diet Sprite!"

They burst out in fresh peals of laughter. My gratitude for his optimism dissipates slightly.

When they calm down again, I pipe up, "I'd like to go out to dinner."

Mom and Katrina look at each other skeptically.

"You go and climb a few stairs. When you get back," says Mom, "we can go to dinner."

Dean comes by to escort me to the emergency stairwell. I walk confidently beside him, without a walker or cane. "This is going to be a lot harder than you think it should be," he cautions. I listen, but ever since Thanksgiving I've been very mobile—walking farther every day. I'm not nervous about a few stairs.

Lifting my foot at the base of the stairwell, I feel the weight of my shoes on my calves. I press my left foot down onto the first step, trying to lift my right one up to meet it, and beads of perspiration flick off my chin onto the railing. My face is red with heat. I feel condensation collect on my back, my chest, and in my armpits. Finally, I pull my second leg onto the step. My bones feel like gelatin and my knees nearly buckle under the weight of the rest of my body. I start on the next step, but Dean stops me—"I think that's enough for today." He helps me down the steps and I collapse into a wheelchair in the hall. My body is so drained of energy that I feel like my soul is on the outside, looking back at myself—just like when I decompensated with Richard in ReSCU. I had hoped I'd never feel that way again.

Maybe I'm not ready to go out. There are no nurses on call in a restaurant. No techs or doctors. I want to get out of this hospital so badly, but right now I hardly have the energy to think, let alone breathe on my own. A terrible thought crosses my mind . . . *Maybe I'm not ready to go home.*

But this is the first hall pass I've really received here and I'd be the most ungrateful patient in this hospital if I didn't use it. I put away my misgivings for later. "Where should we go?" I ask.

Mom and Katrina exchange concerned glances. We've come so

far but so many things could still go wrong. Swine flu is blanketing the country and the airwaves. Even a common cold could kill me. But the doctor *did* just tell us to go out. So, reluctantly, they help me into my wheelchair. I put on a mask and we're off.

We wheel our way through the halls toward the restaurant—part of the hotel attached to the clinic via a skyway. Mom and Katrina banter back and forth while I sit in my chair feeling like a small child. There are so many people! I doubt nudity could make me feel any more exposed than I do. Each time we pass a full hospital room or lobby, I hold my breath. Finally, we walk through the dimly lit restaurant's glass-paneled doors. Dark wood and silver chairs are packed with businessmen, socialites, and fashionable young people. But the din of dinner conversations quiets as Mom rolls me through to our table. I feel every eye focused on our little delegation, and—for once in my life—I don't like the attention.

Mom parks my chair next to the booth. Auntie Katrina questions in a low voice, "How is she going to sit down?"

I just want to get this over with. I push myself up in my chair and pivot to sit down in the booth. But as I do, I step on my loose shoelace and tumble to the ground. Real or imagined, I feel a collective intake of breath as the entire restaurant gasps at the scene I've created.

"Charity! Baby, what are you doing? Are you OK!" Mom cries as she and Katrina help me up and into the booth. Though I'd smacked my arm hard on the armrest of the wheelchair, I nod my head yes.

This is not as fun and freeing as I had hoped it would be. As the minutes pass, I feel increasingly unwell until finally, I look up at Mom pleadingly.

"Do you want to go back to your room, Chary?"

I nod yes.

She gets the check and helps me back into my chair. We leave the restaurant, and the eyes that saw us in follow us back out. This time, I don't feel well enough to care. Something is wrong. I feel awful. And this time I know it's not just nerves.

We make it back to the room and with help I get back into bed.

A nurse attaches me to an apparatus that hisses freezing-cold humidified oxygen down the hole in my neck from the tracheotomy. Supposedly, it's an intermediate stage of coming off the vent, but to me it feels like a form of torture.

I ask for a blessing.

Mormonism has a rich tradition of blessing the sick, the downtrodden, and those in need of direction. Some blessings are for healing, others are for comfort, clarity, and guidance. Priesthood blessings are an access point for divine wisdom and understanding—like a prayer dictated through the soul instead of dictated by one's own perceived needs.

It's late at night, but Mom calls the leader of the local Mormon congregation, Bishop Todd Albrecht. Todd has become something of our own personal saint—taking time from his family and his job (being a Mormon bishop is not a paid engagement) to foretell the miracles and challenges I've met during my coma and since. Within the hour, he's there with another young man from the congregation. They anoint me with a few drops of oil and place their hands atop my head.

"Charity Sunshine Tillemann-Dick," they begin, opening the blessing in the name of Jesus. Frequently, blessings carry peaceful, calming messages. This one is different. It states that I'll regain my singing voice and return home. Then it continues to caution me and my mother to hold our ground in medical decision-making and to not be afraid to demand help when we need it. It warns of imminent challenges. When he's done, I feel no difference.

The priesthood brothers leave and I stay in my seat, hoping that sitting up might ease my breathing on this awful new device. Mom keeps calling the nurses, asking if there's any way they can make me more comfortable. One after another replies no.

"Mom . . . Mom!" I call. My oxygenation is dropping faster than the monitor can keep up with.

"I need a nurse," Mom shouts, but there's no response. "I need the doctor immediately!!!" She's screaming now. Just as she does, every alarm in my room sounds.

―――――――

"Hey, baby," says a voice to my left. It's Yoni.

Instead of sleek cream walls, I'm surrounded by gray curtains again. "Where am I?" I say, but no sound comes out. I look down to see a vent tube trailing out of my neck. I'm mute.

"You're in the NICU—it was the only place they could fit you in."

My mind is racing—*What happened? Why am I on the vent? In the neurological ICU?!* "Where's Mom?"

"Dr. Avery is helping her organize a bed for you in the right ICU. She'll be back soon."

Yoni and I sit in concerned silence until Mom returns.

"Why am I here!?" I mouth to Mom.

"You had what they call a major decompensation, sweetheart. The nurse who ran into the room bagged you for almost two hours—he was drenched in sweat by the end of it, but he saved your life."

"Well," Katrina says, exchanging a knowing glance with Mom, "I'm glad things ended up OK. But I don't think they'll be discharging you this weekend after all. I'm afraid I have to run and catch my plane."

She and Mom walk out together. It's the first time in a long while I've seen Mom with someone who knows her almost like Dad did. I'm overwhelmed that she has to go through this without him; that I have to go through this without him. As soon as the curtains of my room close, tears begin to well. *How on earth am I back where I started?* I see the same cycle playing out again: I rotate from unit to unit, and then some unfortunate mishap indefinitely prolongs my stay. Yoni pulls up his chair.

"Chary, baby, what's the problem?" he asks, taking my hand.

"I want to go home!" I mouth. "I want to get married and I want to sing. I want to live my life. I don't want to be here anymore and I want to be off of this machine!"

Yoni kisses my cheek and climbs into the hospital bed with me. He wraps his arms around me and turns his face toward mine. "Chary, you'll get off the vent. You'll get out of the hospital. We'll get married and have . . ." he trails off, teasing out a smile from me. Both of us know that sentence wasn't going to end with "kids." "Everything will be OK. You just need to rest for another day, then you'll start breathing on your own again."

Resting my head on his shoulder, I hope he's right. A mischievous smile sneaks its way across my face. "What if I told you I was pregnant?" I mouth slowly.

"I'd think it was an immaculate conception," he says, straight-faced.

I begin to silently laugh. "No. What if my whole virginal thing was a ruse and I'd been having other relationships on the side?"

"That's not funny," Yoni says blankly. Even the suggestion tortures him a bit, which is exactly what I need at the moment.

I begin listing off the names of my potential sidepieces. Only then does it really become evident how much Yoni's lip-reading skills have improved.

"That's not even . . . You would never . . . Shhh . . ." He puts his hand over my mouth and turns on the TV.

———

"Get *out* of that bed!" a firm whisper rouses me to consciousness.

"Annette," says Yoni, rolling off my bedside onto the floor, "we were just watching a movie! We fell asleep!"

"Well, *you* managed to fall asleep in *her* bed," points out Mom. I decide I can best diffuse the situation by pretending to still be asleep.

"Annette, I think I've proven . . ."

Mom interrupts. "Nothing. You've proven nothing. You think just because Charity's in the hospital that you're some kind of knight in shining armor for sticking around. Charity has never wanted for admirers. When she gets out, she'll have her pick of whom she ends up with. It *might* be you. But until the two of you are married, you are not to cross the lines I know she has outlined for you. Do you understand?"

"That goes without say . . ."

"I expect you to say it."

"Of course, Annette, of course," he says. "I don't think you know your daughter very well if you think she's going to abandon her beliefs for a night of passion in a hospital bed."

"It's not *her* I'm worried about," she scoffs.

With that, I hear the metal legs of two chairs scrape against the floor. Mom and Yoni sit down, and an uneasy silence falls over the room.

I'm glad I kept my eyes shut.

Yoni was right on a number of counts, and certainly about breathing. The next day, doctors begin weaning me again and I'm allowed to walk around the room.

One day, Mom comes in with her arms filled with Styrofoam takeout containers brimming with *kapsa* and baklava—offerings from the Saudi Arabian and Qatari ladies who are staying in her hotel while their husbands receive treatment at the clinic. Most of them have large families and Mom's a natural addition to their ranks. They've quickly become part of her ever-extending Cleveland "family."

She gives me a bite of the food. The chicken is plump and moist, the rice fluffy yet crunchy. I could eat this all day! Before I know it, I'm licking honey and rosewater off my fingers—the last remnants of my Middle Eastern feast. Mom hasn't been this happy in a while.

When I go home, I will find food like this and eat it until I'm fat.

Within a few days, I'm transferred back to the step-down unit in preparation for discharge. My legs dangling off the side of the bed, I can think of nothing but how happy I am to be off of the ventilator once again. I bow my head in a prayer of gratitude when the door swings open.

Slim with a short bob, the nurse is attractive and probably in her midfifties. "I'm Barb. I'm going to be your nurse while you're here."

"We're so happy to meet you!" says Mom.

"I'm not *your* nurse. I'm hers," Barb dismisses Mom, nodding in my direction. Turning back toward me, she continues,

"Trust me. By the time you leave, you're going to be happy you had me." She wraps a blood pressure cuff around my arm, gives me a handful of pills, walks to the sink, and fills a glass with water. "Mom, discharge is one of the most stressful parts of transplant," she says as she works. "When she's ready to go, you aren't going to believe it. When that time comes"—she looks back to me—"I am going to be *your* bulldog. Not your mom's. If need be, I'll have her dragged out of here by security. I've done it before."

Mom and I glance at each other uncomfortably.

"So just keep that in the back of your mind. Call if you need anything!"

The door closes behind Barb, leaving a pregnant silence trapped in the room. This whole period of recovery has been like experiencing the different stages of childhood in hyper lapse. From waking up to eating to learning to walk. On to trying to be responsible for my own body and my own care. For heaven's sake, there's even been drama with boys! In some ways, I fear that letting me live my own life is going to be almost as painful for Mom as staying in this hospital—it's just a different way to lose me. But this is the first time that someone has acknowledged the dynamic that has been slowly building between us. Up until now, it's been more like my great-grandma Dick's Jell-O salad—we both know it's there and we'll have to eat it soon enough, but we'd prefer not to think about it.

A doctor comes in to check on us. "Well, Charity's doing extremely well, isn't sh—"

Before she can finish her sentence, Mom pounces. It's clear that Barb struck a nerve. "Excuse me, Doctor, but a week ago we were told that 'Charity's doing extremely well.' Later that night, she had a major decompensation which sent us back to the ICU for nearly a week. If you even mention discharge, I'll have a very hard time taking your medical advice seriously."

"Well," the doctor falters, blindsided by Mom's furor, "that *is* why Charity's here. She's preparing for discharge. Maybe in days, maybe weeks. Either way it's getting close and we'll have to talk about it."

"But not in some sort of imminent way," Mom clarifies. "We almost lost her."

Silent, tense stares are exchanged between Mom and the doctor, the doctor and me, and Mom and me. For a few moments, we sit frozen in a sort of psychological Mexican standoff. Then, wordlessly, we all agree that now isn't the time to talk about "it" or anything else, and we each retreat to our respective corners of the hospital.

<hr>

Each day since returning from the ICU, I visit the stairs. It's great physical exercise, but it's even more important mentally. What was the most physically strenuous and draining activity I'd ever engaged in is now something I look forward to. It's a very real reminder that, if I'm determined enough, I can accomplish the impossible.

It's December. For me, tucked away in the heart of the hospital, the weather is always the same—on the chilly side of tepid. But the scene through the window looks blustery. Liberty, Mercina, and Glorianna are in town for winter break. They accompany me to the hospital staircase. Liberty holds one of my hands as Glorianna stands beneath us with a video camera. Today, I'm going to climb the entire flight. I pull up one foot followed by the other, and the steps come almost easily. Soon, Mercina trades places with Liberty and I go for a second flight. I go until we run out of stairs.

Discharge is becoming more and more inevitable. I'm hoping, praying, that I'll be home in time for Christmas in Colorado.

On December 20, Kelynn, the discharge nurse, walks into my room. Tall with dozens of black braids neatly combined into two massive twists, she's at once friendly and in control. "Charity," she says, in a warm, mezzo voice. "You're going home soon . . ."

"Not that soon," interjects Mom.

"She has to gain two pounds, but then she'll be ready. Theoretically, she could be home before Christmas."

A flash of excited energy shoots down my spine. *Home for Christmas!?*

"Oh, no," Mom insists. "That's impossible. Kelynn, I'm sorry, but look at her."

I feel my heart crumple. In the past four years, I've spent roughly half of all major holidays in the hospital. If I add another to the tally, I'm afraid my spirit might just curl up and die.

"Annette, we've been going over her paperwork carefully," Kelynn explains. "She's off of the ventilator and off of oxygen entirely. She's walking. She has use of her hands and arms. Her balance is improving. She eats on her own. She's off of nearly all pain medication and her vital signs are normal. The social worker said that once she could climb stairs, she'll be ready to go home. And I've heard she can climb a lot of stairs."

Mom is furious. She's heard this sermon too many times before, and it's never ended well. She stalks out of the room and attempts to slam the door behind her, but hydraulic stops leave it to squeeze shut gradually.

After a few moments, I turn to Kelynn. We both know I need to get out of here.

"This is your microspirometer," she says. "You blow into it every day and it measures your lung volume."

Microspirometers; incentive spirometers; positive expiratory pressure devices—Kelynn takes me through the breathing exercises I'll have to do daily when I leave. Then she starts on my dozens of medications and when precisely I have to administer them. There's Prograf at 8:00 a.m. and 8:00 p.m. sharp; Noxafil with meals; antibiotics, steroids, antivirals, antifungals, magnesium, folic acid, oxycodone as needed for pain. In all, there are over thirty pills a day. There's so much information, my head starts to spin. Kelynn stops herself midsentence—

"You know, this is a lot. How about I come back tomorrow to finish up?"

I nod gratefully and she says goodbye. The door shuts behind her and, for the first time in months, I'm actually alone. Thinking about everything *is* overwhelming. *How will I learn it all in a couple days? Maybe Mom is right. Maybe I'm not ready. But if I stay here much longer, I'll either get sick again or go crazy. Maybe both. May the best option win.*

Step-down is like a mini Middle East, but less healthy and more peaceful. My neighbor to one side is a famous Kuwaiti businessman. On the other, it's an Orthodox rabbi. A Saudi princess is recovering from surgery at the end of the hallway and her entourage fills half of the hospital wing. Then there's Mom and me. We're both Ashkenazi, but Yoni lends us some Semitic cred.

One night, I'm on a walk with Yoni around the ward. We pass a young woman and I smile at her—as is my habit. She smiles back as our paths cross. Then, just before reaching the door at the end of the hall, she doubles back.

"I am so sorry," she says, with the faintest accent. "I'm Huda. Your names?"

We introduce ourselves.

"Oh!" says Huda. "Yonatan—that's Hebrew for Jonathan, right? Are you Israeli? My grandfather—the only woman he ever really loved was Jewish. He was going to take her as his third wife, but his first wife forbade it . . ." She pauses. "Well, anyway, my father—he's here. He's— I think he's almost next to your room."

"How long has he been here?" I ask.

"Let's not even go into that," she says with a sad smile. "I love it here, though. I have a brother in Washington, DC, and another in Aspen. The Cleveland Clinic is just our third home in your country."

"That's like my family," I say, smiling at our similar geographies. "I'm from Colorado, but my family lives in DC and Denver!"

"What a tiny world in this hospital." She shakes her head in happy disbelief. "Will you be home for Christmas?"

My eyes fall slightly. "I'd love to, but I doubt it. And I feel terrible because we always have a wonderful holiday party on December twenty-third. But since I'm in the hospital, my family is going to cancel it so we can spend Christmas here."

"No, no, no!" insists Huda. "You cannot miss your party! We'll just have to have it here instead."

We immediately delve into plans together. When Huda walks off an hour later, Yoni smiles. "It looks like you've found a kindred spirit."

Over the next days, the entire family arrives in Cleveland. Zen arrives on Monday with Shiloh. Corban follows with his girlfriend, Narae. Levi, then Kimber and David and their daughter arrive next, and, finally, Tomicah, Sarah, and their two sons join the melee.

Just like we planned, we have our party on the twenty-third.

The girls set up in the lobby of our wing of the hospital, decorating with paper chains and popcorn garlands. The party is a reunion of some of my favorite people I've met during my stay in Cleveland. Michelle, the nurse who brought me the matzo ball soup; Rodney and Raven who've transported me all of the way from surgery to where I am now; Nick and Laura—nurses from the ICU; Russ and Bill, my respiratory therapists. Some of our neighbors stop by and a few members of the princess's entourage come too. Huda has conjured the most amazing Middle Eastern food I've ever tasted, and my siblings come with dishes whipped up in our hotel room's kitchenette. There's sparkling cider, beautiful cheese, and fruit. There's even music! My nurse Katie brings her six-year-old daughter along to serenade us with "Silent Night." Her crystalline voice reminds me of mine and my siblings' caroling parties back when we were kids. It's not Christmas in Colorado, but it ain't too shabby.

Just as the party is winding down, a magnificent "Ho, Ho, Ho" rings out into the room. Then the swinging white doors open and Santa Claus walks in. *Who set this up?* I glance at Mom and my siblings, but they all look as delighted and bewildered as I feel.

"Ho, Ho, Ho!" he calls out again.

Santa's suit is the most beautiful I've ever seen. Shining black leather boots rise past his knees, where they're met by the deep crimson velvet of his pants. Heavy brass buttons snuggle into pristine white fur to close up the front of his sumptuous jacket. Behind him, he carries a large velvet sack. One by one, he removes gifts from it with white-gloved hands, giving a gift to everyone in the room. When he gets to me, I notice a few stray black hairs peeking out from underneath his beard and gold-rimmed bifocals frame friendly black eyes.

Turns out our Santa Claus is a prince!

Somehow, this dreaded hospital holiday has climbed the ranks in my "Most Magical Christmases Ever" list. But I still tire easily. Sensing my nervousness, Yoni helps me back into my bedroom, closing the door behind us.

He turns on some Christmas music and takes me by the hand, placing his other hand on the small of my back. Together, we dance. Twirling me slowly, we manage not to get caught in my monitors, cords, and tubing.

"Let's go downstairs to the chapel, just you and me, and get married," he whispers into my ear.

I laugh.

"I'm not joking! Let's do it!" he repeats, this time more emphatically.

"Yoni, do you know how angry my family would be if we got married downstairs without inviting them?"

Blushing slightly, he looks down at his feet.

I lean in and whisper in his ear. "But even if we don't get married now, you get bonus points for being romantic."

Eventually, the music ends, leaving us in silence. All of a sudden, I realize how tired I am. Yoni takes off my shoes and lifts my legs into bed, and tucks me in. Then he pulls up a cot along the left side of my bed, takes my hand, and falls asleep beside me.

I'm not going home for Christmas. It's disappointing. But I think of a night, many years ago, when another virgin was far from home with the man she loved. Since Mary is the now-celebrated mother of Jesus, it's easy to forget how hard she had it. Life for me certainly isn't easy, but I'm here and, right now, that's enough.

Overnight, Mom, Liberty, Mercina, and Glorianna have turned the hospital room into a Christmas dream. Stockings hang, lights twinkle, and exquisite paper snowflakes drift through the air. It's lovely. My godmother, Suzie, has sent giant boxes of gifts for everyone here. Old friends visit and we exchange gifts with the other patients on our floor. In the evening, Grandma Nancy and Auntie Margot arrive with an extremely pink hat covered in glittering LED lights. There are plenty of reasons for gratitude, but I can't help feeling like a failure for once again dragging my family to a germ-infested hospital for yet another celebration.

When Yoni leaves for New York late on Christmas Day, I don't know how I'm going to cope. Mom's nervousness has crescendoed into a full-throttled protest against our imminent hospital departure. In my idle moments, I daydream about dosing her with my Vicodin to calm her down. She's convinced that if we leave the clinic, I'll die. I'm convinced that if I don't get out of this place soon, I just might kill someone.

Act II, Scene 3:
Leonora

After an impossible journey, Leonora rests in the safety of a convent.

Sono giunta! Grazie, o Dio!	At last I am here!
Estremo asil questo è per me!	I give thee thanks, O God!
Son giunta!	This is my last refuge!
. . .	I am here!
	. . .
. . . a Dio sui firmamenti,	. . . to God in Heaven!
inspirano a quest'alma fede,	May this music bring comfort,
conforto e calma!	comfort and peace to my
	troubled soul!

—GIUSEPPE VERDI,
LA FORZA DEL DESTINO

I t's the morning of December 30, my 107th day in the hospital. I'm finally going home.

Bundled up like a leftover Christmas present, Zenith rolls me out into the cold darkness of morning. Glass doors slide open and a wall of freezing air hits me. My eyes widen and my heart quickens. It feels like I'm waking up all over again.

Mom and Zen help me into the car as quickly as they can, scared that I'll catch cold. Then we're off to the airport.

Mom is uncharacteristically quiet in the front seat. While I'm thrilled to be leaving the hospital, she's not. On one level, I understand why: My limbs are scary spindly and my gait is insecure; I'm not eating enough; my entire body is covered in partially healed wounds. Mom is sure that I'm too vulnerable to leave and she's furious at me for telling the doctors otherwise. But in my heart I know I'm ready. I *have* to be, because I couldn't have stayed in that hospital a moment longer without going completely crazy. And now we're here, on our way to Denver, no matter how angry it makes Mom.

The head of airport security meets us at the curb with a wheelchair and helps us navigate through the morass of holiday travelers. Everywhere we go, Mom loudly clarifies my fragile condition: to check-in agents, police, and TSA officers, flight attendants, restaurant employees, fellow travelers. I start to suspect she's actively directing her attentions elsewhere—it seems she can hardly stand to look at me for more than a moment at a time. Finally seated on the plane, we sit beside each other in silence. *Why isn't she saying anything?* I try to quell my unease by looking out the window.

We arrive at Denver International Airport. The vista that greets us upon landing is powdered-doughnut white—freshly dusted with dry Colorado snow. We make our way through the airport and exit the terminal. The door of an old red Range Rover swings open and out steps a lanky man wearing a plaid shirt and a cable-knit cap. *Dad?* For a moment, there's a harsh dissonance between what I see and what I know. But I quickly realize my mistake. It's Uncle Justin, Dad's younger brother. I'd never noticed how similarly the two of them carry themselves—Justin's height, his gait, his laugh, his voice, even his dry sense of humor. It's uncanny.

The drive home feels a bit unfamiliar after being away so long. I'd been back to Denver almost two years earlier for the funeral, but that felt more like a bad dream than a homecoming. This time, it's different.

I take a deep breath as we exit I-70 just past Federal Boulevard. The street is lined with honey locust trees guarding rows of eclectic little homes—modest ranch-style walk-ups, tiny Tudors, and bungalows. Then, you see it. Set atop a hill, its stately lawn spreading across most of the block, stands our Beaux Arts-style home. Neighborhood kids call it a mansion. A long brick walkway meanders toward a double-stairway leading up to three sets of French doors topped by massive, arched windows. We pull into a parking spot by the back door of the house, where terra-cotta topped porticoes tower over us and naked wisteria vines snake up around the second-story kitchen window.

The big white house in Denver is almost like another member of the family. My parents even gave her a name—Theopolis. Built in 1908 by the prolific Denver architect J. J. B. Benedict, the three-story stucco edifice has led a number of lives—serving as a farmhouse, a convent, and even a dentist's office. Before my parents bought it, a childless divorcée who'd succumbed to dementia owned the house. The property had endured significant neglect—you could look straight down from the second story to the first through holes in their respective floors and ceilings—

and it hadn't been updated since a trend-heavy makeover in the late 1960s. But my parents weren't easily intimidated.

When they found Theopolis, Mom and Dad had themselves, nine kids, and three dogs crammed into a three-bedroom Victorian a few blocks away. My parents were committed to staying in the neighborhood, but there weren't many homes big enough for the entire brood. The old mansion was in complete disarray, but it was exactly the kind of space Mom and Dad had always imagined for us. Enough room. Lots of green space. Plenty of nooks and crannies. And all of the work needed—outside and in—would be ideal for keeping nearly a dozen growing kids occupied. We spent my adolescence tackling one massive renovation project after another, laboring to make the grand old house into a *habitable* home.

Growing up, Theopolis was always full—with children, animals, exchange students, guests zooming in and out and around without cease. Now, though, the driveway is still. Without the usual din of ambient chaos to fill up its empty spaces, the house seems massive.

Mom, Uncle Justin, and Zen ferry bags into the house. "We'll be out to help you in a sec, sweetheart!" Mom calls out as the back door swings shut behind her. *I don't need help getting out of the car,* I think to myself, half insulted, half aspirational. *I can do this by myself.* Heaving myself against the car door, I push it open and swing my legs around the side of the seat. As I'm getting onto my feet, though, I feel my shoes begin to slip on the icy driveway beneath me. To keep from crashing onto the ice, I twist my torso back toward the car, face-planting into the passenger-side seat. Still sliding, I reach out my hands to grip the console on the far side of the seat, all the while still trying to gain my footing. But it's no use. I can't get any traction. Still grasping onto the cup holders, I'm left to consider my predicament. I'm fine, or at least physically unharmed, but I can't change positions without crashing to the ground. *Mom is not going to be happy when she sees this.* Hopefully, Justin finds me before she does.

"Charity!" I hear her mortified cry. "What have you done to yourself?! Zen! Justin! Hurry!"

Too late.

"I'm fine!" I mutter adamantly, my face still buried in the velour seat cushion. I hear someone running toward me. Before I know what's happening, Zen hoists me over his shoulders like a sack of flour and carries me into the house. From my upended vantage point, I can only see the floor as it passes by. We go past the brown tile of the laundry room, up the cobalt-blue back steps, across the worn wood slats in the kitchen and the dining room's elaborate Persian carpets, then back down the dark wood of the main staircase. Finally, Zen sets me down onto a large bed—

"Chary-bear, you've gotta promise me that you won't get up without calling me for help, OK?" he censures. I nod yes, my face a little flushed from some mixture of gravity and embarrassment.

Looking around me, I see I'm in my great-grandmother's old suite. It opens onto a half acre of frozen, unkempt grass and, out of the bank of windows lining the main room, I see my mom's growing herd of white dogs roaming happily out back. The apartment is part of an addition I helped build as a living space for my great-grandmother Mamcsi the summer I turned fifteen. I dug holes for the foundation, poured cement, framed the exterior, laid down radiant heating lines, stripped paint. It was a true labor of love, a comfortable place for us to look after Mamcsi as she suffered from late-stage Alzheimer's. I never imagined I'd be the one convalescing in it.

Everything about this place is large: the mountains, the dogs, the yard, the house, my room. I've become accustomed to the efficiencies of East Coast living, and my hospital accommodations were even more cramped than my small apartments. But my single space in this house is twice the size of my place in DC and big enough to host a dozen ICU nooks. I settle into it as Mom and the others go to check up on the status of our newly unabandoned house.

That evening, Mom's anxiety escalates to hysteria. She storms around the house, slamming doors and shouting ominous curses at no one in particular. Finally, she stalks into my room.

"How could you do this to me?!" she howls. "How, when I've given you everything?! I brought you into this world, then I dragged you *back* into it when you were on the brink of death! All I wanted was to stay in the hospital for one more week! One week! But you just *had* to leave!"

"Mom," I counter, almost excited to engage, "with all of the infections swirling around there, it was far more dangerous for me in the hospital than here at—"

"More dangerous?! You're covered in *open wounds*, Charity! Who do you think has to care for those!? You have more medications than both of your great-grandmothers combined. I'm not a trained nurse, Charity—I don't understand these things! But do you know who's responsible if you go into septic shock now? If you stop breathing?! I am, Charity! *I am!*"

"Mom, I was going crazy!"

"*Crazy* is better than *dead*!!!" She turns on her heel and slams the door behind her.

Nurse after nurse warned me that leaving the hospital was one of the hardest things for patients' parents. But I didn't expect it to be this bad. Later that night, my oldest sister, Dulcia, knocks on my door. She sits beside me and starts combing my hair.

"What Mom said earlier—she's just lost so much in the past years. She's scared of losing you too."

I know Dulcia's right, but that doesn't make it much easier to bear.

"She's been in the hospital a long time too, you know? She has almost as much to adjust to as you do. Just give her some time to cool off. You know she always does. Eventually."

She shoots me a knowing smile. Mom and Dad had always subscribed to the proverbial "it takes a village" approach to raising children. And, as they did with so many other things, they put their own twist on it. They built and maintained an entire village right here in our crazy old house. Kids, foreign exchange students, guests, pets. There was always chaos, but, somehow, that chaos was accompanied by an uncanny equilibrium—like a gyroscope spinning wildly to maintain a steady center. Whenever someone was out of line, someone else could always balance out their craziness. Somehow, though its numbers have dwindled, the house still holds that same magic. Tonight, Dulcia is my village.

Despite everything, it's good to be home.

Sitting in my room the next morning, I'm restless. It's New Year's Eve and the rest of the kids are out doing who knows what, so it's just Mom and me in the house. I decide to use the opportunity to get a head start on my resolutions.

"I'll be back in about an hour," Mom calls down the stairs. "We need some bread for the fondue. You just stay put, sweetheart."

Resolution #1: Be More Independent

Pushing myself up from the reclining armchair downstairs, I begin the long and perilous trek to the kitchen. I go to the door and I push down the cold brass handle. The door slowly swings

161

open. Hand against the wall to guide me, I walk through the dark hallway. My foot bumps something furry and I look down nervously—it's Nori, our Great Pyrenees. The gargantuan animal seems unbothered by the interruption. Edging my way around him, I reach the bottom of the staircase. Wrapping my arm around the banister, I observe the task confronting me. These aren't the emergency stairs at the clinic—I much prefer the warm chestnut wood to the clinical gray plastic to which I've become accustomed—but, structurally, they aren't much different. I summit the flight without incident. Steadying myself on the wall at the top, I head down the hallway to the kitchen.

Resolution #2: Be More Helpful

Upstairs, it doesn't look like anyone has started preparations for tonight's festivities—our traditional New Year's Eve Fondue Extravaganza. I go to the fridge and find a Costco-sized wedge of Jarlsberg sitting inside. I squint at it, determined. I can't do much, but I can do this. I manage to peel off the cheese's tight plastic wrapping and then go to the cupboard to retrieve a rickety metal grater. I slide the enormous chunk of cheese up and down it until my arm begins to burn. Soon I have to rest, but after a few minutes I'm back at it. This is as pedestrian a task as exists, but it's important to me. I'm contributing—giving instead of receiving for what seems like the first time in months. I know it's only grated cheese, but at least it's *something*. I've missed this feeling.

The back door jingles open as Mom arrives back home. "Hello?" she calls up the stairs.

Biceps aching, I respond lightly—"Hi, Mom!"

"Chary, what are you doing up here?" she asks as she climbs

the stairs. Seeing the small mountain of creamy yellow cheese piled on the cutting board in front of me, she smiles and shakes her head. "Oh, sweetheart, you didn't need to!"

Yes. I did.

Resolution #3: Gain Weight

That evening, the boys light a fire while Mom sets dozens of candles aglow. We eat bread and cheese until our bellies ache. Illegal fireworks whiz up from across the neighborhood, welcoming the New Year. As I admire them from the front steps, I'm overwhelmed. We've made it. *I'm alive. I'm home. And, boy, am I full.*

On New Year's Day, we host Uncle Justin and his family for brunch, then lapse into idleness. Everyone has fallen asleep on the couches across the living room, except me. I figure I'll go do my breathing exercises in my room. I make my way over to the stairs and start down confidently. But my foot slips out from underneath me on the fourth step and I fall, slamming my way down the staircase. Desperately, I try to grip the banister as it slides past me—all the while praying that my bones don't shatter with each new impact. Finally I crumple to a stop on the bottom landing.

I stay there for a few minutes, trying to assess the damage to my body. Already, I feel a vicious soreness creeping into my muscles and can see that my arms and legs have been tie-dyed with deep purple, green, and blue bruises. But as I carefully squeeze each limb, I can tell that that's the worst extent of the damage. Eager not to be found in this pile, I crawl down the hall to my room on all fours and pull myself into bed. Then I clasp my hands together in prayer:

> *Dear Heavenly Father, I'm grateful my bones didn't break on the way down the stairs. I'm so grateful I don't have to go back to the hospital right now . . . and I'm sorry. I'm sorry for my pride. I just want to be able to care for myself—to support myself. I realize that I've never done it all on my own, dear Heavenly Father. Please help me to admit what I can't do and embrace everything I can. Help me to show gratitude to my family who have done so much for me and help me to make all of this up to them . . . one day. I say these things in Jesus' name, Amen.*

It doesn't take long to settle into a routine. Once a week, a home nurse comes to take my blood to monitor my medication levels. Every three or so days, my physical therapist visits to show me new exercises and give me new goals—ride for this long on the stationary bike, climb that many stairs. Every morning, my alarm goes off at 8:00 a.m. and I take my first round of pills. Then Mom comes down to debride my wounds from the drainage tubes and the bedsores.

Debriding is an awful process, but essential to both prevent infection and reduce scarring as my many wounds heal. After scrubbing up to her elbows, Mom painstakingly picks off dying cells from the raw skin covering my back with tweezers and dresses my tube sites with ointment and antiseptic. It's painful for me and stressful for her—I feel the tension in her grip as she picks and dabs with as much precision as she's capable of. Both of us are glad when it's over.

But other than the pain, there isn't much to stem the monotony. Flu season is particularly virulent this year and, with my immune system being actively suppressed by transplant meds, my visitors are limited: family, nurses, and a few carefully screened childhood friends. I can't walk far. I don't like watching TV. It can get dreary.

Meanwhile, life outside of my room forges on. Now sixteen, seventeen, and nineteen, respectively, Glorianna, Mercina, and Shiloh have all continued the family tradition of early college attendance. When the semester starts up again the first week of January, they're either in school or studying for it. Zen and I begin to spend more time together, just the two of us. While everyone else is in class, we study, cook, and watch movies together in my little apartment.

The weeks pass, and I get stronger. But with every improvement, a terrifying reality confronts me: *I can do almost everything a regular person can by now. But can I still sing?* The question haunts me and my progress, keeping me awake at night.

It's a Tuesday morning and Mom has just finished wound care before going to run errands. I'm alone. I close the door to my apartment and Google the words to an old song I first heard in a musical called *Nat King Cole and Me*. As I scroll through the results I think back to the night I saw it—Mom had won tickets for the whole family years ago, quite soon after my diagnosis. Written and performed by Gregory Porter, the musical was his memoir, told through the songs of Nat King Cole. The stories he shared onstage were profoundly difficult and intensely personal, yet, as Porter sang "Unforgettable," "Star dust," and "Mona Lisa," I couldn't keep empathetic tears from brimming in my eyes. I remember looking down the row during his rendition of "The Very Thought of You" to see my entire family, everyone from Dad to Zenith, sobbing alongside me. Through those hopeful, longing, melancholy tunes, we felt the thrill of ephemeral joys and the sweet sadness that settles into our hearts when they pass.

One of the songs from that night stuck with me longer than any of the others. Whenever my life got particularly bleak, I'd think back to "Smile"—written by Charlie Chaplin and performed most famously by Mr. Cole, then Mr. Porter. Recently, I've been listening to that song almost daily, its simple tune carrying a powerful message.

Inhale. Exhale. I start to sing:

Smile though your heart is aching
Smile even though it's breaking . . .

I continue until the song is over. The sound barely resonates; breathy, small, and thin, it wouldn't be heard over a piano, much less an orchestra. I gasp for breath every other word, messing up the meter of the song terribly. When I sing the final phrase, I'm breathless. It's about as far as it could be from the big, bright, focused sound I know as my own. Still, it's something. Sitting on my bed, I make myself a promise: in a year, I'll have retrained my voice. *That seems reasonable enough.* One year to practice, perfect, and recalibrate my expectations for my career. By then, I'll have made up for the time and skill I lost to my surgery. A year from now, I'll stop playing catch-up and start moving forward again.

The next night, Mom comes down to my room. "I've gotten three calls telling me you're on an advertisement for *American Idol* this week," she says, her brow knit in concern. "I thought you told me you didn't make it to the TV rounds?"

"I didn't!" I insist as my stomach drops through the floor.

This can't be good.

Two months before my transplant, I was in Chicago visiting

Yoni. Waiting in the middle of an endless queue downtown, I was riddled with uncertainty. In front of me stood a doe-eyed teenage girl fiddling with the floral-embroidered guitar strap slung over her shoulder; behind me, a six-foot-four man decked out in full drag. I was auditioning for *American Idol*. *How did I ever let Yoni talk me into this?* During the ten months we'd been dating, he had tried to get me to audition for the show three different times, to no avail. It just wasn't my kind of gig. But I had almost broken up with him over the phone a week before, and this audition was my ill-advised attempt at an apology. As I stood in line, I felt sick—well, a different type of sick than usual. I knew my voice wasn't the right fit for the show. I didn't sing pop or rock or folk. I sang opera. But Yoni insisted that, with all the classically trained singers doing gangbusters over at *America's Got Talent*, the producers would be salivating over me. I was not convinced.

Still, Dr. Girgis had barred me from traveling for work for almost a year, and I really did miss singing for an audience. I convinced myself that—since I'd be in town to visit Yoni anyway—auditioning for a silly TV show couldn't really hurt anything. Maybe it would even be fun.

After hours of waiting, I got in front of the first trio of judges—not Randy, Paula, and Simon, but rather three assistant junior producers. Singing for them, I finally felt comfortable again. My voice filled the arena to bursting and, as I finished my performance, both the judges and the 12,000 spectators behind them broke into exuberant applause. After breezing through the next two screening rounds, I went back to Yoni's apartment wondering how I ever could have doubted myself.

About a month later—just before my transplant—I received another callback. Mom begged me not to go. She thought the entire thing was crazy. But by that point I was so sick, I felt like I had nothing to lose. So I went. Again, I was advanced by all the junior producers. Gathered together in a room with the other contestants who had made it that far, our handlers explained that we wouldn't get on TV if rejected by this next judge, an executive producer, but we should still act as though we were performing on the actual show.

The room I walked into for my audition looked exactly like the *American Idol* set I'd seen on TV—bright colors, microphone stand, flimsy backdrop emblazoned with the *American Idol* logo. Except where the judges should have been, there, instead, sat a middle-aged man with long sideburns, a round face, and a plume of gray hair. After starting and stopping my performance several times, he dismissed me—"Not the right fit, hon." As I left the room, I felt more self-satisfied than disappointed. I was right, Yoni was wrong, and everything was right with the universe. After that, my life got so crazy I didn't even think about the audition again.

This can't be good.

I go to YouTube, already feeling ill. The advertisement isn't hard to find. There I am, belting out a high C at the end of the Season 9 Chicago auditions promo. The girl on that screen—me, six months ago—was dying. But she still wanted to be Great. At the very least, she wanted to be remembered. To be known and appreciated for doing the thing she loved most. If she didn't have the time to be ad-mired at the Met or La Scala, she could at least get 20 million viewers to tune in to watch her from the comfort of their own living rooms. Only as I sit in front of my computer six months later, the promo reel on loop in front of me, do I realize what a terrible mistake I made.

I never should have given them that high note, I taunt myself with crystal-clear hindsight. Regardless of the note's being clean and right on pitch, it was *different*. And that meant, in the hands of the right video editor, it was mockable.

Sitting in front of the television the next night, my entire body is tense. As segment after segment of the show passes, I begin to hope they've cut me out altogether. But then it happens. After a gag reel of zany, off-pitch, off-color performance snippets, I swoosh onto stage in a sunshine-yellow dress. Amputated from the rest of my performance, my high C bellows out from the TV's speakers. Then the tape deftly splices to a close cut of Simon Cowell's signature blasé scowl. Unhurriedly, he states in an uninspired British drawl—

"That was a complete and utter waste of time."

The scene cuts back to me. The Charity on screen smiles, says, "Thank you," and walks off happily—probably because she hadn't just been pilloried by Simon Cowell on the top-rated prime-time show of 2010. But current-day Charity isn't so lucky. I am utterly mortified. My head starts to spin, dizzy with embarrassment. Apparently, Mom feels similarly—

"Charity," she laments beside me, "I begged you not to do it! I begged you!"

And how I'm now paying for not heeding her advice. The opera world does not look kindly on unorthodox disciples of the antiquated art form. On the list of unforgivable sins in the classical universe, being ridiculed on a reality television show for performing one's craft is probably pretty near the top. Without a hint of my typical exaggeration, I can honestly state that I've never been so humiliated in my entire life. The fact that the interaction portrayed on-screen never occurred in reality doesn't make it any better. In fact, it might even make it worse. If I try to explain the circumstances to anyone, they won't just think I'm pathetic—they'll assume I'm a liar too. Talk about hitting a girl when she's down.

I feel my world imploding. Simultaneously, all of my family's phones begin to ring. My Facebook, voicemail, and email are jammed with notifications from friends, frenemies, acquaintances, and strangers letting me know they had just witnessed my professional downfall along with millions of other people. Hours later, the phones still haven't stopped ringing. People begin telling me I have to sue for defamation. I go to my room and fall onto my knees in painful, humble prayer.

For a week, the Facebook posts, voicemails, and emails pile up. I dig a pit of self-loathing so deep I can't see daylight anymore. Then, almost as suddenly as they started, the calls and notes stop. The next episode of *American Idol* airs and establishes a new lineup of unwitting human punch lines. I delete everything and decide to move on from this catastrophe the way everyone else already has: by forgetting about it.

As my wounded pride and my wounded body begin to heal, I begin training in earnest. With half a decade of intensive vocal training and without the stamina for an hour, let alone a half-hour, lesson, I feel like I can at least start the process on my own. My breath always feels a little shallow, but every moment I practice, I feel my new lungs growing stronger. Each song I sing makes my new lungs seem more at home. After every session, the pressure around my scar diminishes. The act of singing makes me feel more complete—more whole. Each day, it seems my breath carries me a little farther in a musical phrase.

And it's not just in my head. The doctors confirm that my lung function is improving steadier and more quickly than before. As is my voice. While I still never quite feel like I'm taking a full breath, my body begins to belong to me again. But not *just* me. Now, I'm a collaborative endeavor; a partnership between the lungs, their former owner, and me.

I've taken up painting since my surgery—reading and TV give me headaches while I'm on my meds, but painting brings a sort of productive relief from the monotony of getting better. While I paint, I listen to master classes with the Greats: Callas, Tebaldi, Freni, Carreras, Horne. Blue, yellow, and green strokes dance across wood boards to Sumi Jo's Ophelia; droplets of ivory speckle a robin's-egg blue sky as Fleming sings Marguerite's arias alongside Domingo's Faust. As my hum crescendos and decrescendos along with these masterful performances, my brush ebbs and flows its way across my canvas—it's an encompassing sensory experience.

I could do this forever. The stakes are low. It's less public. And I have purpose, of a sort. Slowly, I begin to feel content. Then, on a Friday afternoon in February, I hear a knock on my door.

"Charity," Mom invites herself in. "Today are the regional finals for the Met auditions. It's at the new opera house. Should we go and listen?"

The Metropolitan Opera's National Council Auditions are the *American Idol* of opera. They take place annually across the country for singers under thirty. Local winners advance to the regional finals and regional finalists advance to the Metropolitan Opera House at Lincoln Center for the final competition. Thousands of singers participate every year. A lucky few are catapulted to national and international careers in opera.

The prospect of going torments me. I miss opera terribly, and I've always dreamed of singing at Lincoln Center. But watching others on their way to accomplish *my* dream might be a special kind of torture. Even if I ever had a chance to be the next Great opera singer, how could I expect to now—after everything I've been through? I've begun to love painting, but deep down I know it's not mine. A single image can capture glamour, pain, joy—a thousand different words. Music captures nothing; it sets sound free.

As I contemplate whether or not to attend the auditions, my heart starts pounding in my chest. My life can never be a work of art hanging static in a bare gallery space. *Because it's already an opera*. Dramatic. Dynamic. Loud. Cast with exquisite, imperfect people—together with their wrinkles, fat rolls, and flat notes. Virgin priestesses who long for love and the men who misunderstand them; fishers of roles and menders of people, either trying to hook their next big break or save a life worth dying for. Somehow, this cacophony of noise and humanity comes together in transcendent highs and ecstatic lows—strong enough to create waves that pull people back across centuries, just to hear for themselves the sound of being alive.

"Let's go. It will be fun," Mom goads me back into the real world as I shake myself out of the strange reverie into which I've ascended.

"Yes. All right," I agree.

A pile of Purell wipes accumulating in my lap, I sit in the theater listening to the young singers who have devoted so much of their lives to this esoteric art form I love so much. Their voices are beautiful—some more polished, bigger, brighter, darker, fuller, or flatter. But none of them are mine. Until I'm singing where they're singing, I refuse to be content.

So, the joke goes: A tourist asks violinist Mischa Elman how to get to Carnegie Hall. Elman tells him, "Practice." It's not bad advice.

I start to practice in earnest. Every day, I double my singing time. Soon, my body begins to quake with exhaustion. It doesn't matter. I am going to do this until my voice feels like my own. But returning to the world of opera requires more than a voice. Eventually, I'll have to start functioning like a human being again. Changing out of my sweats seems like a good place to start.

It's a more challenging task than I'd anticipated. My sisters have brought me piles of clothes, but Double Zero skinny jeans sag on me and every single one of my ribs is visible through their old T-shirts. Looking through drawers in my mom's room, I find a pair of black leggings. I pull them on. They're loose, but they'll do. I tug an oversized Scotty dog sweater over my head and move toward the vanity in my room. Putting on makeup, I attempt to fill out my sunken cheeks and eye sockets. The results aren't exactly convincing. These days, looking in the mirror is depressing. My face is so thin I can hardly recognize it. My legs are sticking out of the bottom of my sweater like a pair of black fleece chopsticks. As I wrangle my hair, trying to cover the bald spots and bedsores on my scalp, a tear runs down my cheek. I don't want to subject other people to looking at me. As if on cue, Zen strolls into my little suite, sees me standing at the mirror, and begins to laugh.

"Don't tease me!" I wail.

"I'm not teasing you," he rejoins. "I'm giving you some much-needed fashion advice. Scotty dog sweaters are *not* your look."

"I don't have any other options!" I throw my hands up in frustration.

"You would if you'd eat more."

I glare at him. Eating used to rank as one of my all-time favorite activities, but now it's one of the most unpleasant things I do. Every meal begins with a caloric tour de force: a full-fat-and-sugar root beer float and a cheese quesadilla topped with green chili and sour cream. A couple of Lindt truffles, and, then, an entire meal on top of that. And this happens for Every. Single. Meal. But no matter how much I eat, it never sates my family's expectations. As long as I'm underweight, they'll remain unimpressed. Nothing I do is ever enough for them.

I start to cry in earnest.

"Dude. Charity. You can't just cry every time anyone tells you anything," Zen scoffs, walking back out of the door.

Zenith should have been an only child, I think contemptuously to myself as he leaves. Nearly six feet and thirteen years old, he's too tall for his age and too handsome for his own good. To make it worse, Zen's charming too. Girls flock to him in indecent numbers, and no one except Zen can quite figure out how to manage them. He gets what he wants and has no respect for authority—expertly tugging emotional threads to torment or delight others as it suits him. The rest of us have always been responsible for someone or something—a sibling or a pet, a chore or exchange student—but somehow Zen has never fallen into the regular Tillemann-Dick chain of command. In his eyes, he's either equal or superior to everyone else—mother, brothers, sisters. Church leaders and doctors and soccer coaches. It makes no difference. Zen is on their level—or at least he can talk like he is.

"You just don't understand," I mutter after him.

"No, I don't"—he spins around, agreeing with me. "To me, you seem totally nuts. Like, kind of emotionally unhinged."

I am a little unhinged. I'm twice Zen's age, living at home, and dependent on my family. I can't walk on my own, I can't cook on my own, and apparently I can't even dress myself. I can't sing—really sing—anymore. I don't look like I used to. I can hardly take a deep breath. I'm not myself right now and I'm the first to admit it.

In the hospital, every single one of my nurses would tell me how well I was doing every time we interacted. Each therapist would comment on how strong I'd gotten during each of our sessions. Whether I needed it or not, there was always a "You're doing great!" or "I can't believe how far you've come" just a few sentences away. At home, though, I can't help but feel I'm doing something—maybe everything—wrong. Now surrounded by teenage siblings, snarky asides and eye rolls have replaced glowing commendations and high fives. I'm still working as hard as I ever have, but somehow I keep coming up short to everyone around me except Mom. At the hospital, I felt like an athlete training for some epic feat of physical prowess. At home, I feel more like the embodiment of disease and its inconveniences.

I've been training my voice in earnest for almost a month, but it's still a shadow of the instrument I had planned to build my life around. If I could only get Zen to understand what I've lost—

"You don't know what it's like to have spent your whole life working for something, *fighting* for it, and then losing it all for no reason—to complete arbitrariness. It's really painful, Zen. It's hard."

"You're talking about singing?" he asks, an eyebrow raised.

"Yes, I am."

"Then you're a selfish idiot," he states matter-of-factly.

"*Excuse* me?"

He continues—"Dude. You had a mom and a dad when you were a kid. Guess what? I'm pretty much an orphan. Me. Glorianna. Mercina. Shiloh—we were orphaned because Mom ran off to take care of you and Dad died. I mean, grow up a little, Charity. We didn't have anyone to raise us and we figured it out. But you're crying because you can't *sing*? *That's* why you're a selfish idiot."

He slams the door behind him as he saunters out of the room. I'm aware that my illness was hard on my siblings, but it's not a walk in the park for me either. Frustrated, confused, and, for the first time in years, PMSing, I face-plant into my pillow and sob.

"What did you do to your sister?!" I hear Mom ask Zen in the stairwell.

"Nothing!" Zen exclaims. "Charity's just crying again because she's insane."

"Zen . . ."

"Really! Nothing!" He pauses. "Nothing to merit this kind of response, at least."

"Zenith. What happened?" demands Mom. "Your sister wouldn't be crying like this for no reason."

"Maybe it isn't 'no reason' but it's a stupid reason . . ."

I could scratch out his eyes right now.

". . . She's in there whining—sobbing—because she says she's never going to sing opera again," he finishes in a mocking voice.

"That's very hard for her, sweetie," Mom rejoins calmly.

"Yeah, well, it's dumb. For a few reasons: First of all, she already sings better than 99.9 percent of the world's population. My guess is that she'll be doing whatever the heck she wants a few months from now. But, Mom. She's in there mourning like, like, Mimo died because—one month out of the hospital—she's not singing as well as she did when she was working as a professional opera singer in Italy. That's just unreasonable. In my opinion, it's crazy."

"Well, when you say it like that . . ." Mom concedes.

"How else are you going to say it? She's already down here all day belting like Barbra Streisand. So what if she doesn't sing opera again? No one really likes that crap anyway! She's probably better off singing something else."

Mom takes a deep breath and they both walk back up the stairs together.

Guilt has been my constant stalker. There's been no way to avoid the drain my disease puts into our trough of family relationships. But whether I am conscious of it or not, listening to

Zen helps me begin to unravel a paralyzing culture of perfection within the opera world, my understanding of faith, and of family. Theoretically, all three hold an appreciation for what makes something different. But all Zen wants me to do—all that my family wants me to do—is to sing and be happy; however, wherever, and doing whatever I can. That is the only thing they want for me. It doesn't matter if it's opera, musical theater, or children's songs. When I sing, I see judgment and inadequacy. Zen sees a miracle.

I'm just curious, *what will happen?*

Turning on the water in the sink and the shower to muffle the noise, I brace myself against the counter and begin to sing. I've chosen Puccini's simple yet exquisite tomato-sauce aria: "O mio babbino caro."

The first notes sound thin, but all right. Then, I go up for the high A natural.

Just air.

I try the phrase again. Same result.

If I just sing the A alone?

Nothing.

I'm humiliated, but at least only privately. Opera obviously isn't working out. Maybe Zen's right. Maybe it's time for me to try my hand at folk or jazz or musical theater. Maybe there just isn't room in opera for someone like me.

Putting on makeup is exhausting. *How haven't I realized that before now?* Lining my upper eyelid, my right bicep gives out and I rest my arm on the vanity when Mom walks into the room.

"Chary," Mom croons, "how are you?"

"Better today. Sorry about my little breakdown yesterday," I reply.

"Don't be silly," she insists. ". . . Chary?" The tone of her voice becomes sheepish all of a sudden.

"Yes?"

"Well," she continues, "I got a call from Jeanne at the Cleveland Clinic."

"Oh! I hope you gave her my love!"

"Of course, of course . . ." Mom trails off. There's a beat of silence.

"Why did she call? Just to catch up?" I ask.

"Not exactly," she responds cautiously.

I leave the bathroom door open as I apply mascara to my other eye. Mom speaks a little louder.

"She asked if you would come back to Cleveland to perform for your doctors . . ."

"Of course!" I say. "I'd love to. Maybe in a year. I think I'll be ready in a year."

"She was hoping you could do it a bit sooner," Mom goads hesitantly.

"Mom. I'll never be taken seriously again as a singer if I'm not at my best for my first major performance. And anyway, people will enjoy it much more if I'm really in shape vocally," I say, moving on to my hair.

"But Jeanne's been so good to us—she was so good to you!"

Of course, Mom's right about that . . .

". . . I told her you'd perform at the clinic in three months."

I turn to face her, eyebrows raised.

The words tumble out of her now. "Chary, the clinic has been very good to us and I think we owe this to them. If it wasn't for

Dr. McCurry and Dr. Budev, you wouldn't be alive! And I have a feeling this could be a very important opportunity for you."

"Mom, you know, I wasn't planning to perform for a while."

Quiet for a moment, a tired smile makes its way across her face.

"Charity," she says, taking my gaunt shoulders in her hands, "I know if you have something to work toward, you'll do it. I know you'll do it. And these people were so good to us! They did so much for us. We owe this to them."

Looking into Mom's glistening eyes, I see the pain of her father's death. Of Dad's death. Of my illness and transplant. I see hours spent on her knees making pacts with God to win back my life. I see nights spent crying. I see months spent away from her home and her young children. I love my doctors—I respect what they've done for me—but I don't need to sing for them. Nor do I need to sing for some faceless, hypercritical musical intelligentsia. I need to sing for Mom. I need her to know that she didn't just keep me from dying—she saved my life. And that means I need to sing.

"OK, Mom. I'll do it."

I'll do it for you.

If I'm going to perform in three months, I need to move up my timeline. I email my old voice teacher, Cathy, and we schedule a lesson. The night before our first session, I pick up a call from Yoni. Finishing up his final semester of grad school in Chicago, he calls me in between his classes and before he goes to bed.

"Are you nervous," he asks, knowing how wary I am of fellow singers' judgment.

"I'm just so worried I'll go in there and she'll tell me not to do this performance. I mean, Mom would be so disappointed," I add, unwilling to admit that I've begun to look forward to it too.

"But you trust her?"

"Totally," I reply, recalling her fateful advice for me to stay in Hungary so many years before.

"Baby," Yoni says after a pause, "I miss you. So much."

"Oh, Yoni. I miss you too. I'd like to talk all night. But my lesson is early and you have class in the morning . . ."

". . . What if we just don't hang up? I can wake you when I get up for school?"

I smilingly consent and slowly drift off, phone still pressed to my ear.

"Chary? Chaaaaarity . . ."

I stretch out and rub my eyes. *Where's Yoni?*

"Chary! You have to take your meds!" Yoni is now shouting at me from the receiver, which has become tangled in the sheets beside me during the night. I pick it up and, finally, we say a hurried goodbye to each other. Then I rush to take my medications and dress for my lesson with Cathy.

I haven't had a proper voice lesson in over a year and a half. Headed south on I-25 toward the University of Denver's Lamont School of Music, I'm a ball of nerves—equal parts dread and excitement. When I exit onto University Boulevard, my angst materializes in a knot lodged between my shoulders. Snaking through the monumental building, I finally make my way down the second-floor hallway to Cathy's studio. I wait in front of her heavy wood door for just a few extra moments.

Cathy welcomes me into a studio with sparkling wooden floors and soaring ceilings. Large windows overlook the school's grand atrium while score-filled bookshelves line the walls. Framed portraits of past students smile down at Cathy as she sits in the back corner of the room, just like she'd sat when I first met her a decade earlier. Looking at me, her big brown eyes flash. "Charity!" she exclaims. "It is *so* good to see you!"

I feel nervous. Awkward—like it's my first voice lesson all over again. It's as if all the concert halls I'd packed and the orchestras I'd performed with never even existed. But maybe this isn't terrible. *Maybe this will be like starting with a vocal blank slate. But in a good way. Maybe I'll just relearn everything even better than I had before.* I'm so wound up in my own thoughts I nearly forget to greet Cathy.

"... Charity?"

"It's good to see you too!" I offer quickly, still distracted.

"You're ..." she pauses, "... so thin!"

"Oh, well—there's nothing like organ failure for weight loss!" I reply without thinking. For a moment, she looks mortified. Then we begin to laugh together, still not altogether comfortable.

"Well," she says resolutely. "We'll have time to catch up later. Shall we vocalize?"

We make our way up and down the scale. Before the transplant, I'd had a range of over four octaves. Now, my voice cracks a full octave below high C. I used to know every note I sang just by the way it felt. Now, I can't even tell when I'm off-pitch. As I gulp down breaths in the middle of the short five-note scales, I wonder how on earth I thought I could ever do this again. I'm already twenty-six. It will take years to regain what I've lost. By then, I'll have aged out of every young artist program or competition. And returning to Europe? Out of the question. It was a mistake to think otherwise.

Cathy stops me. "Do you know 'Home,' from *Phantom*?"

"I've never heard of it," I admit.

"It's not *Phantom of the Opera*. It's the one by Yeston and Kopit. Take a look. I think it will fit your voice nicely right now."

She opens the book and I sight-read through the song. It tells the story of a girl who only feels at home in the midst of music. While it's extremely different from the arias to which I'm accustomed, Cathy's right. Somehow, the tessitura—how the music sits in my vocal range—is perfect for me exactly where I am. Even a cursory read-through makes me feel like a singer again. It's not as complex as Bellini, but, singing it, I feel confident. I feel at home.

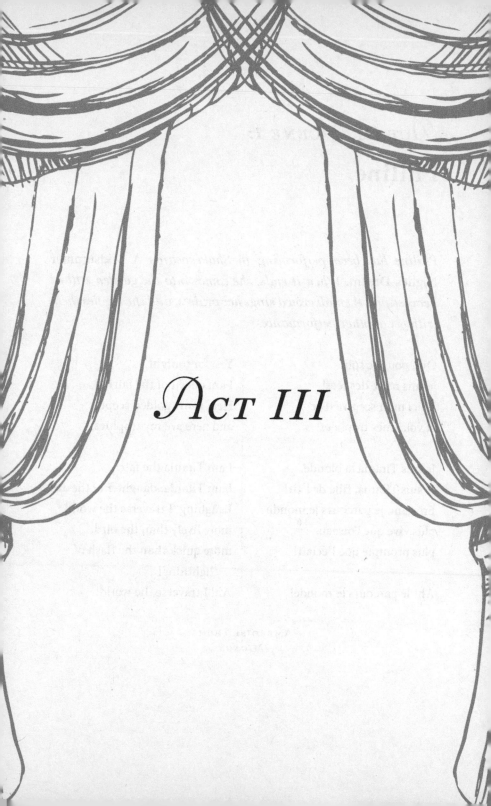

ACT III

Act III, Scene 1:
Philine

Philine has been performing in Shakespeare's A Midsummer
Night's Dream. *When it ends, she comes into the garden still in
her costume. A small crowd sings her praises, and she regales them
with yet another performance.*

Oui, pour ce soir	Yes, for tonight
je suis reine des fées!	I am queen of the fairies!
Voici mon sceptre d'or	Here is my golden scepter,
et voici mes trophées!	and here are my trophies!
Je suis Titania la blonde.	I am Titania the fair.
Je suis Titania, fille de l'air!	I am Titania, daughter of the air!
En riant, je parcours le monde	Laughing, I traverse the world
plus vive que l'oiseau,	more lively than the bird,
plus prompte que l'éclair!	more quick than the flash of
	lightning!
Ah! Je parcours le monde!	Ah! I traverse the world!

—AMBROISE THOMAS,
MIGNON

I t's 3:00 a.m. and I can't sleep. Today, May 25, 2010, I'll perform for the first time with my new lungs. Today, it will be the first time an opera singer has performed with someone else's lungs.

Mom and I arrived yesterday evening. I think of the last time we were in Cleveland together—of our tiny ICU nook, her lounge chair, and my hot hospital sand mattress. She now sleeps beside me in the king-size bed, snuggled into downy hotel pillows. But I can't get my heart to slow down. It's been a long year and so much has been lost and regained. The work required to get here is almost unfathomable and now that I've arrived, my body doesn't want to miss a moment of it—not even to sleep. I feel ready, but I also feel nervous and terribly excited.

The performance for my doctors is a much larger event than I anticipated. Every year, the Cleveland Clinic holds a Patient Experience Summit. Scott Simon from NPR and I will close out the festivities. The clinic flew Mom and me out from Denver together. Mercina, Shiloh, Zenith, and Glorianna are following behind us by car.

My cell phone rings. It's Mercina. *They're here!* Trying not to wake Mom, I tiptoe out of the hotel room and make my way down to the mezzanine to let the kids in through an unmanned side door. Creeping back toward the room, we do our best to be inconspicuous. Crammed into the previously cavernous hotel room, everybody falls slowly to sleep. Everyone except me.

Inhale. Exhale.

Finally morning. I sneak down to the lobby for breakfast, careful not to wake any of the snoozing bodies surrounding me. Undressed and unshowered, I put the hood up on my sweatshirt to mask my appearance. A beautiful buffet has been spread for the summit's attendees; I start helping myself.

"Excuse me," chimes one of the organizers, tapping lightly on my shoulder, "this is a private event." I turn my head, smiling broadly.

"Oh! I didn't recognize you!" She steps back in shock.

"I'm hoping that no one else does, either!"

As she walks away, I fill my kangaroo pocket with pastries, fruits, muffins, rolls, jams, and butter. On the elevator, fellow riders regard me—standing in the corner, hood up, pockets bulging—suspiciously. As the floors tick off, I remember how, as a little girl, it so humiliated me when my grandmother would sneak food from galas and receptions into her purse. I smile at my own ridiculous (and obviously inherited) display of food hoarding.

Back in the hotel room, I arrange the pilfered breakfast on a windowsill. Then I pull on some slacks and head down to my dress rehearsal. Just as I reach the door, Mercina begins to rouse.

"There's breakfast on the table," I whisper. "If Mom wants to come, tell her I'm practicing downstairs."

My sister groggily nods and I make my way down to the dress rehearsal. There, I meet Joela for the first time since I was in the hospital. Among other things, Joela is the principal pianist and keyboardist for the Cleveland Orchestra. Expert in everything from organ and celesta to harpsichord and accordion, Joela was a child prodigy and remains a virtuoso. We met in 2005 when I debuted at Severance Hall and have been dear friends ever since. It is wonderful to sing with her again and she goes over every note with me to be sure my voice is sitting in the ideal place on each pitch.

I walk back to my hotel room, invigorated. I coat my lips in a rose lipstick, then layer a gold shade on top of that. I line my eyes and rouge my cheeks. I pull up my burnished gold skirt and button the matching jacket, then bring my now-plentiful hair back into a simple chignon. As I pass the full-length mirror, I have to stop. It's only been three months since I got out of the hospital, but it seems like a lifetime ago. Three months ago, I could hardly breathe, I could hardly eat, I could hardly walk, and I certainly couldn't sing. Three months ago, I was sure I would never get better. Looking at the reflection gazing back at me now, though, I can only think that I've never looked prettier.

Stepping onto the platform, Dr. Pettersson—the senior lung transplant surgeon at the clinic—helps me onto the stage and I take care not to trip. This is only the third time I've been in high heels since the surgery and my feet constantly tingle from nerve damage. Greeting the old surgeon with a kiss on his cheek, I turn toward the audience. Bright lights blind me and, for a moment, the stage and I are the only things in the room.

The pinched introduction of the piano begins and I know Joela is once again by my side. As the broken VII chord sounds, I breathe in. Just as the dominant note plays, I say a silent prayer: *Oh my dear Father. Bless me to sing gloriously.*

With that, I begin "O mio babbino caro," the aria I had tried to sing so unsuccessfully in my bathroom three months before. As I navigate the octave jumps in the score, I understand Lauretta's dilemma for the first time. There are things we each know belong in our lives and, sometimes, it doesn't matter whether they make sense or not. With Lauretta, it was a man. I'd started off caring about my music, but my list was growing. The older I got, the more I realized that my entire life was a series of things that—to an outside observer—made absolutely no sense. My faith. My career. My boyfriend. But life isn't lived through observation.

You don't perform by sitting in the audience. Love is a noun and a verb. It is something I just have to *do*. Same as Lauretta. To anyone else, her devotion seems like the definition of recklessness. But actually *experiencing* love is the only thing in this world that makes any sense. As this epiphany fills my mind, I sing the last, pleading words of the aria. Approaching the final note, I'm filled with gratitude for these lungs, for my family, for my doctors, for my donor. My life. I hold the final note for as long as my breath carries it, coming off just as Joela finishes the final arpeggio.

A brief moment of silence, then the audience jumps to their feet and applauds seemingly endlessly. Only now do I realize how enormous the room is, and there's not an empty space in it. There are over a thousand faces looking up at me—many striped with tears.

I sing a few more songs. The crowd's reception is heady. I thank my doctors, my nurses, and my mother, then exit stage right. Waiting for me outside of the ballroom, production crews and journalists descend with questions, cameras, flashes, and microphones. An avalanche of people floods out from the hall, joining the well-intentioned melee. My little brothers and sisters buffer me against the press of the crowd as we stumble toward a quieter room away from the fray. As we walk off, a man with white hair and a goatee grabs my hand, placing a card in it—

"I have an amazing performance for you this fall. It will change your life."

I nod, smiling halfheartedly. With so many people, I'm nervous about germs. *Wouldn't it be ironic if I caught a virus while singing for my doctors?* My brothers and sisters must be thinking the same thing, and their collective pace around me quickens.

"Email me!" the man shouts as my siblings push me away from the crowd. "Don't forget!" he calls, shaking his finger.

Within days, my performance has gone viral—showing up in newspapers and newscasts across the globe. I have to admit, it's exciting. Mom and I unwittingly collected a giant pile of business cards after the performance. Back in Denver, I go through them, sending promised emails to each one of the well-wishers. Most of the replies come from administrators, doctors, and hospital workers. And then I get a note from a senior executive at Yamaha Music Corporation.

> *Hey kiddo. I'm the guy with the goatee from your performance the other day. Just so you know: in a few days, you'll be receiving an email from the producer of a major event taking place this fall. He works with the founder of TED. They're working on TEDMED and you'll be amazing for it. Make sure to get back to him. Look for me at the conference. I'll still be the guy with the goatee!*

I have two important questions. Marching upstairs to the living room, I announce: "I think I'm going to sing for someone named Ted. Just 'Ted.' But who is this guy anyway and why does he spell his name in capital letters?"

"Wait. Did you say TED?" Glorianna, rarely star struck, looks at me like I'm from another planet.

"Yes?" I say nervously.

"Like, capital T-E-D? *That* TED?"

I nod.

"Oh. TED's awesome. That's awesome. You'll be awesome . . . or you'll suck," she concludes with a snort.

The information, though minimal, is at once exciting and

discouraging. Later, on the phone with Yoni, I look up the TED website. Turns out he's an "it," not a "he." TED is an acronym for technology, entertainment, and design—an elite conference that brings together experts, artists, and luminaries for one giant show where everyone performs in eighteen minutes or less. TED-MED is its medically oriented counterpart. The list of presenters reads like a who's who of medicine, business, music, the arts, and design. And the conference isn't just expensive, it's exclusive. There's a long, involved application process for any person already willing to spend thousands of dollars for the privilege of attending. I've attended my share of Washington soirees with my grandfather, but this is an entirely different animal.

Just as he promised, TEDMED's producers, Marc Hodosh and Richard Saul Wurman, email me after a few days. Two phone calls later, I have my first real booking. Then there's a gala performance in Cleveland and a keynote for a huge organ donation conference in Dallas. As the invitations pile up, I start to get excited. It's not a return to the stages I've dreamed of, but it's a start.

July Fourth in Washington, DC. Yoni will arrive later in the afternoon from New York. He has just finished graduate school and we'll finally be able to spend significant amounts of time in the same city. The prospect thrills me, but I can't help but feel some apprehension as well. Yoni left job offers on the table in Chicago, and DC is as saturated a job market as exists right now. Because of concerns over health insurance, we've decided to not get engaged until Yoni has a job with benefits for both of us. I'm concentrated on moving toward that goal, while Yoni is more concerned about literally moving closer to me. But today, I try to put aside those concerns. The Fourth is kind of our anniversary and we finally get to celebrate together. I can't wait.

Yoni spends his days on the job search, but the market is still sluggish. Washington is inundated with NYC refugees of the Great Recession, and finding a suitable position is difficult. In contrast, my fall schedule is packed—I have a number of well-paying performances and speaking gigs—but I can't help but feel dissatisfied. The path to Lincoln Center is through young artist programs and opera companies, not the conference circuit.

By the end of the summer, Yoni has finally secured a spot on a campaign. Temporary and in another state, it's far from ideal. But we've done long distance before and I know we can do it again. We rendezvous two, three, four times a month—meeting for a quick bite or for a walk in a park. The work is good for him and he's good at it. Yoni isn't a showman like me, but he has a knack for politics and he thrives on the campaign's constant hum of activity.

Meanwhile, I'm trying to ready my voice for the upcoming performances. I haven't yet summoned the courage to go and see my New York contacts yet, but I know I'll soon need to. Joan Dornemann, the grande dame of the Metropolitan Opera, has recently gotten back to me and asked me to come see her in September. While I've been improving, she needs to know I'm ready. I'm determined not to disappoint her—or myself—but it's going to take a lot of work.

There are a few weeks in New York where summer seems to forget fall is on her way. There are hints: the air is drying out and a few errant yellow leaves grace most trees. But it's when we forget life is always changing that the most drastic transformations take place.

"This weekend. Eleven a.m. I want to show you another piece," Joan says, bidding me farewell after our first lesson in over a year. "Charity, you are very fortunate. Your voice—well—you sound better than when we were together two years ago in Israel. And your breath is coming along nicely. I'll see you soon."

I kiss both of Joan's cheeks and step into the elevator. As the door closes, so do my eyes in prayer, *Dear Heavenly Father— thank you. Thank you so much.*

"It went well?" Yoni asks, leaning against the car door as I exit the building.

"She called my voice a Stradivarius," I whisper, tears running down my cheeks.

I'm so very happy. It's been one year since my transplant and I'm right on schedule. Nine months earlier, I thought this day would never come. But now, I can sing! I can *really* sing. My desire to return to the opera stage isn't some pipe dream—it can still happen. I'm just now starting to believe it again. Driving home with Yoni though, I realize this small success means I have a lot of work ahead.

My coaching with Joan sets the tone for the whole season. Early autumn is cloaked in a kind of peaceful, creative energy. While we've had a lovely interlude in New York, Yoni has to go back to the campaign in Delaware, and I start a self-directed vocal boot camp. Joan sends me to Renée Fleming's voice teacher, Gerald Martin Moore, and an amazing breathing coach named Deborah Birnbaum. I reconnect with singers, directors, and conductors I haven't seen in years. Simultaneously, I'm preparing for my presentation at TEDMED. They send me the final dates toward the end of summer. My performance falls on the one-year anniversary of awaking from my coma.

I mention the unexpected anniversary to Marc Hodosh

during a conversation about the progress of my talk. While trained as a doctor and engineer, Marc has an unexpected gift for showmanship. A few afternoons later, he calls me.

"Charity," he explains, "first, I want you to know that we've decided you should open the whole event. You'll come onto stage. You sing an aria and everyone in the room is going to be saying to themselves, 'That was great, but why is an opera singer performing to open a medical conference?' And the first thing you need to say is: 'Exactly one year ago, I woke up from a monthlong coma after having undergone a double-lung transplant.' The rest of the talk sounds perfect and I love that you'll end it with a song. But if you start it like that, their jaws will drop to the floor. It will be amazing."

He's right and I know it.

My collaborations invigorate me. Knowing Yoni is only a few hours' drive away eases a great deal of stress. We talk multiple times a day about everything happening in our lives. It's a magical, easy season of kinship and wonder, which, it seems, is only going to get better.

———

L. Frank Baum wrote much of *The Wonderful Wizard of Oz* in the Hotel del Coronado, and more than a dozen movies were filmed on the resort's sprawling property. Pulling up to the hotel, I understand why. Memories of black-and-white movies turn Technicolor; blue sea, golden sand, white walls, and iconic red roofs dominate sight lines while the grand pagodalike turret looks like a dream come to life. The whole place is something out of an American fairy tale. I've spent the past weeks performing in Cleveland and Milwaukee and, as I step out of the taxi now, I feel prepared for tonight's TEDMED performance. Mike Bates—the

Yamaha executive from my March performance in Cleveland—greets me at the door.

"Welcome to paradise, kiddo," he says, spreading his arms wide and smiling.

Mike escorts me inside. The old, dark wood interior contrasts against the airy exteriors. As we walk through the spacious lobby, Mike chats absentmindedly—

"I almost got myself in big trouble with this one," he explains. "I called to tell them about you and how great you were gonna be, and Richard called me back and says, 'F— you!' about twenty times, telling me I'm not his producer and they aren't going to have you. But, kiddo, you wowed 'em both when you guys talked. And you'll wow them now!"

The insight makes my stomach somersault as we make our way into the grand ballroom, where we meet Marc. He helps me onto the stage, and the room is buzzing with activity as nearly fifty members of the production team and hotel staff prepare for tomorrow's big event. I wish Mike had kept me in the dark about Mr. Wurman's response to me—now, I can't help but feel I might be in hostile territory.

I begin to rethink. I had wanted to start off a cappella—no accompaniment. But while the effect is much more dramatic, it's also treacherous. If I start flat or sharp or go off-key during the cadenza, there's no way to hide it. *No. Whatever the risks,* I assure myself, *the impact will be worth it.* As I step onto the stage, one of the sound engineers hands me a microphone.

"Thank you, but I don't generally use microphones," I explain.

I have a pet theory that the placement of microphones too close to the face is a major reason opera has fallen from popular favor. Close amplification of opera singers flattens sound waves that carry the classically trained voice great distances, but sound technicians with backgrounds in rock and pop tend to put a disproportionate value on volume. I want this audience to feel the sensation of a raw voice vibrating against them—just like I had when I saw *Hansel and Gretel* as a little girl. I know how transformative it can be.

"Ha. You must not understand, lady," the technician shoots back. "The sound, it all gets lost under this rotunda—it's a huge room. And it will be filled with nearly a thousand people!"

"Would it be all right," I ask, smiling as broadly as I can, "if I just tried it once without the mic first?"

"We need to record . . ." he begins to protest, shaking his head.

"Just once! I promise I'll turn the mic on if you still think it's necessary afterward."

He relents and I begin to sing. As my trill lands on the high B-flat, the entire room freezes. People stop speaking midsentence. I continue, and several take seats in the semiconstructed audience space as my voice coats the room's every surface with sound. As I finish the aria, a white-haired man I don't recognize approaches me.

"Opera in blue jeans! Why hasn't the Met thought of this?" He wipes a tear from his face as he walks toward the stage. "You'll have to wear this same outfit tonight. People are going to be in a state of total disbelief. Disbelief!" he repeats, grasping my hands in his.

Who is this man and why is he telling me what to wear?

"This is Richard Saul Wurman," introduces Marc, "founder of TED." *Ah. That answers that.* I tense for a moment, remembering my earlier conversation with Mike. Briefly introducing myself and thanking them both, I'm grateful when our conversation is cut short—

"I've gotta steal her away, guys," interrupts the sound engineer.

"She obviously doesn't need the mic, but we still need to figure out how to record her."

We settle on a recording mic with dead speakers, and I head back to my room to prepare. The dress I had planned to wear is much more casual than my usual evening gowns, but blue jeans it ain't. I decide it can't hurt to take Richard's advice. Mercina, who arrived with Mom during my rehearsal, is skeptical. Eminently presentable from the moment she could button her own buttons, we sometimes joke that she was adopted because she's so different from the rest of us, her haphazard family. Mercina has a special gift for making things lovely—however hopeless the task seems at first. Immediately, she undertakes to make me shine.

I smile as she pulls out the hotel ironing board to starch a plain white oxford shirt, then moves on to selecting shoes and jewelry. Grateful to have Mercina managing my image, I focus on my speech—repeating the talk to myself over and over again in the bathroom, figuring out my emphases and intonations.

All of a sudden, it's showtime.

Glimpsing out from behind the curtain, I mostly notice the cameras. They're everywhere: one on a giant arm that swings up, down, left, and right; a few on platforms in front of the stage; several wandering around backstage—they're inescapable. I take a seat and continue to recite my words to myself. I'm not nervous. Of course there will be mistakes, but I'm as prepared as I'll ever be. I stand and practice pacing back and forth on my five-inch heels, hoping I won't fall during the talk.

"Two minutes," calls the stage director.

Dearest Father, I am so grateful to be here. Please bless me to bring glory to thy name by singing exquisitely and performing in a way that touches the hearts and souls of those who are in attendance today.

"Exactly one year ago, on October twenty-sixth," I begin, "I woke up from a monthlong coma after undergoing a double-lung transplant."

Audible gasps are followed by applause. My cadenza is pitch perfect and the opening line hits the audience just how Marc had envisioned. Weaving my tale of medicine and music, I feel simultaneously terrified and invigorated. I can't spot Mom in the crowd, so instead I look to the front row, where Sonia, a woman I chatted with in the washroom just before my performance, sits beaming. Every time I feel nervous or unsure, her smile encourages me through the next paragraph.

Soon, I'm giving my final pronouncement—a critique of fear-based medicine. I conclude with a message to Dr. Barst, the New York doctor who forbade me from singing after my diagnosis. Death comes to everyone, I declare, and no one can know when. A diagnosis isn't a death sentence, and doctors *and* patients should aim to live whatever life they have meaningfully—placing a higher value on happiness than on any pill.

When I finish, the crowd jumps to its feet, remaining there until I begin to sing again. I feel like my voice is as resonant as it has ever been.

After the performance, the group around me parts as Richard approaches. "I know TED. I founded TED. In all my years at TED, this was, without a doubt, the best opening I've ever had." He's glowing. "Tonight, you will come to my birthday party. It's very exclusive, but you can bring your mother."

I guess that means he likes me now?

That night, Mom and I walk into his birthday party. Elton John staples ring out from his fire-red piano. As I walk toward the table, I feel a tap on my shoulder. "Could you hold this for me," requests a man in a dark suit.

As I grasp onto the nearly empty wineglass, the bottom begins to feel hot. Then, with a twist of the goblet, the stem bends into a knot.

"How did he do that?!" Mom exclaims beside me.

The man smiles enigmatically and steps back into the crowd. Later, we learn he's a famed mentalist. Continuing into the room, exotic foods, performers, and beautiful artwork fill every space. I stand still for a moment, taking in this fantasy-come-to-life.

"Excuse me," a man's voice interrupts. "I have to introduce myself."

I do a double take. Strapping, Asian, and obviously older than me, the man is handsome, but perhaps not double-take handsome. No. I'm shocked because I've met this man before. During my coma.

"My name is Lee." I nearly stop him to explain I already know his name, but I realize that might come off a bit strong. Instead, I do my best to act normal. "I know you get this all of the time," he continues, "but I find you extremely attractive."

I blush at his forwardness. "It's nice to meet you too," I stammer, nearly dumbstruck.

My post-transplant coma was like a portal into an alternate universe. And in that universe, Lee and I had built a life together with my career as its centerpiece. As we speak now, it's undeniable there's something electric between us. Almost otherworldly. After a few minutes, I'm pulled away from our conversation to sing a birthday song. As Mom and I leave for the next party we've been invited to, Lee grabs my arm and places his card in my hand.

"How can I find you?" he asks.

I jot down my info for him, but really I'm relieved to go.

As we make our way through the vast resort, we pass a few of the parties we've been invited to join. Popping our heads in to say hello, we make slow progress toward our final destination—a dinner hosted by a famous venture capitalist. We step inside and find our seats.

"I thought I'd lost you!" shouts someone from across the room. It's Lee.

We're seated at different tables, but a knot starts to form in my stomach.

"Mom," I whisper, "can I leave early?"

"Why?" she demands. "We're having such a lovely time!"

"Yes," I agree, "but I was asked to sing again tomorrow morning. I should get to bed." It's a thin excuse, but it will have to do.

Lee catches my eye from across the dining room, but I avoid his gaze. It might only have been a dream, but I know where this leads, and it's not to happiness. I walk back to my room as quickly as I can.

"How'd it go, baby?" Yoni asks from the other end of the phone. "Martha Stewart, Steve Case, *everyone* was tweeting about the talk. Word on the street is you're amazing."

"Seriously? That's crazy!" I take a breath. "My night was— well—interesting . . . I met this guy from my dream."

Yoni pauses. "At least he's not the guy *of* your dreams?"

I laugh.

"What's his name?"

"Lee something or other."

Yoni responds with his full name.

"How did you know that?!" I ask.

"I didn't, but he's been all over the financial papers in the past week." Yoni pauses again. "You know, he's one of the wealthiest people in the world?"

Silence. Then Yoni scoffs.

"Why am I barely even surprised?" he says, sounding almost defeated.

I gave up on really breaking up with Yoni after it landed me in the hospital. We make so little sense as a couple, I figure fate is the only thing strong enough to keep holding us together. I know Yoni doesn't believe that. He's always been worried that we'd date for years, abstinently working our way toward marriage when, just before we make it official, I'd leave him to be someone else's trophy wife. Considering we regularly almost break up and it's never about anyone else, I find this fear ridiculous. But for the first time, I understand his paranoia. There's silence on the line for a few more moments.

"I love you," I say.

We say good night.

My performance the next morning is a big hit. In this little world of big people, I feel like a celebrity. This conference is like a fantasy grown-up version of summer camp, and like summer camp, it feels like it ends too soon. But I have to get back to work, with performances and auditions spread across the country.

I'm not performing in the operas I've been trained to perform. Instead, I'm performing the opera of my own life, using the great arias to articulate what words alone could never say. It's a different path than the one I'd imagined for myself, but, in the same breath, it suits me. I still hope to return to the opera stage one day. But, at this moment, I can't imagine being happier.

$\mathcal{A}$CT III, $\mathcal{S}$CENE 2:

Tatyana

Tatyana sits down to write a letter, pauses, and reads it back to herself.

Я к Вам пишу, — чего же боле?	I write to you, —and then?
Что я могу еще сказать?	What more is there to say?
Теперь, я знаю, в Вашей воле	Now, I know, it is within your power
Меня презреньем наказать!	to punish me with disdain!
Но Вы, к моей несчастной доле	But if you nourish one grain of pity
Хоть каплю жалости храня,	for my unhappy lot
Вы не оставите меня.	you will not abandon me.
Сначала я молчать хотела;	At first I wished to remain silent;
Поверьте, моего стыда	then, believe me,
Вы не узнали б никогда,	you would never have known my shame,
Никогда!	never!

—PETER ILYICH TCHAIKOVSKY,
EUGENE ONEGIN

November 7, 2010

Dear Charity,

This morning, I saw you on the television when I woke up. I know it was taped some time ago, but for me to wake up, turn on the TV and hear you sing and speak about what it was like after your lung transplant, and especially your singing "Smile when your heart is breaking . . ." by Charlie Chaplin was the best medicine for me!! Absolutely the best medicine!

I doubt you know that I have advanced non-curable, lung cancer that cannot be removed nor able to undergo lung transplantation. I never smoked, ate healthy my entire life, exercised—like your own history—something really bad happened and why? I don't know. But I responded to treatment for about a year and now no longer respond . . . I am starting experimental treatment which seems very bizarre as you know I spent more than 30 years of my career developing experimental medicine for pulmonary hypertension. I have to keep telling myself to believe in what I always told you and so many more of my patients, we will keep you stable until we have better treatments.

Enough rambling—and I haven't opened up to anyone like this since my diagnosis over a year and a half ago, but somehow hearing your voice this morning has had the most inspirational effect on me since being diagnosed.

My request may seem silly, but I would so appreciate a CD of your singing "Smile when your heart is breaking . . ."

as I keep singing it over and over in my head today. And I
believe that if you can do that, I need to as well!

With very warm regards,
Dr. Robyn Barst

S hame begins to course through me. The news clip came from an interview I did with CNN after my TED talk. In a few months, TED will push out a video of my talk. While I don't mention Dr. Barst by name, my speech's thesis is an indictment of her patient philosophy and bedside manner—even though this woman devoted her life to finding a cure for the disease that nearly took my life. I feel sick with guilt.

A few weeks later, Election Day has come and gone and Yoni's candidate won. They're still closing up shop, but Yoni has a bit more free time. Together, we drive out to Westchester, New York, to visit Dr. Barst. As we battle rush-hour traffic and icy roads, I warn him about her personality.

"She's extremely intense."

Yoni laughs. "I'm planning to marry *you*, Charity. I think I'll be OK."

"She makes me look mild!" I insist. "She's like a more intense Mom. But *all of the time*."

"Yeah," says Yoni dismissively, "I think I can handle it."

"You just don't understand," I say, shaking my head. "This woman haunted my treatment for half a decade. She'd call Didi to rile him up and try to insist I shouldn't sing."

"Charity," advises Yoni. "She's sick. If you're going to have a bad attitude, we should probably turn around now."

"No!" I protest. "I want to go! Honestly, I just feel really terrible about my TED talk." I pause for a few moments. "... Thinking about it, I don't know that I would have been so insistent about singing if it hadn't been for her."

"What do you mean?" prods Yoni.

"Well ..." I stop to gather my thoughts. "I suppose nothing is as encouraging as a worthy adversary."

I grew up in a family that values healthy disagreement. Dr. Barst was a remarkable person, responsible for putting my disease on the map. When I was diagnosed with PH, I wasn't in control of anything. In a way, it was empowering for me to disagree with this luminary. Even more so because I ended up being right. If I could prove one of the best doctors in the world wrong about my singing, maybe—just maybe—all of those other doctors were wrong about my disease. Maybe everything would be OK. Maybe I'd recover.

Just then, we pull into a long driveway. Together, we walk to the door. I hold Yoni's hand tightly, bracing myself for the acerbic doctor I met so many years before. Then the door opens to reveal a tiny woman wearing an enormous smile.

"Hello!" she says, bursting with warmth and wrapping her thin arms tightly around me. She holds the embrace a few moments longer than I anticipate. When she lets go, she's still beaming.

"And *this* must be Yoni!" She takes hold of him next as a handsome white-haired man steps out beside her.

"This is the other doctor in our house," she gestures, introducing her husband. Together, they show us around their home; family photos, and the inlaid piano that belonged to her grandmother. Then we make our way to their farm-style kitchen where a platter of charcuterie awaits. Over the next hours, we swap stories about the people we love and our dreams for the future. Dr. Barst wants to see her first grandchild born and her daughter's wedding. I want to sing at Lincoln Center. We both want to see pulmonary hypertension cured and rejection-proof, 3D-printed lungs.

"The first time I ever saw PH was in the early eighties. The patient was so sick, so young, and no one could figure out what was wrong with her. Everyone had given up, but I stayed beside her all night. She died in my arms after three days. The next time I saw the disease, I was able to diagnose it. I explained that the patient needed to be careful, but we'd treated some of the symptoms and he was feeling better. The night after he was released from care, he went out dancing with friends and dropped dead. When I got that call . . ." Tears begin to well in her eyes. "These patients—they just wanted to live their lives, but I was so scared for them. They didn't have to do anything *wrong*. Just being normal was enough to kill them. I decided I never wanted to see another young person die because of this disease. There were no treatments approved for PH at that time, but I dedicated my life to changing that. Today, there are ten approved and another twenty in the pipeline. Patients have choices now. But being so close—sometimes I couldn't see what it was like to live with a disease like this; with a sickness I know is going to . . ." she trails off.

Before we leave, I sing "Smile" for her, my voice vibrating the crystals on the living room chandelier. Back in the car, Yoni turns to me—

"Chary, you were just off," he says, shaking his head and smiling. "I know this woman. She's an overly protective Jewish mother. She cares so much about the people around her that she doesn't care what they want. That's what she is to all of her patients—and to you. That's why she's such a great doctor."

Yoni's right. She accomplished as much as or more than anyone in her field of study because she *cared*. Almost too much.
Caring doesn't make you omniscient and, sometimes, worry can
blind you to reality. But in most cases Dr. Barst's concern brought
about major progress for the patients for whom she so cared.
Maybe, on an individual level, her drive could be oppressive. But
on a systemic level, that intensity was transformative.

As I ponder, we cross the bridge into Manhattan, headed back
toward Yoni's own overly protective Jewish mother.

Thanksgiving again. This year, I'm out of the hospital and we certainly have a lot to be grateful for. It's a feast of epic proportions:
salmon, turkey, tofurkey, multiple stuffings, fresh bread, and
sides galore, over a dozen pies and cupcakes on top of that. One
would expect the games and guests and merriment from a family deprived of celebration for decades. It's a wonderful evening.
But over the past month, I've been getting nausea-inducing migraines. Midway through dinner, I have to excuse myself because
of the pain. Before the night is through, I've lost the contents of
my stomach twice.

Shortly after Thanksgiving, I catch cold. My sputum samples
and blood tests come back normal and I want to stop worrying,
but I can't. While my breathing measurements haven't taken the
dramatic drops I've been warned about, they are trending lower.
I call to explain my concerns to Travis, the nurse assigned to my
post-transplant care.

"Well," he says, "sometimes you just have to wait these things
out. Just remember the general rules: if you're coughing less
than a tablespoon of blood or measuring less than a ten percent
spirometry drop in a week, you're probably all right."

I know the guidelines, but still, something feels off. Waiting out an infection without medication seems to go against everything my nurses taught me. If I allow my immune system to deal with the bug in my upper respiratory tract, it's likely to attack my new lungs too. And that can lead to rejection.

I follow up with Travis a few times, but soon I just feel like a pest. It takes another two weeks before I feel like myself.

"Well, Chary," says Mom after the cold is finally resolved, "you should be grateful your body can get rid of a disease on its own. I never would have anticipated that after the transplant."

But during the quiet of night, I hear the faintest wheeze. An almost imperceptible rattling. *It's just my imagination,* I assure myself in the dark. But weeks later, my spirometry still hasn't returned to where it used to be. I'm starting to get nervous.

I return to New York. I love the city and the experiences I have here, but I dread the spirometer's downward march. Every four or five days, it drops again. Not enough to be considered statistically relevant, but it's not normal. I email Travis again and hear nothing back. *It's all psychosomatic,* I think, privately chiding myself for hypochondria. But each day, as I walk the blocks to my music lessons, my breathing gets heavier.

Fear is the side effect they never mention in transplant literature. The constant anxiety that the next thing to go wrong has already happened—that there's already a disaster under way inside you, just no way to measure it yet. My doctors have promised I'll get used to it—that I'll learn when I need to worry and when I can relax. *So why do I feel so ill at ease?*

The night before I go home for Christmas, my friend Katie and I carry a Christmas tree from the Upper East Side back to her apartment in Midtown. Decorations twinkle on brownstones as snow drifts down from a rose-colored sky. After cramming inside the elevator, we place the tree into a holder. We trim the Tannenbaum while listening to carols, then sip hot cocoa together in front of the twinkling lights. But I'm nearly too exhausted to appreciate the yuletide wonder of it all.

That night, I blow into my spirometer. Wheezes and moans squeeze out from my lungs. I start to cough. Spitting phlegm into my sink, I see blood—like a pin dipped in red ink dragged through the viscous mess. It's less than a drop, let alone a tablespoon. *Sometimes, you have to wait it out,* I repeat Travis's words in my head, trying to reassure myself. But in my gut, I know there's a problem.

Yoni picks me up the next morning and we begin our drive to Denver. (Flying home on a plane jammed full of strangers during flu season just isn't going to happen right now.) As a child, riding in the back of our family's repurposed Blue Bird school bus, I had always loved Kansas. Turns out I still do. The plains surrounding the highway are stunningly beautiful; even when the landscape is a mess of dirt and snow, the flatness surrounding us reflects light with an almost opalescent pink-yellow glow. Soon, we've crossed the border of Kanorado—an aptly named town that straddles the state line—and immediately the landscape changes. Past Colorado's threshold, we begin the climb to a mile high.

Within an hour and a half, we're exiting off I-70 and turning right on 46th Avenue. We park in front of Theopolis. Cloaked in snow, wreaths twinkle in every window. As Mom's herd of white dogs bounds out to meet us, the house looks straight out of a Currier & Ives picture print.

I'm so grateful to be home. But almost immediately I feel myself running out of breath as I climb the stairs to my room. I decide to call Dr. Budev.

"Charity, are you all right?" she asks, her voice tinged with concern.

"I don't know," I admit.

"Why didn't you call me when you got sick? I would have made an appointment that week!"

I try to explain—"I called my coordinator . . ."

"I don't care about the coordinator, Charity. This is your *life* we're talking about. If you're worried, you call *me*." She sighs before continuing: "You sound scared. Your appointment is in a week. Do you want to come in before then? Because I can bring you in to see me tomorrow."

"No. A week is all right."

"Well, just remember. Call *me*," she makes me promise before I hang up.

Young, ambitious, and pretty, Marie Budev is equal parts doctor and kindred spirit. A sharp dresser with a soft bedside manner, when she metes out medical advice, it feels more like input from a valued friend than preaching from a medical professional. Maybe because she really acts like a friend. She'll put off personal plans, vacations, or holiday arrangements to make sure her patients are cared for. That said, she has scores of patients and I'm wary of taking advantage of her dedication. Still, wheezing here in Denver, I'm grateful she knows what's going on.

Christmas in Denver can't help but be magical. It's been six years since I've been home for the holidays. We have our annual Night Before the Night Before Christmas Party. I spend most of it tucked away from the crowd in the study, but it's the first time in years I've seen a bevy of my old friends. My oldest siblings have stayed in DC with their own families, but there are still enough brothers and sisters around to make it really feel like Christmas. Not to mention the snow, crafts, carols, and food. But

underscoring the festive hum of the season is the distinct dissonance of my subtle health decline. *It's just the altitude*, I tell myself
as my spirometry ticks down yet another point. It's still slow, but
ever more noticeable.

Like a dog before an earthquake, Mom's always had an extremely keen sense for impending family disaster. As Christmas
Day nears, she's becoming increasingly tense. And, while Mom
doesn't always know *what* exactly is making her nervous, she can
almost always pinpoint *whom* her unease concerns. This time,
she's decided the source of her worry is my imminent engagement to Yoni, and she whispers entreaties to me to really carefully
consider my choice of partner. I'm too preoccupied by my numbers to even care about her attempted meddling.

Christmas Eve, I stay up with Mom and my sisters to prepare
for Santa Claus's visit. It doesn't matter that we're all too old for
the full Santa Claus experience. It's tradition. We wrap gifts, stuff
stockings, write love notes from elves, sing songs, and eat the
milk and cookies we'd set out for ourselves a few hours earlier.
Finishing as the sky begins to lighten, Liberty, Mercina, Glorianna, and, finally, Mom all go to bed. I sit alone on the couch,
gazing at the tree. Sprinkled with lights and ornaments my family
has collected over three and a half decades, I'm overwhelmed by
a flood of memories: getting tucked in by Dad; being so excited
I couldn't sleep; waking my parents at the crack of dawn; the
avalanche of gifts and stockings filled with the stuff of dreams;
dropping off sacks of gifts for families in need. *This is what home
feels like.* Over the years, I've missed this place so much. At times,
I've been willing to sacrifice everything just to come back. Being
here is my own personal Christmas Miracle. I have a nagging
feeling it won't be repeated next year, though.

Our giant Great Pyrenees, Nori, shoves his head into my lap.

I give him a good scratch. Whatever happens next, I'm glad to be here now.

On Boxing Day, Yoni and I need to get back on the road. I have a much-needed appointment in Cleveland, closely followed by lessons in New York and a performance in San Diego. There's a lot of ground to cover and not much wiggle room in my schedule. But goodbyes are never easy, and Mom has grown particularly weary of them. As Yoni and I prepare to leave, she has a full-blown meltdown.

"You can't do this!" cries Mom hysterically in the driveway as we pack bags into the car.

"Annette," says Yoni, "Charity *needs* to go to Cleveland. Driving is safer than flying. We have to go."

"You're going to kill her!" she wails, already certain there's something wrong.

"Mom," I protest vehemently, "this isn't fair. You know I have to go to the doctor." Mom knows my spirometry has been falling since November. But she's decided Yoni is the problem—not the fact that I've had an untreated infection for nearly two months. As we drive off, she's still fuming in our rearview mirror.

We arrive in Cleveland late the next day, a storm nipping at our tail. A familiar routine greets us. First, my blood is drawn by my usual phlebotomist, Anita. She takes sixteen vials. Next, an X-ray, and then spirometry with Gerry the singing respiratory therapist. Placing my lips over a white plastic tube, I wait for his command: *Inhale. Exhale.* We repeat the exercise twice. Three times. Five times. Eight times. Finally, after twelve tries, I'm dismissed with my spirometry analysis. The numbers themselves are consistent with what I've been seeing at home, but, looking at the different points plotted out on a graph, it's worse than I'd expected. During the month following my hospital discharge, the line has a steady upward trajectory. Beginning in November, it takes a sharp turn downward.

How did we get here? I wonder. I'm six days shy of my sixteen-month anniversary—well outside of the most common period for rejection within the first year after transplant. I thought I was safe.

"Charity Tillemann-Dick?" calls a nurse.

She takes my blood pressure and tests my oxygen levels. They're lower than I'm used to seeing. Then Dr. Budev opens the door—

"I'm so glad you're here," she quickly moves on to my prognosis. "I think there's an infection in your lungs. I have an appointment in the bronch suite for you, but something looks off. There's a strange sort of . . . mothiness in the lungs which shouldn't be there," she explains. "First things first, we'll get a clearer picture with a CT scan. Then, you'll go for the bronchoscopy."

We race to fit in a CT scan before heading to the bronch suite. This will be my fifth bronchoscopy. Before they snake the camera down my throat and into my lungs, I have to inhale a lidocaine nebulizer for twenty minutes to numb my trachea. Puffing away on the soap-flavored gas, I lament. They used to say I wouldn't need to have these procedures anymore. Now I wonder if I'll ever reach a new normal.

When my gag reflex is totally numb, I'm rolled into the surgical suite. The space looks straight out of a sci-fi flick: stark white and gray interrupted by screens, medical machinery, and tubes. It's cold, so I've been wrapped in thin blankets. The nurses and doctors strap on their colorful aprons, confirm my name and date of birth, then administer anesthesia. As I drift off, I'm not nervous about surgery; that's become routine. I *am* nervous about what it might reveal about my lungs.

The scene blurs to black. I wake up hours later in the hotel room.

"Hey, honey, you want something to eat?" Yoni asks, sitting beside me.

I'm starving. I haven't eaten a real meal since we left Denver. But nerves combined with nausea mean I'd rather forgo food than throw it up an hour from now. Instead, I fall back asleep. At 2:00 a.m., I wake again, disoriented. My temples feel like they're being squeezed together as a giant lead ball rolls back and forth between them, banging into my skull on either end. Saliva pools in the back of my mouth and I start to hiccup uncontrollably. Yoni rolls out of his bed on the other side of the room.

"Chary," he says groggily, "what's the matter?"

He stumbles after me as I run to the bathroom, grabbing my hair for me as I retch into the toilet. Pulling my hair back into a ponytail, he calls the hospital.

We drive to the ER in the faint morning light, where we're rushed into a dark room. Doctors inject painkillers, but nothing helps. For three days, there's no relief. The constant pounding shatters inside my head, sending shards of pain to the farthest reaches of my body.

"I think she may need a lumbar puncture. We'll go into the lower back to extract fluid from your spine," explains the young doctor on call. "If it's meningitis, we'd like to deal with it immediately."

I've never heard of a lumbar puncture before, but—even in my desperate state—it sounds like something I want to avoid—

"Is there anything else we can do?" I ask faintly.

"Well, we can do an MRI. It will rule out a number of other potential causes—like a brain tumor," suggests the doctor.

I nod my head in consent.

Around midnight, the nurses arrive to take me for an MRI. Loading me onto a gurney, they roll me into an impossibly white room, then transfer me to a narrow plastic plank curved to cradle a body. The machine hums to life and my body slowly descends into its sterile white maw. Once inside, deafening knocking, buzzing, and pounding surround me. But somehow, as these noises cancel out the rest of the world, my pain breaks. It's not gone, but there's a decrease in pressure. The nausea and discomfort abate. A nurse returns me to my hospital room and, for the first time in four days, I sleep.

Early the next morning, I hear a familiar voice—

"Good morning, sweetheart."

My eyes flutter open. Mom is here.

"Honey, I'm sorry about everything," says Mom. "I was just so worried something like this would happen . . . Don't worry. Yoni's resting back in the room."

A few moments later, Dr. Budev walks in.

"Well, it's not acute rejection," she starts. "But you have a terrible infection in your lungs. It looks like it's been growing for weeks."

We speak for a few minutes. I should be relieved. Infections are treatable. But I can't help but feel the doctor is skirting around something serious. A much more ominous diagnosis.

"Mom," I whisper after Dr. Budev leaves, "she didn't rule out rejection."

"Don't be silly," says Mom. "She *just* said it's not rejection!"

"She said it's not *acute* rejection. But it could still be chronic rejection!" I say, almost frantic now. While I'm fuzzy on the pathological details, I know there's a vital difference between the two types: Acute rejection is reversible. Chronic rejection isn't. The latter implies cellular fibrosis of the transplanted organ—in other words, permanent damage. Some people live with that damage, using the rejected organs for years—even decades. But those are best-case scenarios. And once chronic rejection starts, there's no stopping it.

Before Mom can respond, the door edges open—

"Knock, knock!" chirps the bespectacled doctor from before. "We're here to perform the lumbar puncture!"

"You're here to do what?!" demands Mom.

"A lumbar puncture," he repeats. "We go into the lower back to extract fluid from—"

"I know what it is," interrupts Mom. "Why on earth do you want to give my daughter a spinal tap?!"

"Well," he says, "we think she might have meningitis."

"Doctor, Charity has a history of vomit-inducing migraines after anesthesia or painkillers. She was numbed and put under for her bronch. This latest episode was an admittedly extreme case of a typical reaction for her," explains Mom. "So I'll repeat my question: Why on earth would you subject my daughter to this painful, unnecessary procedure? And after she's already been through so much," she finishes, finally taking her crystal blue eyes off the doctor to shake her head in exasperation.

"Look, miss, we're going in circles. We still haven't ruled out meningitis," he declares more insistently. "So we're going to do a lumbar puncture and we're going to do it now."

There's a moment of tense silence.

"Then I refuse treatment," I state calmly.

"*You refuse treatment?*" He raises his eyebrows at me, visibly peeved.

"Yes. I refuse."

"Turn it around, folks," he says to his nurse who is holding the medical instruments. "The patient refuses treatment." They trundle out of the room.

Glad to avoid another battle, I am nervous about how I will make it to my next performance in California. Had it not been for the infection, I would have returned to New York after Christmas. I am supposed to fly out of JFK to San Diego for a performance in Balboa Park. Changing the ticket will be complicated and expensive. And there's no way Mom will let me go alone now.

I ask for my phone to text Yoni about scheduling. Glancing at my email, there are over one hundred new messages. "Congratulations!" reads one subject line. "You're amazing!" says another. Facebook reveals that the video of my TED talk was released two days earlier when I went into the hospital. People seem to like it—it already has nearly a quarter million views. I should be thrilled. Instead, I wonder if Dr. Barst has seen it. *When she does, will she forgive me?*

"Charity," says Mom, almost shaking me from a trancelike state, "they're going to release you tomorrow. Isn't that wonderful?"

Looking up, a doctor stands in the doorway, smiling. But darkness clouds my senses; *there's something missing.* I smile back uncomfortably, trying to think of what could be wrong. "There isn't anything else I should know?" I ask, hoping he may relieve my sense of foreboding.

"You just need to make sure you're taking those new anti-fungal meds," he says seriously, referencing a noxious slurry I swallow to protect my lungs from infected spores. "Frankly, I don't know why they stopped that in the first place. It probably could have prevented this infection before it started . . ."

A knot forms in my throat. I pled with my doctors for months to remove the antifungal from my regimen. It tasted awful and I had to eat fourteen grams of fat with each dose—equivalent to nearly half a stick of butter every day. That was fine back when I was a hundred pounds soaking wet. But, edging my way toward a fifty-pound weight gain, I was eager to rein it in. Now once again sitting in a hospital bed, guilt washes over me. *I've done this to myself.* Could my vanity lead to chronic rejection?

"You think you can handle that?" asks the doctor, recapturing my wandering attention.

"Yes," I reply distractedly. "Yes. But will a nurse go over everything again before my release? I'm not feeling quite like myself right now, and I wouldn't want to miss anything."

"She'll be fine," Mom declares. "She'll come back to Denver where we can take care of her properly."

We say goodbye to the doctor before I begin to protest.

"Mom, I can't come back to Denver. I have a performance in California in two days."

"Charity, this morning you were going to get a spinal tap! You're not flying to California the same day you're discharged from the hospital to perform the day after that. That's insane!"

I know she's right. But that doesn't mean I'm wrong. Sometimes when life refuses to be reasonable, you're forced to respond in kind. I am so constantly dogged by drama that my situation will probably never be ideal. If I try to relaunch my career by canceling after every medical mishap, there soon won't be anything to cancel in the first place. I can either take opportunities as they're given to me, or resign myself to sitting in a hospital bed forever.

I pause, trying to read Mom's mood. Then I pull out my phone and show her the video of my TED talk—

"Mom. I've been given a second chance. But you know show business—if I can't perform, I'll be written off. Nobody will be willing to risk booking me."

"You're crazy," she reiterates, unmoved. "I am calling whoever is putting this on to cancel. Give me the number."

"I don't have it here," I stall. "Look at it this way: it's January. It's cold everywhere except for San Diego. You know how much I love performing—this will be more like a vacation than work!" I see her softening, so I keep going. "Either I have to leave now and drive cross-country—"

"No way."

". . . or I have to fly."

Mom averts her eyes in frustration.

"Mom, what's the difference between flying to Denver or California? I'll wear a mask. I'll wear three!" I assure her.

". . . Well, I'm coming with you," she declares after a pause.

"Mom, I'd love that, but tickets are really expensive," I start to protest.

"Then they'll use the money you're making from this performance to get me one."

Stopping for a moment, I feel my blood pressure rising. *Can't anybody treat me like a grown-up?* But the more I think about it, the more sense it makes. I call Yoni and ask him to book the tickets. This time, Mom's right.

San Diego is a big success, leading to two more performances there less than a month later. Following those, I meet Yoni in Cleveland for my follow-up appointment. When we arrive, a camera crew from the hospital's PR department shadows us. They've been trying to schedule a sit-down for months and now that my TED talk has gone viral, they're more eager than ever to include my story in their media package. I don't mind it. I'm feeling somewhat better—my spirometry has stabilized, though it's yet to return to its pre-November levels; I'm still coughing up blood, though with less frequency than before.

We go through the usual routine, but this time with film cameras recording each step. Then—

"Charity?" calls the nurse.

We follow her into the checkup room and I squeeze Yoni's hand. The film crew follows behind us. Pushing open the heavy wooden door, Travis, my transplant nurse, enters.

"Would you please excuse us?" Travis asks the film crew. As they leave, he turns to face me.

"I'm worried about you and noncompliance," he says sternly.

"What are you taking about?" I flinch at the suggestion.

"You've asked me to change your Monday blood draws at least two times—maybe more."

"Yes," I respond. "And you've always said yes. I don't see how that's noncompliance."

"Compliance would be getting your blood drawn on Monday. Not Tuesday or Wednesday."

"Wait," Yoni interjects. "You're telling us that when you say, 'Sure, Charity. You can get your blood drawn on Tuesday!' getting her blood drawn on Tuesday is actually noncompliance? That makes no sense."

"Look. All I'm telling you is—And look at you!" Travis interrupts himself, gesturing at my feet. "You're crossing your ankles!"

"No one ever told me not to cross my ankles!" I say, my voice rising.

"Well, *that* can lead to rejection."

I quickly uncross them, bewildered. All of a sudden I feel like there's a secret checklist and, if I don't guess what's on it, something terrible will happen. In the wrong circumstance, almost anything can spur rejection, making guidelines for transplantees involved and convoluted. After discharge, patients are given a lengthy list of instructions: avoid large crowds, wash hands regularly, take your meds on time. Don't eat grapefruit or soft cheeses, do use straws, don't attend events where people buy tickets in advance, never wade in a lake. Some of the things are universal. Others depend on where a patient is transplanted. Some rules are written down, and others are left to the discretion of the coordinating nurse to communicate with their patient.

"I just want you to be safe. That's all," Travis says. But his words are far from reassuring. As he walks out, my brow furrows. *Crossing my ankles causes rejection?* Sitting beside me, Yoni looks as confused as I feel.

After a few minutes of perturbed silence, Dr. Budev walks into the room.

"Charity," she says, sitting at the computer and pulling up that morning's scans, "we need to look at the results of your CT. See these diamond-ring shapes?"

I nod. As she scrolls through pictures of my lungs, there are occasional silhouettes of a swelled-up diamond ring.

"Those are bronchial oblasions. They were there when we saw you last month, but we couldn't do anything about them until the fungal infection was gone."

"What can we do about them now?" I ask.

Dr. Budev looks at me seriously. "Charity, the oblasions mean you have chronic rejection."

I put my face into my hands. *Chronic rejection.* The words roll through my head like a migraine. It feels like a family member has died and I'm to blame. I rescheduled the stupid blood draws. I was late taking my medication—more than once. I'd crossed my ankles. Clearly, I've done this to myself. I am responsible.

"What about retransplant?" asks Yoni after a long silence.

"It does happen occasionally. If candidates are young, well-qualified, and compliant," she says, reaching over to squeeze my shoulder. "But that's a long ways off."

There's a tap on the door. It's the film crew.

"Could we get a few shots of you guys together?" they ask, unaware of what's just transpired. In a daze, I watch as Dr. Budev points to different parts of my X-ray on a light board.

"So we'll see you across the street at two?" asks the cameraman.

I nod yes listlessly as the crew packs up.

"Chary, are you sure you want to do this interview?" Yoni whispers. I nod again in a daze. "But . . . we need to call your mom—your family."

"We'll figure that out after my interview." The gray clouds coordinate with my psychological state as we walk back to our dingy hotel room.

Sleet begins to fall. As I ascend the stairs to the interview, I feel the weight of my feet. By the top of the staircase, I'm out of breath. I sit in the large, sparsely decorated room and share the story of my transplant and recovery, barely even conscious of what I'm saying.

Afterward, Yoni hands me my phone.

"You need to call your mom," he urges.

I start to cry. Yoni wraps his arms around me.

"This is my fault, Yoni. If I had just been more careful—"

"Stop, Charity. Don't say that. Don't even think that. Sometimes bad things just happen and no one can do anything about it. It's awful. I know. But right now, you have to call your mom."

"I just— I'm hoping if I don't say anything, it will go away—that it won't be real."

He holds me in silence for a few minutes. After nearly a decade, I am so close to independence. I'm managing my own medications. My own health care. I am supporting myself with my performances and have a full schedule lined up. Now, everyone could respond just like Travis—entitled to point out all of the mistakes I didn't even realize I was making. *Inhale. Exhale.* I press the call button.

I tell Mom first, then my brothers and sisters, then my grandmothers. They're as supportive as they can be in the midst of the news. Yoni calls his family. He says, "It feels like we got the wind knocked out of us" over and over. *If it were only that.* For me, it feels like I've had my lungs ripped out of my body and someone else's sewn in, all for nothing. If I had died quickly, at least my family could have gotten on with their own lives. Instead, I've tortured them through a decade of disease and disappointment.

We finish the miserable work and Yoni takes my hand. Back in our room, I shut myself in the bathroom to change into PJs. I brush my hair and floss, avoiding my defeated eyes in the vanity mirror.

Yoni tucks me in and kisses my forehead before crawling over into his bed on the other side of the nightstand. He reaches across the gap between us to grasp my hand.

"I was so proud of you today."

I begin to weep again, stirring up more hurt, disappointment, guilt, regret, fear, and pain than I ever knew I had inside of me. I tear my hand away from his and roll out of bed, crumpling onto the floor as my shoulders heave silently. He hurries over to pick me up and lay me back down in my bed.

"No!" I cry, clinging to him. "Please! I don't want to be alone! I don't want to be alone!"

He sits down and I drape my sweatpants-clad legs over his knees, clutching onto him like a frightened child.

"I love you," I gasp out between defeated sobs.

As he softly presses his lips against my head, his tears wet my hair. "I love you so much," he whispers.

Crying in each other's arms, we lose track of time. Then an alarm sounds, reminding me to take my evening medications. Getting up from Yoni's lap, I navigate in the dark to the bathroom and swallow the handful of pills with a swig of tap water. Making my way back to the bedroom, I sit cross-legged on the bed facing Yoni.

"What do you want to do now?" he asks.

After a long silence, I nestle my head into his shoulder. "I want to marry you," I say quietly.

Yoni pushes me back by the shoulders, looking into my face by the light of the street lamps outside. He's grinning as tears spill from the outer corners of his eyes.

"Really?" he asks.

Sitting in the dark, something changes. Big performances in big venues, fame, recognition. They all seem so small from where I am. Right now in this dark, crummy Cleveland hotel, only one thing matters. If I can do nothing else before I die, I want to be with Yoni. I want to be sealed to this man—to fall asleep in his bed at night and wake up by his side in the morning. My hopes, my dreams, my fears, my body. Whatever I have left in life, I want to share it with him.

After years as an opera singer, I'm still not used to rejection. After breath, it's one of the first things singers learn about. Every professional musician knows its sting. For each audition that goes well, there's one or two or twenty that come to nothing. Some mistakenly tout talent (or its absence) as the mechanism by which some reach success and others do not. But chance is heavy-handed, redirecting many excellent singers to business or academia, jobs as parents, teachers, or real estate agents. The only reliable difference between a music major and a performer—the amateur and the professional—is in their ability to face rejection. It's not the callback that makes you a singer. It's what you do when the callback doesn't come. Do you give up, or do you head to the next audition?

I've always tried to approach professional rejection with a certain amount of honest introspection, trying to separate what I can improve (like breath control) from what's out of my control (like other people's personalities). It's never a pleasant exercise, but at least there's the potential for growth. The chronic rejection of my lungs has no comparable silver lining. The only direction to go is down.

After my appointment in Cleveland, I return to Denver. I feel doomed. Every day is the Great and Terrible Day spoken of in Revelations—just without the greatness. My body is hosting its own judgment day and playing the roles of judge, jury, executioner, and accused in an awful, angry parody of God.

We all host our own body god. It rests inside of each of us, waiting for a chance to exercise its engulfing power. The body god teaches us that we are inadequate and unworthy of love. It is the voice of *cannot*; the spirit of hopelessness, impotence, and indifferent observation. The body god knows our every weakness, misdeed, and misstep and it unceasingly whispers into our ear that those are *all* that matter. When we look in the mirror, our body god condemns fat and scars and wrinkles. It demands perfection while only acknowledging the imperfect. Where I find breath, my body god condemns Other. It is not the God of Abraham, Isaac, Jacob, Jesus, Mohammed, or anyone else. This is the God of Rejection and it knows my lungs don't belong.

Even here, back in my beloved home, I can't help but feel out of place. My apartment has been filled by an exchange student, so I'm staying in my brother's old room on the top floor. A wall of windows looks onto a vast azure sky and Parrish blue mountains peek out from behind February's naked gray trees. I exhale into my breathing machine. *Maybe, if I do everything right from here, the rejection will stabilize.* Maybe I can stop it by sheer force of will. Even if I can't, I can take care of myself long enough to finish my performance season. Long enough to marry Yoni.

I've had a good life. My family loves me. I've followed my passion and experienced a great deal of goodness. I could complain about any number of things, but no one has ever wished me real harm. My problems aren't the result of unkindness or ill will. All anyone has ever wanted to do is help me. My body just won't be helped. *That,* I tell myself, *is a pretty charmed challenge to have.* There's a knock at my door.

"Chary, sweetheart," Mom says as she cracks the door open, "can I come in?"

"Of course!" I wave her into the room, crawling out of bed to clean up.

"No, no, no. Don't do that. You rest. I just brought you some clean towels," she says, offering me a short stack of linens. "You're not too lonely up here, are you?"

"No," I insist. "This is perfect. It gives me a little breathing room."

We both smile at the unintended pun, then sigh.

"Charity," Mom continues, "do you want to think about canceling the events in Florida and Milwaukee?"

"No," I respond resolutely.

"Charity. You're sick. You should be resting with your family."

"Mom, I don't have a house or an apartment. I don't have a dog or a cat. Even if Yoni and I get married, I don't have kids and I probably never will."

"Don't say that," chastises Mom.

"—But I have my voice, and there is nothing I want to do more than sing."

"Well, that's just silly, Charity," she says. "You can sing here. And there are lots of other things you can do too."

"But, Mom, I'm a performer. You know it's true. It's been true since I was a little girl."

She takes a deep breath. She doesn't want an argument. "Well, I've made lunch. Come downstairs whenever you're ready."

Over the next weeks, my return to dependency is emotionally draining. But it is wonderful to spend time with my family, and Mom, Shiloh, Mercina, Glorianna, Zen, and I have some wonderful adventures together. I miss Yoni, though, and once again, we're thousands of miles apart.

Finally, we meet in Florida where I'm opening for a large conference. The night before my performance, our hosts take us out to dinner. Usually, I try to socialize minimally before a performance. It allows me to focus and avoid germs. But we've already accepted the invitation and I don't want to back out. As the sun sets over the Gulf Coast, the wife of the conference organizer asks me about the subject of my talk from across the table. She knows I'm an opera singer, but that's all. Not wanting to spoil the surprise, I explain the thesis of my talk instead of telling her my story—

"I'm going to speak about how physical challenges shouldn't stop us from pursuing our dreams."

"Stop right there," she commands. "That is not going to go

over well with this audience. This little beauty queen up there onstage telling successful people twice her age—people who've seen parents die, who've probably had hip replacements or even pacemakers—telling us about how we should live with all that crap?" She shakes her head. "No. It's just totally inappropriate. If you want to hear about hard times, you should *listen* to the people in this audience. They don't want to hear about your so-called challenges and they *certainly* don't want to be lectured on how to be better people. I mean, these people have given more money to charity than you can even imagine."

"Well, I've never seen a penny of it," I say, not skipping a beat. The joke falls flat.

It's said that 80 percent of people think their story would make a great book. Many people have had challenges every bit as heart-rending and dramatic as my own. But my ordeal has been made significantly less frightening thanks to others who have been willing to share their struggles with me. I've never before felt so inappropriately ridiculed. Here I am, volunteering some of what little time I have left, and being talked down to by an aging dilettante. I'm furious—

"Extra decades do not give you or anyone else a monopoly on heartache," I say, trying to restrain myself. "There are children who see their families ravaged by war and soldiers who lose limbs. While I respect the wisdom that can come with age, it's foolish to assume that just because someone is young or attractive that they haven't faced true hardship."

"You're not exactly a limbless child soldier," she scoffs back. "And I am telling *you* that if you give that kind of crap to this audience, they will laugh you out of the theater—and so will I."

I'm silent for the rest of our meal, leaving Yoni to navigate this situation as amicably as he's able.

That night, her words echo in my dreams. I wake up early and unsure. Maybe I should just sing musical theater? Maybe I should drop my talk and speak off the cuff? Maybe I should talk about rejection instead? Yoni interrupts my list, grabbing me by the shoulders.

"Charity," he pleads, "stop. That woman last night? She was probably drunk and, regardless, has no idea what she's talking about. Sometimes, people just like to make themselves feel important. What you have to share—it's a miracle. I mean, if Martha Stewart loved it, so will these schlubs. You just do what you do best. You'll be great. You always are."

When I make my way onto the stage, I see my dinner companion from the previous night sitting front and center, arms folded across her chest. I sing like it's my debut at the Met. My cadenzas are cleaner, legatos smoother, my fortes fuller, and trills more delicate. The talk is the same way. Within minutes, half of the audience is in tears. With my final pronouncement, I point directly at her—

"I want to tell *you* that disease shouldn't divorce us from our dreams. When we live the lives we're supposed to, patients don't just survive; we thrive. Some of us might even sing."

She jumps to her feet in applause and the rest of the audience follows.

My performances continue with stops in Colorado and Washington, DC, in between. After going to Milwaukee on my own, I realize that Mom is right: I need support. Shiloh accompanies me to Monterey during his spring break. He's a natural at these conferences—garrulous, brilliant, and eager to learn whatever he can from every person he meets.

The morning of my performance, I awake to a vomit-inducing headache. But a performer's job is to get onstage and leave everything else behind—nausea included. Still, singing and telling my story while ignoring the drama currently unfolding inside of my body feels like a lie. *No one wants a sad ending*, I remind myself over and over. Ovations greet me as I crisscross the country, but they offer little comfort. I'm too distracted, mourning my future death.

By April, it seems everyone wants to tell my story. CNN reruns the piece produced at TEDMED and the Oprah Winfrey Network contacts me about a TV show. Reader's Digest is working on a cover story, and I know that telling them that my wonderful tale of triumph is just a tragedy waiting to happen will sour their interest. But there is another story I want to tell. One much bigger than my own.

Transplants trade one chronic or terminal disease for another. It's a lifeline, not a perfect solution. Every year, twenty-eight thousand people don't realize how little research is being done on how to keep their transplanted organs healthy. While part of me wants to discuss the challenges and shortcomings of transplantation, I don't want to discourage people from donating their organs by making them think it's ineffective. I also don't want to discourage people from moving forward with a transplant if they need it. I am so grateful to be alive, I just hoped I'd have a little longer than eight months of relative well-being before getting thrust back into a long-term medical crisis.

In mid-April, I receive a message on Facebook. It's an invitation to debut at Lincoln Center. *Inhale. Exhale.* This must be a joke. I mean, who invites someone to sing at Lincoln Center over Facebook? But it turns out the note is actually from a major producer. As we communicate more, it becomes clear that this won't be just any debut. I'll be a headliner alongside some of my own musical heroes. And they don't want me to talk or tell my story, they just want me to sing! Afraid I might jinx it, I don't tell anyone for a while. But I already know, even if it's the last thing I ever do, I'm going to get there.

My health-care company, Kaiser Permanente, has been amazing through all of my medical woes, but they don't have a syndicate in New York, so Washington becomes home base. I can't live alone, but it quickly becomes obvious that staying with family isn't a perfect solution, either. The constant volume of babies and dogs and visitors leaves me vulnerable to germs, and my regime of perpetual sanitization is not sustainable.

Shortly after I return, I go to lunch with a friend, JaLynn Prince. An advocate and arts patron in Washington, DC, she asks if I'd like to take up residence in her and her husband's sprawling, Italianate home in Potomac, Maryland. I jump at the offer. The Princes have a piano, plenty of space, and fresh air galore. I'm so grateful for their graciousness. But they travel frequently, leaving me with only my wheezing lungs for company in the spacious mansion.

Levi treks up to visit me from DC every week or so. Immediately beside each other in the sibling lineup, he's the black sheep and I'm the family zealot. But the devil on his shoulder and the angel on mine are fast friends, and we've always shared a special affection for each other. He works in the kitchen as we talk. Then he invariably comes around the counter with a smoothie—each more delicious than the one preceding it. Little do I know that, worried about my gradual weight loss, Levi has made it his personal crusade to stuff as many calories into me as he can muster. Artfully masked by fruits and ice creams, the shakes are filled with everything from whole pieces of pie to raw egg yolks.

The good news is that Yoni has finally found a job in DC. For the past two and a half years, we've lived in different parts of the country. Initially, the distance wasn't terrible. It gave us both the space we needed to decide whether we really wanted to be together. But now that we're committed, it's become a nuisance. We're both eager to live near each other and officially check the last item off our list of things that need to happen before we can get engaged.

Yoni needs to go to New York to get some things he'd been storing at his parents' house. I need a lesson, so we drive up together. But that's not the only reason we're going to New York.

We walk into his parents' house side by side, fingers laced. Sitting down in the sunken living room couch, my palms begin to sweat. Yoni's parents, Marsha and Eldad, sit facing us. About five foot three inches with a mop of curly brown hair that makes her look taller than she actually is, Marsha is a Long Island schoolteacher. Eldad, a hair shorter than me with a giant black mustache, loves nothing more than a good argument—often happy to play devil's advocate if he thinks it will enliven a conversation.

Yoni begins, "We just want you guys to know now, we're planning to get married."

Eldad looks at Yoni, then Marsha, then back to Yoni. Over and over again. "What about religion?" he says, his Israeli accent sounding thicker than usual.

"Well," I say nervously, gripping Yoni's hand more tightly, "we want to share a religious identity."

His father stares at Marsha uncomfortably.

"Charity's already Jewish," Yoni clarifies. "We do Shabbat a fair amount and celebrate the holidays together. I go to church with her on Sundays. It makes us happy."

"And the children?" asks his father.

"It's a little complicated," I admit. "Because of the transplant, it's very unlikely I'll have children myself. I'd love to adopt, but the germs make everything more complicated. I know children are a very important part of a marriage and that you both must be worried—"

"Stop right there," Marsha interrupts me and I feel my shoulders tense.

"I don't want to hear anything about that," she continues, leaning forward. "That can happen to anyone—anyone. It can happen to the healthiest person in the world. It is the last thing I want you two to think about. It shouldn't have anything to do with your decision to get married." Marsha sits back on the couch, almost defiant in her conviction.

I feel myself relax and my lips spontaneously rise in a smile. For all of our differences, it's moments like these that give me a deep appreciation for Yoni's parents. Their aspirations aren't complicated—they want their kids to be able to support themselves and their families, to honor their cultural traditions. But most of all, they want them to be happy.

As Yoni and his parents banter back and forth, I realize that, for all of my lofty dreams of great stages, that's all I want too. I just want to be happy. A verse buried deep in Mormon scripture states that "Men are that they might have joy." Everything else boils down to this short sentence. It's comforting to see that our families' deepest dogmas align so effortlessly.

The next morning, Marsha joins Yoni and me around the kitchen table. "I have something for you," she says. "I saw the post on your blog with all of those awful gaudy rings you like and I called my sister and said, 'Carol, those look just like our mother's, don't they?' So we dropped by the safe deposit box this morning."

With that, she spreads a slew of old rings across the counter, and I see it. A gold filigreed ring with a pale white stone inlaid. Immediately, the artistry and craftsmanship grip me.

"Thank you, Marsha! I love it!"

It's perfect—a part of Yoni's past that could have been something I chose for myself. It will be an honor and a pleasure to wear it.

Back in Washington, Yoni and I leave Mimo's apartment after a visit. Standing in the courtyard outside of her condo, he shifts his weight nervously.

"Um, Chary?" he hems and haws. "What are you doing next weekend?"

"Not sure. I think I might be getting engaged, though," I respond giggling.

"Stop—you're not supposed to know!" Yoni pouts in exasperation.

I feel a little guilty, but we've been planning the wedding for months now. Still, Yoni is a stickler for tradition, and wants to present a ring before anything is official. I know to expect something low key. Yoni's not an exhibitionist. He doesn't need to broadcast his love for me, because he's already proved it a dozen times over.

The next Saturday morning, Yoni meets me, a picnic basket in hand. As we drive into Rock Creek Park, mist rises from the river and the trees seem to drip with green. We park and begin our trek through the verdant landscape. Walking up hills is once again a challenge but, unlike our first date in Manhattan, Yoni goes slowly and stops frequently to make sure I'm all right. Passing over a particularly pretty footbridge, I feel magnificently content. I don't need fireworks or a flash mob. This moment couldn't be more perfect. I stop and gaze out over the creek, waiting for Yoni to turn toward me.

"Come on!" he shouts, grabbing my hand and dragging me to the other side of the bridge.

He spreads a checkered tablecloth over a log and arranges an assortment of cheeses, breads, berries, sweets, and garnishes in front of us. As we make our way through the delicacies, I find myself preoccupied. This can't happen here. Not on this muddy, rotting log. *We're probably going to walk while he talks, then finish up with the ring on the footbridge.* Because our marriage was going to be a magical footbridge. Not a muddy, rotting log. He knows that, *right*?

Midway through dessert, Yoni begins reciting a speech. "Charity"—he says, taking my hands in his—"when I first met you, I joked you were an alien because you were so different from anyone I had ever met. You were this tall, beautiful woman and I couldn't get my head around you—where you came from, who you were, what you were. It was so completely foreign and I knew I wanted to learn more about you." We're still seated firmly on the blanket, *but he's just started.* He continues, "When we lost touch, I knew I'd remember you forever. Then I found you again in DC, and I felt so lucky. I didn't think it'd be possible you'd ever want to date me but still, that Fourth of July, I was just kicking myself all night for not asking you to come on a walk with me. I thought I'd lost you again." *Still, no sign of movement.* I'm really beginning to worry. "Then, of course, there was your transplant, and I was worried that I'd really lose you—permanently this time." My tear ducts begin to fill up at his words, but I also know that, somehow, I need to get us over to that footbridge. "Charity, I love you and I don't ever want to lose you. Come rain or shine, I want to know you are by my side."

"Charity Sunshine Tillemann-Dick," he says, shifting onto one knee—

"*Stop!*" I gasp through happy tears. Yoni looks at me, startled. Maybe nervous that I've changed my mind.

"Not here," I plead, pointing to the bridge over his shoulder. "There!"

True to form, Yoni doubles down. "But don't you like this?" he asks, perturbed.

"No!"

"But . . . but this is nice?" he says, half statement, half question.

"But that's so much nicer!" I insist, still gesticulating toward the bridge a few feet away.

"Mmm. I like this." He's obviously made up his mind.

"Yoni, do not make me beg."

He doesn't respond, aggravated that I've interrupted him.

"I am not asking for Paris or Disney World—I don't even care about a fancy restaurant. But so help me, if you do not take me over to that footbridge right now, Yonatan Avi Doron—"

"OK, OK. I'm walking!" he says. Then he pauses and we both begin to laugh. Then we start to cry. He takes my hand, escorts me to the bridge, and gets back down onto his knee while pulling a small box out of his back pocket.

"Charity Sunshine Tillemann-Dick, will you marry me?"

Most little girls dream of their wedding, but I always had other things to imagine. Things like costume jewelry and great debuts. Most of the weddings I grew up attending were homespun operations held in the gym of our local church. I never thought that I'd actually marry but if I did, my dream wedding was no wedding at all. I'd always wanted to elope like my parents; maybe later in life while I was living and performing abroad. But that wasn't going to cut it for Yoni and his family. Naïvely, I'm certain we could find a way to make everyone happy.

During the next few weeks, I start dreaming up an actual wedding. Having spent much of the last decade being paid to traipse around stages in expensive ball gowns, I have little desire to pay tens of thousands of my own or my family's dollars to put on a show. I want to exchange rings under a chuppah in the backyard of our Denver home. It's already May, so we'll miss the lilacs, but by September Mom's cosmos will be in full bloom. Next, we'll parade over to the historic theater a few blocks away for dinner and a show put on by the guests—many of them fellow performers and musicians. Then dancing, then cake. My favorite Mexican restaurant will cater from a truck outside of the theater and my sisters can do the flowers. The venue and the caterer are available and their prices put us way under budget, leaving extra money for music and travel. We'll be able to invite everyone, but having the wedding in Colorado will cut the number of attendees in half. That will leave us with the people who really want to be there. It's going to be magic.

At first, Yoni is fine with—even excited by—the idea of a Colorado wedding. Sitting in my car in Potomac, I call him to confirm before sending my account information to the restaurant and the theater. But suddenly he's less sure than he'd been a week before.

"So you want *my* family to spend all of the time and all of the money to go all of the way to Colorado for the wedding?" he asks in an exasperated tone.

"Yes. Yoni, we don't have much time. I don't think I can plan something else."

"My family would prefer it if we get married in DC," Yoni states.

"You should have told me that two weeks ago!" This entire conversation is confusing me. "And why should my family travel instead of yours? There are so many more of them! A Denver wedding will cost half as much as the same thing in DC. We can use the savings to help your family pay for transportation if you want," I say, trying to reason with him.

"So just because there are more of you, you just get to ram whatever wedding you want down my throat?" Yoni snarls back at me. I'm speechless; activist grooms are not something I'm used to. Yoni knows I'm sick. Since he can't fight the rejection, he seems to be opting for a proxy that will make his family proud. Over the next weeks, he'll become the ultimate wedding warrior, fighting me tooth and nail over every decision and making an enormous mess of the entire affair. He doesn't realize how the stress of that combativeness will accelerate my physical degeneration. Back on the phone, I again try to conciliate—

"I've always wanted to elope?"

"No. No, no, no. I won't stand for it. I just won't. And my sister says she won't come."

"Well, she already had her wedding!" I say, half wondering if Yoni understands what, exactly, an elopement entails.

"My sister's wedding was beautiful! And she planned the whole thing with *her* mother-in-law!" he hollers instructionally.

"Planning a wedding with your mom could just about kill me right now," I retort, only half-joking.

"Look, I might be willing to forgo table service for a buffet, but I want a traditional wedding and I don't think it's fair to have it all the way in Denver," Yoni says, a pretentious air of magnanimity dripping through the receiver.

"You're 'willing to forgo table service'? How good of you, Yoni."

Having a wedding is an enormous compromise for me. But even my most gratuitously revised plans can't match the eminently standard, monstrously overpriced celebration envisioned by my husband-to-be.

Finally, after days of conflict, we decide to get married in DC. I find a historic theater an hour outside of the city that is large enough to accommodate the bigger crowd we're likely to have. Instead of Mexican food, I settle for Chicago-style hot dogs, and my conservatory friends agree to perform. The wedding will be the grand finale to a vaudevillian ruckus, and then we'll dance. It won't be intimate, but it will still be magical. I find a restaurant to cater. The venue is available on the right weekend. Everything looks good.

Hoping to avoid any more conflict, I drive out to the theater with Yoni. He loves it as much as I do. But now, he wants us to double-check with his parents, whom we're going to see that weekend.

Perhaps I should be more willing to embrace my inner diva. As a rule I've always thought that as long as a couple sticks to a budget, the bride should get whatever she wants. Merging two families is more than enough stress to manage. Piling joint party planning on top of that is like asking an orchestra to follow two conductors simultaneously. It's just a bad idea. But my illness makes me extremely high maintenance as is. I take twenty pills a day; people have to use antibacterial gel before shaking my hand; I walk more slowly than everyone else. The last thing I want is to turn into a bridezilla. So I relent.

Sun streams through the windows onto the Dorons' breakfast table on Long Island.

"So," says his father, gruffly, "what is the plan?"

I sketch it out for Marsha and Eldad in broad terms.

"What, you're going to feed them hot dogs?" Eldad barks out skeptically. I can already see the excitement beginning to sap from Yoni's eyes.

I smile. "Chicago style! Yoni and I had them all the time when we started dating. And we'll serve corn on the cob, kettle corn, cotton candy, and gourmet snow cones. I thought we could have fresh doughnuts instead of cake—my cousin did that at her wedding and it was a big hit!"

Marsha wanders over from the sink. "No," she declares. "Absolutely not. I'm not inviting my friends to drive down to Washington, DC, to eat hot dogs." She pauses. "My guess is your mom won't like it either," she adds, hopefully.

"My mom wants me to be happy."

It's true. Mom is a big believer in marriage over weddings. To her, the typical focus on weddings has always distracted from the importance of joining one life to another. She thinks cluttering up an eternal companionship with party planning is a waste of energy. While some other brides might want their mother to be more involved in wedding planning, I was exceedingly grateful for her hands-off approach to my nuptials. Especially when contrasted to the Dorons. An alarm goes off on my phone and I toss a handful of pills into my mouth before continuing—

"We have a few other options too. I've always wanted to elope."

"Over my dead body," interjects Marsha. "My dead body."

"All right." I sigh. "Then we could do only family but no one else. There are so many people who have done so much for me and my family, and if I include one person, I have to include them all. But something small could be beautiful. We could do it in the Shenandoah Valley?"

"Mmmmm," groans Marsha, "I don't much like that either."

"Well, then I hope it's not presumptuous, but you could host it here, on Long Island. You could invite anyone you wanted. My mom would come, then we'd have another party in Denver a few months later."

She and Eldad glance at each other, then Yoni pokes me under the table. He doesn't want a Long Island wedding.

"Or we can continue with this plan. Everyone is welcome, the music will be world class, and it should be great fun. Maybe it's not a typical wedding, but what fun is a typical wedding anyway?"

"Eh. We'll think about it," Eldad says after a pause.

"We don't actually have time to think about it." I'm about to explode; it seems Marsha feels the same way. Looking across the table at her, I can almost see her blood pressure rising.

"Look," she spurts out, "you're young, you're healthy, and you get to spend the rest of your lives together."

"Well, not really 'healthy,'" I reply, stunned by the comment.

"Quiet!" she's almost shouting now. "You're young. You're healthy. This is one of the last chances we'll have to see some of these friends who would come, and I don't want to make them trek halfway across the country for a county fair."

"You have options," I say firmly. "But we need to know how to move forward within the week." I excuse myself, panting as I rush up the stairs. I'm furious that Yoni's parents don't seem to grasp how quickly my health is declining. I'm even more upset at Yoni's unwillingness to stand up to them for me.

The week comes and goes with no compromise. The DC venue is booked by someone else and Yoni, his parents, and I fall into a wedding-planning stalemate. Months pass with no progress and intermittent performances. I unintentionally lose a dozen pounds even as my siblings sneak hundreds of extra calories into everything I eat. Beyond frustration and sicker every day, I decide to go back to Denver.

Already well into the process of being relisted for a second transplant, I know that my travel will soon be seriously limited. I want to see home once more. But even I don't realize how sick I've become. As I board my flight, my N95 face mask grips my face like a large hand, covering my mouth and nose. It's not comfortable, but I've never gotten sick on a flight and now's not the time to start. As the plane begins to climb, though, the mask seems to tighten around my face, making it almost impossible to breathe. But I can't take it off—if I contract another infection, there's no way I'll be listed for a second transplant. *Inhale. Exhale.* I focus on pushing down my diaphragm, one breath at a time. Near exhaustion, I ask the flight attendant how much farther to Colorado.

"About two hours," she chirps back.

Should I ask them to land? Why—so I can be hospitalized again? No. I've faced bigger challenges than this. Focusing on a white spot on the bulkhead, I relax my body into the seat cushion. Arching my back, I bring my shoulder blades together on inhalation, manually expanding my lungs. Then, I collapse my chest forward to force the air outward. I ache after an hour, still, I have no choice but to continue. I begin counting my breaths. *Seven hundred . . . seven hundred one . . . seven hundred two . . .* When the pilot announces our final approach, I switch to praying. I don't know how much longer I can go.

A great sound of thunder marks the opening of the plane's landing gear. After waiting endlessly on the tarmac, the door pops open and I hobble onto the Jetway. I rip off my mask and I lean against a steel beam as I gasp for air. But it's not the relief I'd hoped for. Breathing is easier, but the air is dry and thin. I brace myself against the beam, finding it difficult to stand. Finally, my wheelchair arrives.

Mom meets me at door 606, her car packed with dogs. I fall asleep in the passenger seat, only waking to stumble into bed when we arrive home. The next morning, I try to explain the plane ride to Mom. To the person experiencing a challenge, Mom always underplays its significance—

"Well, I'm glad you powered through, sweetheart. Just keep up with your breathing exercises and it will get better." But after we speak, she quietly calls to schedule a home nurse visit, concerned I might not be well enough to get to a doctor's office.

That night, our unofficial sister, Pinky, comes over with an arsenal of crafting supplies. Together, we make a bevy of mock wedding announcements. I whip them out, each more ridiculous than the last, until they number over thirty. It's exactly the pressure release I need for my wedding-related angst and I go to sleep laughing so much that tears soak my pillow.

The doorbell rings, waking me. No one else seems to hear it, so I make my way to the front door, nearly fainting on the way. Steadying myself on the door frame, the home nurse comes in and guides me to a nearby chair. She places an oximeter on my finger to measure my blood oxygen levels. Pulling her head back in alarm, she inquires—

"Do you have any nail polish on—" Seeing my unvarnished nails, she revises, "maybe just a clear coat?"

"No," I assure her.

"You need oxygen immediately. Excuse me."

She steps into the other room and makes a call. I put the oximeter back on my finger. The numbers waver between 69 and 75 percent. When oxygenation dips below 90 percent, a patient is usually hospitalized. It's a wonder I lived through my flight. It's a wonder I'm still conscious.

Within hours, the insurance company delivers an oxygen machine. They roll in the suitcase-sized contraption and the nurse slips a cannula over my head. My heart sinks. This isn't supposed to happen again. Certainly not so soon. But as the machine hisses and grumbles, I'm grateful to feel better. I guess a bedridden trip home is better than wedding planning and replanning with my beloved groomzilla in Washington. Still, I wish I could just catch a break.

Yoni's visiting his sister in the hamlet of Hamilton, New York. As I dial him, my hand shakes with nervousness. "Yoni?"

"Hey," he says as he picks up. "I wish you were here with me. It's so beautiful up here."

"Honey," I explain, "I'm getting sick faster than I thought."

"What's wrong? Are you OK?"

I explain my latest ordeal.

"Babe, why don't we just have the wedding here, upstate? You'll love it. And you won't have to worry about a thing," he promises.

"If we do it in DC, my sisters can help. They'll make it beautiful."

CHARITY TILLEMANN-DICK

"No. Let's do it here!" he pleads.

"I don't want to ask my entire extended family to spend the time and money going to the middle of nowhere New York if they're going to have to do all of the work to pull the wedding together at the last minute, Yoni." I'm already feeling serious trepidation. "That's not fair. If we do it in your sister's town, you and your mom need to make sure it's nice."

"Mom *wants* to," he insists. "It will be beautiful. You, your family—you won't have to do a thing and the food will be great!" he assures me with all of the enthusiasm of an eight-year-old boy persuading his parents to take in a stray dog.

Reluctantly, I agree to his plan. I know this is part of why I love him so much—his enthusiasm. His positivity. His willingness to let me be me. Yoni doesn't always understand what I do, but he understands why I do it. It's the same "why" that makes me want to spend my life with him. It defies logic and explanation. It's love. Our wedding day, the earthly trappings of our union, will doubtless leave a lot to be desired. But our relationship is already so much more than seating charts and flower arrangements. In a few weeks' time, Yoni and I will be sealed together for time and all eternity. As I inch my way closer to mortality's edge, as my sphere of concern necessarily narrows, I know more than ever that nothing else really matters.

———

Boarding a dual propeller plane in Boston, the pilot tucks my suitcase of medicine in the rear cabin. Yoni and I are on our way to a private party with Anita and Toby Cosgrove, the CEO of the Cleveland Clinic, on Nantucket Island. The ocean glitters below like the sequin dress I've brought for my performance this evening. With Yoni's arm around me and a small condenser wheezing oxygen into my nose, I feel immeasurably safer than I did flying to Denver a few weeks before. We land and debark. An airline employee heads into the plane to unload the few pieces of luggage in the cabin, but when he finishes, a few of us remain luggage-less.

"If your luggage isn't here already, it will be waiting inside," calls the young man.

"But we need her bag," Yoni insists nervously. "There's important medication in there."

"It'll be inside," the young man repeats nonchalantly.

"It was in the cabin," reiterates Yoni, more adamantly. "I would rather get it now."

"Inside, sir," the kid responds with a New England chill.

"I don't think you understand—she'll die without that medication—"

"Honey," I interrupt as sweetly as I can, "I don't think he'd lie to us. Let's pick it up inside."

Yoni looks at me and then the young man nervously. "It better be in there," he mutters as I take his arm.

I'm surprised by his curt behavior. As long as wedding planning isn't involved, Yoni is usually the picture of a nice guy. But you couldn't tell it on that tarmac.

We get inside and, within minutes, all of the other passengers have their bags. Still, my suitcase remains missing. Yoni approaches the young woman manning the door to the runway and explains the situation. She ignores him.

"Excuse me," he says, slightly raising his voice, "I have to get to that plane before it takes off. Her medication was left in the cabin. She'll die without it."

"OK, sir. Just wait a minute," she replies languidly.

"Can't I just go back out there? I can see the plane—it's 100 feet away . . ."

"No," she drawls. "Just go over there and wait."

Yoni comes back over to me, sitting on the edge of the baggage carousel as my cannula wheezes into my nose. We watch as the woman does nothing. Actually, nothing. She's not helping other passengers. She's not using the phone. She's not even fidgeting. She leans, immobile, on her podium. Minutes tick by. Finally, Yoni goes back over.

"I've been waiting for nearly fifteen minutes. I spoke to the pilot. I know he's headed back to Boston today. She will die without that medication!" he's almost shouting now.

"Yeah," the clerk replies, staring at him blankly. "Well, you're going to have to wait."

"I am not going to let her die because you won't pick up the phone!" he yells.

Rolling her eyes, she picks up the receiver. "I'm picking up the phone. *Happy?*"

"Now please dial the captain or security or whoever you need to call," he directs.

Another passenger comes up to me. "Excuse me, but you really need to learn how to control him. This is just uncomfortable for *everyone* here."

I try to explain—"I'm sorry, but I really will die if I don't get those medications."

"Look. You're not in New York anymore." As she says this she casts side eyes at Yoni over by the console. "People come here to go on vacation. Not to deal with your problems." She walks away before I can reply.

Thirty more minutes pass. Yoni's righteous indignation would make Mom proud, but it doesn't seem to be making much progress in getting my meds back. The girl appears to be on hold. In such a tiny airport, certainly there's more someone could be doing to help?

Suddenly, our plane's propellers begin to spin. "THAT PLANE IS LEAVING," Yoni screams. *"She is not dying because of your incompetence!"*

Shocked into actual action, the girl flashes her pass in front of a scanner and walks onto the tarmac, away from the now-departing plane. Unbeknownst to her, Yoni slides through the door behind her and runs toward the plane waving his arms—

"STOP!! I NEED THAT MEDICINE!! DO NOT TAKE OFF!!" he screams over and over again. It's exactly what Mom would have done in this situation.

Within seconds the entire Nantucket Airport police force (all three of them) is barreling toward Yoni. Two of them tackle him while the third cuffs his arms behind his back. As they drag him off of the tarmac, he never stops yelling. "STOP THAT PLANE! *She'll die without her medicine.*"

Nantucket hasn't seen this much action since Hurricane Earl last year. Everyone at the baggage claim freezes as the drama unfolds. On one hand, I'm mortified. On the other, this is as sweet and pure a token of love as I ever could receive from my fastidiously rule-respecting companion. The only problem is now I don't know where my meds *or* Yoni went.

Ever chivalrous, Yoni is holding everything of mine. I have no money, no wallet, no medications, no itinerary, and no phone. I've been waiting nearly an hour, and I start to worry about getting to my performance. If they return my purse, I'll happily post bail for my jailbird. After nearly two hours, a large policeman approaches me.

"Are you here with Mr. Doron?" he demands.

"Yes," I reply.

"I've gotta run a background check—you know, make sure he's not on any terrorist watch lists—but we're probably gonna let him go." I breathe a half sigh of relief, though I still don't know what's happened to my medication. The officer continues, "You know, he can't pull stuff like that in airports. People are afraid enough of flying. But, boy, that kid really loves you."

I smile gratefully. I'm about to ask about my meds when the officer adds—

"Oh. And the plane is turning around now. You'll get your medicine."

With that he walks through a thick white door. Within the hour, Yoni is out of the holding cell and the plane has returned with my suitcase. We'll even make my performance in time.

It's a great success. I'm glad for the opportunity to again thank the institution that saved my life nearly two years ago. After his earlier display of devotion on the tarmac, contrasted against his boorish wedding planning, I wonder if the clinic has saved my relationship with Yoni too.

Details about the Lincoln Center performance have been intermittent and a little sketchy, but as the weeks roll by, more information presents itself. It's a artistic gala, with a guest list of heads of state, CEOs, and artistic leaders. Among others, I'll be headlining with Jessye Norman, Joshua Bell, Steve Martin, Morgan Freeman, and Patti LaBelle. It's beyond anything I could have hoped to imagine.

But back in Washington, my condition continues to deteriorate. Every day, it's harder to breathe. Yoni has a new job at a well-known Washington think tank, but his hours are more befitting an investment bank than an NGO. Mercina and Glorianna have started their first semester after transferring to Yale, and Mom and Zen have temporarily relocated to DC to be with me.

By the second week of September, I can do little more than sit in a corner and try to breathe. Still, inexplicably, I can sing. Once a day. I pull myself up to full stature, belt out the aria from *La Traviata* I'm slated to perform at Lincoln Center, then crumple back onto the couch as soon as I hit the final, resounding high note. I know there's no way I can perform like this.

I call Dr. Budev to explain my situation. I've already been on the transplant list for two months, and she explains that it's unlikely she can help. But she promises to try and do something if I come to Cleveland.

The next morning, Zenith carries me through the cold rain and places me in the backseat of my car with an oxygen condenser. My debut is in a week and my wedding is days after that. Mom carries my wedding dress to the car—just in case we don't get back to Washington beforehand. As Mom drives the seven hours to Cleveland, I'm sure I won't leave again until I receive a match or die waiting.

As dusk turns to dark, I decide to be at peace with having come so close to making my childhood dream come true. We arrive in Cleveland around midnight and I'm immediately given a complex cocktail of steroids, antibiotics, and only God and my medical personnel know what else.

In the morning, I awake to an unanticipated and very welcome visitor: my appetite. Within the next forty-eight hours, something I never expected happens: I get better. I'm still far from well, but by the weekend my doctors are discussing my release. I figure, if there's ever going to be a moment to broach my upcoming performances, this is it. After careful consideration, my doctors decide they'll try to get me out in time.

An intravenous PICC line is inserted into my left bicep and a nurse shows Zenith how to administer my complicated concoction of meds every two hours. We're released from the hospital at 6:00 p.m.—giving Mom enough time to drive us to Philadelphia overnight for a conference opening before heading to New York for my Lincoln Center dress rehearsal.

Violent sheets of rain fall down onto the windshield, battering what little traffic there is to travel at sluggish speeds. It's amazing we're moving at all, but at thirty miles per hour, we won't reach Philadelphia until morning. As we inch along the dark, flooded highway, my mother and I alternate occasional bursts of uncomfortable laughter.

"How did they let us leave the hospital?!" she scoffs, shaking her head.

"Mom," I reply, "I think I need to be institutionalized—I belong in an insane asylum. Honestly, though, how am I doing this to myself—to you?!"

Then the manic laughter starts again before we refocus on the road and Laura Hillenbrand's *Unbreakable* blaring over the car speakers.

We pull into the parking lot of an empty McDonald's and rouse Zenith. He sterilizes the mouth of the tubing and flushes my line. Then he attaches a bottle-shaped container of steroids to the PICC and we roll slowly back onto the highway.

Dawn approaches as Philadelphia's skyline spreads out before us. We pull under the portico of Philadelphia's Grand Hyatt Hotel at 4:30 in the morning. A bellman waits with a wheelchair and Zenith helps me out of the car and rolls me into the ornate lobby.

At 7:00 a.m., the phone rings. I'm set to go on at 9:00 a.m. Still exhausted from the long drive, Mom gets up to iron my salmon suit as I try to nurse my parched vocal cords with lemons, honey, and herbal tea. I groggily put on makeup and pull back my hair into a barely presentable bun. At 8:30, my minder arrives to escort the three of us to the ballroom. I'm sucking down oxygen until the last possible moment, removing my cannulation only as I step onstage. I stand to sing my aria, then sit to share my story of triumph over death and illness. When I finish, Zenith, Mom, and I return to the hotel room and collapse in sleep. Three hours later, the hotel phone rings again.

"Hello," I answer, barely conscious.

"Chary, where are you?!" shouts Yoni on the other end.

"Asleep. Why?"

"Where are you asleep?" he asks more tentatively.

"My hotel room."

"Your hotel room in New York?" he asks.

"No," I say, perking up slightly. "Should I be?"

"Your dress rehearsal is at 5:00 p.m.—that's two hours from now!" he's yelling again.

Only half awake, Zenith, Mom, and I trundle back into the car and weave our way through traffic. Following my phone's GPS, we drive down frontage roads, underneath highways and on side roads, through subdevelopments and residential neighborhoods. The clock is ticking ever closer to five. Occasionally, we'll pass underneath the highway where stationary cars blare horns and brake lights.

"I don't know how we're going to do this," I admit to Mom. Picking up my phone, I call the stage manager at Lincoln Center. "I am so sorry," I say. "We're lost somewhere in New Jersey. I don't think we'll make it."

Just then, the GPS directs us back onto an empty highway. We blaze through the Lincoln Tunnel and, almost before I realize it, we're in the city.

"We might get there," I tell the stage manager, calling again. "But is there any way we could get a wheelchair downstairs?"

Mom rounds the corner at West 65th Street and we pull up

to the stage door just after 5:00 p.m. Zenith runs in, grabs the wheelchair, and I carefully lower myself in, clutching my oxygen condenser. "*Go! Go!* Straight, to the right and in through the big white doors," directs the stage manager.

Zenith zooms down the vast corridors and a stagehand beckons us through a set of huge doors. We head into darkness, navigating a mass of cords and electrical wiring until we see the klieg lights. Just then, the orchestra begins to play the famous introduction for Violetta's aria and Zenith wheels me onto the stage.

White lights glare and, after a moment, I see them reflect off two pairs of glasses in the house.

It's not too late. I'm here. I'm at Lincoln Center.

Sempre libera. "Always free." The irony is palpable. As I extricate myself from the wheelchair, I become tangled in my oxygen tubing. Finally, I stand, tethered to a breathing machine and attached to intravenous medications. My oxygen condenser hisses to my introduction like an offbeat metronome. But as I start to sing, my voice bounces off the pulsing strings behind me. As the sound edges heavenward, I become more open—more free.

About halfway through the first verse, the oxygen falls off my face. But I continue to sing, and it's easier than before. Pulling air into my lungs, I engage every muscle in my body. As I let the air out, half of those muscles relax while the other half keep my rib cage and pelvic floor expanded. Being so sick, I pull out every technique I've learned over the past decade. Each is vital. I finish and the hall rings out with hollow applause from the stage manager, the music director, the conductor, and the orchestra. We run the aria once more and I feel more alive than I have in months.

Afterward, Zen wheels me to my dressing room. There are

famous actors, singers, dancers, musicians, and opera stars wherever I look. It feels like a joyous climax before the heroine's tragic death. *My* goal is to outsmart the tragedy. Finally finished for the day, we head back to check into our hotel room.

The next morning, I realize that the only gown I have with me is my wedding dress. I'm just grateful Mom thought to pack it! We arrive at the theater and the costume director works up a sleeve out of panty hose to secure the tubing trailing from my upper arm. As the makeup artists do their magic, he sews a creamy white pashmina to the shoulder of my wedding dress.

The show's director has gotten me a handful of obstructed-view seats, and they're all filled. Mercina and Glorianna have taken the train down from New Haven. Tomicah arrives after a meeting at the UN. Levi and Liberty are in town for work. Then, of course, I have my indefatigable companions, Zenith and Mom. Altogether, six of my siblings are here with me, and JaLynn Prince has come as Mom's date. Yoni's job has once again kept him from being with me, but I can't even find the time to be sad about it.

My hair is piled high atop my head and doused with spray. I'm ready. Glorianna and Zen, who have stayed in the dressing room, help me into my wheelchair and we make our way backstage. As I wait in the wings, Joshua Bell plays Massenet's achingly beautiful "Méditation" from *Thaïs*. Dancers' footsteps sparkle across the stage like the thousand incandescent lightbulbs which make up the set. I focus on breathing deep into my lungs.

The violin and the dancers skip their way up a delicate cadenza until the sighing, longing upward tenutos beg the bow to hold each note for just a moment longer before tumbling back down the scale. A week ago, this was an impossible moment. And I know I didn't get here alone. I think about my father and my grandfather.

About my incredible mother. My brothers and sisters. I think of all they've sacrificed to help me reach this moment. I think about my friends and teachers scattered across the globe, and I think about Yoni too. I think of my doctors and my nurses, about the IV hanging out of my arm and the young woman whose death brought me back to life. I think of the lungs I'm rejecting. I think of the breath they've given me. I am about to make my Lincoln Center debut. It's a miracle. But it's not just one. A thousand and one miracles have paved this most unlikely of paths. As the violin jumps higher and higher, it resolves downward into exquisite melancholy. It's wondrous to have a dream; to work for it; to fight for it. Catching it—realizing it—can be a treacherous task, often mired in disappointment. The last, sustained note sounds like a beautiful, distant whisper and I realize that for these few minutes, this world has been as perfect as I could have hoped for. This is my dream and I have nothing but peace.

The dancers swoosh past me and I hear the orchestra begin to play. I take off my oxygen, stand up from my wheelchair, and walk onto the stage.

This is no dream. This is real. I begin to sing. There is nothing but the darkness, the music, breath, and air. I know I'm dying, but I've never felt so alive.

The audience erupts in a huge ovation and I exit stage right. As I collapse into my wheelchair, Glorianna helps me place my cannula as Zen lowers my footrests. I did everything I could not to cry onstage, but now tears stream down my face. I think of Éva's pronouncement, uttered so long ago—nearly ten years ago. I know true love. I know death. I know sickness. I know work. As I go on for the final curtain call, Jessye Norman takes my hand.

"That was wondrous. Miraculous. Spectacular!" Sandwiched be-tween Ms. Norman and Patti LaBelle, I am among the Great artists whose ranks I've always aspired to.

On the second anniversary of my first lung transplant—two days after my Lincoln Center debut—I'm back in Cleveland for another performance and activated on the transplant waitlist. It feels like filing for divorce on a wedding anniversary; there's a poetic unkindness about it.

But there's no time to dwell on it. My wedding is less than a week away. "My" wedding. I seem to have less to do with the event by the day. Marsha has picked the wedding planner, the caterer, and the venue. Even relatively small things like the colors or the fa-vors inspire the Dorons' (Yoni included) full-throttled opposition.

"Charity, the rabbi sent over a sample for the seven blessings." Yoni begins to read from the adaptation of Joel Rosenberg's text as we sit together in Cleveland. It's lovely, filled with allegories of the heavens and of nature. I love 98 percent of it. But every other sentence talks about hummus.

"Babe," I say, when he's finished. "It's so beautiful. But could we say 'earth' instead of 'hummus'? I mean, I love hummus, but on chips. Not my wedding vows."

I've unwittingly unleashed a beast who's been snarling in his cage for months. "Why do you have to change EVERYTHING?!" Yoni screams. "Is nothing sacred?! You just have to get *everything* you want!" He's still screaming.

"Yoni! I am getting nothing I want with this wedding! You know that!" I respond, totally bewildered by his vociferousness.

"You said this could be *my* wedding! That's what we agreed to! *I* am supposed to plan this wedding! This is supposed to be *my* event! But, NO. You insist on having your colors. You tell *my family* to wear *your stupid colors*. And this?! What, are you ashamed that we're Jews? That I'm Israeli?!"

I'm totally baffled. Yoni isn't just being mean. He's not making any sense. I don't bring up my family's deaths in Auschwitz's gas chambers or on the banks of the Danube. This argument is so utterly unworthy of them. "Yoni!" I can't keep up with his rage. "You're saying my desire not to use the word 'hummus' repeatedly in my wedding vows makes *me* a self-hating Jew?"

"You certainly wouldn't be the first," Yoni spits.

What has this monster done with my Yoni? I shut myself in the bathroom and splash cold water over my face. I decide the best thing to do is go to sleep. I brush my teeth, get into my bed, and pull my covers over my face.

"You promised never to go to sleep angry," he says to me, sitting on the side of my bed.

Oxygen hisses into my nose and I pause for a moment.

"You just equated my desire to change the word 'hummus'—commonly known as a type of bean dip—to the word 'earth' in my wedding vows with a deep, latent anti-Semitism. Anti-Semitism killed most of my mother's family. I'm going to bed angry."

He gets up and slinks to his bed.

"And, Yoni?" I say. I hear him perk up, perhaps hopeful for some reconciliation. "You'll be lucky if I go through with this wedding at all . . . And there better be no mention of bean dip in my vows."

———

The next morning, I return to the Cleveland Clinic for follow-up treatment. As we drive from the hotel to the hospital, the skin on my forehead sticks to the passenger-side window of the car.

How, after all of this, am I still planning to marry that? As I scoot from the car into a wheelchair, I remember how much we've done together. The things we've experienced, learned, and grown from as a couple. But if this is how he plans a wedding, how can I trust him to face *real* challenges alongside me?

"Can you bring my paints?" I ask him before we go up to my room.

"Are you really going to use your paints in the hospital?" he protests.

"Yoni, I want my paints. You will bring them for me because you know I can't lift them myself."

He takes me and my things upstairs where the admitting nurse directs me to my room. It's in a corner, surrounded by windows and filled with light. I can look out onto Lake Erie and downtown Cleveland. Yoni kisses my head, reminding me that Mom arrives later that day and promising to bring my wedding dress to his sister's house. Then he says goodbye.

"I'm Danielle and—well, don't you just look like happiness and sunshine?" croons the nurse's assistant as I sit on the edge of the bed, the sun's rays warming my face.

I laugh, thinking about the previous eighteen hours. "It's such a wonderful room!" I say.

"Right?" Danielle responds. "Usually, there's someone real important in this room, but it was the only empty bed today so you got it!" she says, smiling. "You know, I heard a Saudi Arabian princess stayed here a few years ago."

Over the next four days, doctors conduct more tests than I'd like to count. But I paint and paint and paint in that light. I end up with eighteen panels—all in my wedding colors. Between tests I see friends: my old doctors and nurses, and new ones I've met on the floor; Huda and her father are still next door; Jeanne drops in occasionally; Nancy and John, my old neighbors from the ICU, come to visit; Joela stops by after concerts. I loathe the tests and the pain, but I value being with all these lovely people. In a strange way, the Cleveland Clinic has started to feel like home.

While I'm here, I pray. A lot. I realize that Yoni is just nervous. His behaviors are inexcusable, but they come from a place of powerlessness. Yoni was there for me when I was mourning the deaths of my grandfather and father. He was there through my first transplant and now, as I face another transplant and the very real possibility of death, he still wants to marry me. He hasn't flinched. On the contrary. From teetotaling to abstinence to my death, his reactions to our lives' biggest challenges are unerringly optimistic—an attitude I've only ever expected from myself and Mom. But Yoni naturally sees the good in almost any bad situation. He only really messes up when the stakes are low—like wedding colors, difficult conversations with parents, and a stubborn determination to win arguments regardless of whether he is right. It is possible that I've found the only man on earth who has both a more positive outlook and a more stubborn disposition than my own. But I know I'd much sooner be annoyed by Yoni than be without him. Despite his terrible behavior, I can't imagine facing the future—however much of it I have left—without him by my side. I dread the wedding, but at least things between us can only improve afterward. For that, I'm grateful.

———

I arrive at my wedding venue in upstate New York and walk into a nightmare.

Freezing rain coats the sidewalks in sleet as we trudge up to the door. The venue itself is beautiful: a nineteenth-century hall with a domed steeple—reminiscent of early Mormon temples—

but walking through the doors, it's colder inside than it is outside. And it's *cold* outside. From the linens to the woodwork, it appears the building hasn't been updated since its construction. *But at least it's charming,* I try to reassure myself. Slowly ascending the antique staircase with my oxygen in tow, I'm hopeful it might be warmer upstairs in the main hall. But as I turn the corner, a lump forms in my throat.

Weeks ago, Marsha's planner demanded a series of "vision boards" from me. I had filled them with pictures of quivering gray-and-yellow aspens and sunflower fields. Somehow the planner has translated that into brown, orange, and red garlands of plastic leaves. Instead of luminarias hanging from posts, stuffed scarecrows leer smilingly from every horizontal surface, with the odd sugar pumpkin thrown in for good measure. It looks like elderly church ladies have commandeered my wedding venue for an ill-conceived Halloween craft night. As the woman who was supposed to be my wedding planner explains that the building does not, in fact, have heat, I'm struck speechless.

At this point, my youngest sister, Glorianna, steps up. The only introvert in the entire Tillemann-Dick family, she typically shies away from conflict. People—especially those not related to her—exhaust her. But here, her sense of loyalty, need for justice, and excellent taste demand action. This will not be tolerated.

"Charity, your colors were yellow, khaki, silver, and white, yes?" she asks.

I nod my head.

"So, my question is," she says, turning to the wedding planner, "what is this mess?"

"Well—I don't know—I thought she'd like it . . ." responds the planner.

"And did you ever speak with Charity or Yoni or Marsha about making scarecrows and pie pumpkins the wedding theme?" Glorianna continues.

"She . . . she said she liked fall," stutters the planner.

"You need to take this all down . . . right now," says Glorianna. "It seems the scarecrows aren't the only ones in this room in need of a brain," she mutters under her breath.

Where's Yoni? Supposedly, we're doing the wedding here so he and his family can organize it, but I haven't seen any of them since last night's rehearsal dinner. I call him.

"We're at the farmers' market. Then Mom and my sisters have appointments to get their hair done," he says in reply to my question.

"You need to get over here. *Immediately.*"

Yoni's voice begins to rise. "This is why we hired a wedding planner—it's my wedding day too and I have things I need to do. The planner will deal with the venue. It's done! Everything is done!"

He hangs up on me.

As I hobble around the room, yanking down the ghoulish décor, I glance out one of the tall, arched windows. There, covered in grass and mud in the freezing rain, stand my sisters. They're gathering wildflowers from the side of the road. Alone in the frigid hall, I begin to cry. My sisters are risking pneumonia, Lyme disease, and who knows what else picking weeds along the side of the highway. My aunt, uncle, grandmother, and brothers are building a chuppah at my sister-in-law's abandoned house. Meanwhile, Yoni is browsing at the farmers' market while his mother and sisters primp for my wedding.

As I wonder how to tell my family that the wedding is off, I remember a story Dad told me years before.

He was young—barely twenty-two—and he and Mom were planning to elope. He'd become friendly with the maintenance worker in his dorm, and, in light of his impending nuptials, the man shared a story with Dad. Around the time of the maintenance man's wedding, his wife went a little crazy. They fought and she transformed into someone he felt he barely knew. The man wondered why he was getting married in the first place. The row was so traumatic that, shortly after their wedding, the couple divorced. The man said he didn't realize that weddings make people crazy, and he looked back at the divorce as the biggest mistake of his life. His warning, verbatim, was: "Don't let a little upset ruin a lifetime of happiness." Dad said that was the best marriage advice he'd ever received.

Inhale. Exhale. Maybe that was what this whole wedding was about. A whole lot of upset.

Yoni's family rarely talks about serious issues. Rejection is too scary—too permanent to talk about. Maybe it's easier for Yoni to be angry about something he feels he can control. Like wedding colors. His work is demanding; my health, deteriorating. Perhaps this wedding is the only thing Yoni can control right now. Even if he's doing a terrible job of it. Silently, I pray that after the wedding the man I've grown to love so much will reappear.

With the wildflowers my sisters collect, flowers my grandmother brings from the market, and 200 sunflowers I've ordered, my sisters transform the hall into something worthy of its own Pinterest board. We head back toward town with very little time to spare. In the hotel room Yoni and I will share that night, there's only one bed. As I slip on my wedding dress, I realize my makeup and shoes are miles away at the B and B where my family has been staying. It's too far to retrieve them before the ceremony. Working her magic, Mercina shares her little pouch of makeup and jewelry, navigating around my oxygen cannula to make me feel beautiful.

By the time we arrive at my sister-in-law's house, we're exhausted. Everyone is abuzz over the chuppah that Auntie Margot,

Grandma Nancy, Uncle Justin, and my brothers have built out of knotted aspen trunks. The rabbi arrives. She has a mop of curly chestnut hair and she's well into her pregnancy. Eldad keeps asking about her husband, but somehow, he always walks away before I can whisper, "She has a wife, not a husband." She doesn't seem to mind, though.

Somehow, a pregnant lesbian rabbi seems about the right fit for this unlikely wedding. Wrapped in his grandfather's prayer shawl, we end our (hummus-free) ceremony as Yoni breaks the glass and kisses me. The rest of the evening leaves much to be desired. But for these minutes, this house is filled with love. I silently pray that love will continue to follow us in our lives together.

"What?!" I yelp, sitting at a table in our tiny apartment.

"I need to look for another job," repeats Yoni. "This just isn't a good match."

The faint hum coming from the yellow light overhead is amplified to a deafening buzz as his words ring in my head.

"What happened?" I ask.

"The hours are insane. I'm the only man in the office and I'm totally isolated. I just don't fit with the team," he tries to explain.

"This woman hired you away from another job," I say, thinking about the impossible economy and all of the people we knew looking for jobs. "We have to make this work, Yoni—for your future. For the health insurance!" I've already surpassed my lifetime maximum and it isn't clear if my insurance will pay for another transplant.

"I know," he says, obviously frustrated. "Please don't tell anyone right now. I just can't take it on top of everything else."

I agree reluctantly, worrying about how much more stress my increasingly delicate system can handle. Yoni is already working long hours. He's often at the office past 10:00 p.m. My family is already complaining that he isn't taking proper care of me. Simultaneously, he's under assault from a mean girl manager—his hours will almost certainly get worse and I won't be able to tell my family why. I try to explain this all to him, but it's more than he can manage.

Usually, members of my church help congregants when they have babies and when they're sick. But it's as if Yoni and I had tumbled into a chasm and everyone thinks someone else has already sent down a rope. My situation is so complex, no one—including us—knows exactly the kinds of help we need. My diet is complicated and one more infection will almost certainly kill me, leaving people nervous about cooking for us or visiting. The one exception are my brothers who've added butter and coconut cream as a vital food group for my very survival. I've dropped nearly thirty pounds since the start of the year and the scale continues its downward march. So Levi and his girlfriend bring me butter-poached steaks, granola, and French pastries. Tomicah and his wife make thick coconut soup and Zenith makes me vegetables that congeal into lumps of butter dotted with veggies when stored. Their efforts aside, I've never felt so lonely.

Each morning, Yoni wakes up at 6:30, showers, and heads to the kitchen to make me breakfast and lunch. Before he leaves, he carries me into the living room where I sit for the remainder of the day, too exhausted to do anything else. When he gets home, he makes me dinner, cleans the kitchen, and carries me back to bed.

Focusing on what I can do despite my illness has always been my saving grace. But now that list has all but disappeared. I don't have the energy to paint, to read, or to play the piano. I can barely crawl to the bathroom, sometimes preferring to sit on the toilet all day so I don't have to worry about how I'll make it there when I next need to.

Mom has traveled with me during all of my engagements, but my grandmother and Mom's grandbabies demand more of her time when she's in DC. Lauri, the mother of one of my dearest friends, has recently relocated to DC. Her son Daniel, a lawyer and a quadriplegic, needs her help in the evenings, but she increasingly spends her days with me. We talk. She cooks for me and keeps me company. Lauri is a stunning model of true, Christlike charity. An angel of mercy during my dark night of the soul.

Yoni's parents join us in Washington for Thanksgiving. The meatless Turkey Day spread is magnificent—balsamic roasted beets with chèvre, cheddar-crusted apple pie, Marsha's famous New York cheesecake—but I don't eat a thing. Before the night is through, Yoni carries me back to the car and drives me home. Marsha and Eldad follow soon after.

After preparing me for bed, Yoni rejoins his family in the living room. I listen through the cracked bedroom door as his parents speak—

"Yoni," says Marsha, "this is too much for you."

"We have help," Yoni insists. "Lauri comes over almost every day. And Annette and Zen are here a lot too."

"No," Marsha continues. I imagine she's shaking her head vigorously as she says it.

I take a deep drag of oxygen, anticipating the upcoming argument with dread. I can't leave . . . *I wonder if I can breathe if I use a pillow to drown out the sound of their voices?*

"You don't understand," Eldad interjects before I can lift the cushion over my ears. "I'm retired. I can come down. Charity *needs* someone here for her during the daytime. And you need someone here for you when you get home."

"And I can take care of myself," Marsha chimes in. "Your father will make wonderful breakfasts and lunches for both of you!"

I drop my pillow to the side of the bed and I begin to cry. I remember Dad's advice: *Don't let a little upset ruin a lifetime of happiness.* Our current situation is excruciating—sometimes I don't even know if I can eke out a day of happiness, much less a lifetime. But the Dorons are a reminder of the things a happy life is built from, regardless of its length. Love. Commitment. Sacrifice. Even if I don't want my in-laws to move into our apartment, I'm so grateful that they're a part of my family.

During the time I spend alone, I think about Dad and my grandfather a lot. I miss them both and I wish Mom and Mimo had them here. In the same breath, I'm grateful that they don't have to see me like this. It's terrible to watch a child die. There is supposed to be an order to these things and when that order is interrupted, desperation causes us to act in unexpectedly heroic and horrible ways. Then again, I wonder if any of this would have happened had they been alive. I've often felt their untimely deaths were what interrupted the delicate medical equilibrium that my body had achieved. But mostly, I miss their voices and the calm reassurance of their presence and protection over me and my entire family.

One warm afternoon in late winter, Mom is with me. She knows my time on earth is growing short; either I'll receive a transplant soon or I won't. Regardless, I need her. I can't talk much, but it's comforting to have her nearby. Sitting on the couch, I realize I need to use the bathroom. I make the mistake of trying to stand up. Even with ten liters of oxygen, my legs crumple under me and I fall backward onto the couch. Unable to catch my breath, I begin to turn blue. Mom calls 911 and, within minutes, a fire truck arrives. They bring in a fifteen-liter oxygen condenser and, after they reattach my cannula to their machine, I feel much better. After settling, though, I notice the wet couch cushion beneath me. During the asphyxiation, I urinated. I have become totally helpless.

During December, I spend more time in the hospital than at home. I've always wanted to die at home, but I had hoped to do it as an old lady. In my mind, death has never been the worst thing. Only now, as a twenty-eight-year-old experiencing the slow deterioration of my organs and body firsthand, do I recognize that the process of dying is a humiliating, excruciating horror show. For the past week, I've been in and out of Kaiser's emergency clinic. At 1:30 a.m. on Christmas Eve, I'm discharged yet again. There's nothing the doctors can do but try to stabilize my blood pressure.

Yoni carries me into the house. He sits me up on the toilet seat while he readies my toothbrush and gives me a cup to spit into. Carrying me to the bedroom, he places me on the mattress. Kneeling in front of me, he unbuttons my shirt, resting his head on my chest for a few moments. Then, cupping my breasts in his hands, he gently kisses the scar from my surgery. He removes my shirt and pulls a cotton nightgown over my head.

As he takes off his shirt and jeans, I feel as though there's a cement wall between our future together and our present. Even so, I can't imagine either of them without him. As I lie down, my diaphragm feels immovable.

"Honey," I ask, struggling to breathe, "could you take me to the couch instead?"

"Is that really more comfortable for you?" he asks, skeptical. I've spent many recent nights on the couch, sleeping sitting up.

"Yes," I assure him.

He brings the down comforter out along with a number of pillows and one of my breathing devices. Then Yoni places one arm under my knees and the other behind my back, picking me up and placing me on the couch. He sits down next to me, and lays his head in my bony lap.

"Honey," I protest, "you need a good night's rest tonight."

"And there's no way I am going to get that sleeping in the bedroom without you," he rejoins, craning his head to kiss me. I say a prayer, we read the Christmas story, and he falls asleep in my lap.

With ten liters of oxygen hissing into my nose, I feel like I felt on that airplane to Denver months earlier. I don't dare go to sleep for fear I'll never wake up again if I do. Blowing weakly into my green plastic breathing tool, my ribs ache from hyper-expanding them over and over again. My arms ache from blood draws. My legs ache from lack of oxygen. My back aches from not having slept in a bed for days. My joints ache from medications.

Inhale. Exhale. It seems if my focus wanes, I'll drop into eternity's abyss. *Is this how a life ends?* It could be worse. At least Yoni is here. But I don't want to die now. I don't think I'm ready. Not yet. There's so much I haven't done. *God wouldn't have me go like this*, I tell myself, forcing my diaphragm up again against the resistance of the breathing aid. About to drift off, a thought jolts through my mind: *I will not ruin another Christmas with my death.* It keeps me going for a few minutes longer.

It's the longest night of a life that has seen many long nights. I fight through every moment of darkness with my entire soul. When dawn arrives, I know I've made it. As the sun rises, I wake Yoni.

"It's so early," he yawns. "We didn't get to bed until nearly two."

"I didn't sleep at all," I confess.

As soon as Yoni hears this, he snaps awake. "Baby, why didn't you wake me up?"

"You were tired," I whisper as he runs to retrieve my blood pressure machine. Placing the cuff around my gaunt arm, it inflates until I can't feel my fingers. It reinflates several times before giving us a final read.

"That can't be right," murmurs Yoni. He goes to get another cuff, then another machine. They all reach the same conclusion: 220 over 200. It's time to go to the ER.

Mom comes to the house and we drive to the hospital together. Admitted emergently, I'm sent directly to triage, where I'm placed on fifteen liters of oxygen. It's a relief to finally be able to breathe. Doctors scurry around as Mom is, once again, by my side. The nurses prepare to move me to a different ward. As they pull me away from the wall, my oxygen stops. I can't move, speak, or breathe. Time seems to freeze as they wheel me away. *Is* this *death?*

A chorus of alarms sounds.

"She's turning blue!" shouts Mom. "Do something! She's turning blue!"

Backing away from me as she runs to fetch a nurse, Mom bumps into my unattached oxygen tank. It crashes to the floor.

"Oh!" whimpers Mom as it lands squarely on her toe.

Grimacing in pain, she yells, "Her oxygen! It's not hooked up!"

The nurse struts in, seemingly annoyed by Mom's histrionics. She grabs at my cannulation, just to be sure. "Oh my goodness," she says under her breath. Stopping the gurney, she quickly re-attaches me to the pump.

I gasp back to life. "Mom," I say faintly, "I am so sorry!" Her toe is broken, I'm sure of it. The injury seems downright gratuitous. And yet, we would not have realized what was wrong without it.

The rest of the day is a blur. Family comes in and out, trying to carry as much Christmas cheer with them as is humanly possible. With my siblings in the room, we begin to sing. "Children Go," "O Come, O Come, Emmanuel," "Hark, the Herald Angels Sing," as many other carols as we can remember.

The doctors decide to medevac me to Cleveland so I can wait for a match there. But the question of who will accompany me on the plane is quickly turning into a major family feud. My mother and my husband both want to be with me, unsure of whether I will survive the trip. One after the other, they visit my room to explain the other's inconceivable nerve, insisting they only have my best interests at heart. If either of them had just left in the car instead of staying behind to argue, they would have arrived in Cleveland before I did. I wish that, for a moment, either of them could be gracious and exhibit a little compassion toward the other. But just as I'm about to ask Zenith to fly with me instead, Mom relents. In truth, Yoni should have done the same thing earlier. I resent facilitating family pettiness over my deathbed. But I suppose even life's bleakest moments deserve an unworthy distraction.

We fly out around ten. When we arrive near midnight, Dr. Budev is there to admit us. She had planned to spend the holiday with her family in North Carolina, but she's delayed her departure to make sure we're taken care of first.

As I'm getting set up in my room, Yoni waits outside. Dr. Budev leans toward me—

"Charity, I need to know, when is enough, enough? When should I tell Yoni and your mom that it's time to say goodbye?"

Despite the fact that I've stood face-to-face with death for nearly a decade, I've never given her question much thought. Sure, I have a living will. Before my first transplant, I told Kimber that if I was ever brain-dead or in a coma for more than three months, it would be time to let go. But now I've *been* in a coma. I've been on a respirator and every other form of life support.

"Marie," I say, "if I'm brain-dead, donate everything you can. But if I'm going to die, it's very important to me that my husband and my mother agree on the best way to move forward."

She nods her head, skeptical yet supportive.

"And, Marie," I add, "thank you for making sure we got here." I don't want the last thing she remembers about me to be our end-of-life chat. "Can I sing for you?"

On the dark Christmas Eve, on fifteen liters of oxygen, I take a deep breath and begin to sing—

Silent night, holy night.
All is calm, all is bright.
Round yon Virgin Mother and Child.
Holy Infant so tender and mild.
Sleep in heavenly peace . . .

A man from the local congregation stops by. He works in the hospital and heard I was inpatient through the grapevine. He gives me a blessing, promising me that my voice will be restored and that I'll live. He tells me I need to be patient, but promises my sojourn on this earth will be lengthened.

Everything sounds great except for the line about patience. My time is running out so quickly—*haven't I been patient long enough?*

A Christmas feast prepared by friends for the whole family sits uneaten on their dining room table; our gifts for each other languish unopened at home. I've scattered the family and left another perfectly good holiday in tatters. Who'd have thought that the Grinch who stole Christmas would have an oversized heart and a name like Charity Sunshine?

Certainly a match will come quickly. But months have already passed, and I'm now at the very top of the transplant list. My situation is growing more desperate by the hour. I've been patient. Now, it's time for my miracle. Every moment I feel like things can't possibly get worse, so how is each previous minute always easier than the one I'm currently facing?

December 26, Yoni returns to work. We've used all of his vacation and sick days for hospital visits and he won't qualify for family medical leave for another month. With all of my physical challenges, it seems like it's only fair if work, insurance, and other obligations would just take care of themselves. But sometimes mercy only plays a bit role in life.

Within the hospital, things are somewhat different. Mom and Zenith stay with me, and they're accompanied by a rotating cast of family members. Kind and long-suffering, they do whatever they can to make me more comfortable. But nothing really helps.

On New Year's Eve, Yoni returns. We watch a concert on television and things are as normal as they can be if you happen to be dying in a hospital room over the holidays. But, over the course of an hour, there's a shift in my condition from general misery to something far more serious. My heart feels like it's choking me. Frantically, I call to Mom, Yoni, and Zen.

"Charity," Mom assures me, "look at your numbers." They've stabilized considerably since I arrived a week ago. "You're fine!" she insists.

Yoni takes my hand. "Baby, she's right. You're OK. Just try to calm down."

But my concern turns to hysteria. I feel my body begin to shut down—my heart, pumping out a few last beats for old times' sake before closing up shop for good. If my doctors can do something to fix me, I need them to know there's something wrong while there's still time. But then again, this feels like it *is* my time. Maybe the only thing that matters right now is the people already around my bedside. As pain closes in around me, I say the only thing that really matters right now or ever—

"I love you! I love you all so much. It's my time now." With that, I lose consciousness.

Act III, Scene 3:
Adriana

As Adriana awaits her entrance, she explains the source of her creative gifts.

Ecco, respiro appena,	Look here; I'm scarcely breathing . . .
Io son l'umile ancella	I'm but the humble servant
del genio creator;	of the brilliant creator.
Ei m'offre la favella	He offers me the words
Io la diffondo ai cor . . .	that I impart to the heart . . .
Del verso io son l'accento,	I'm the verse's music,
l'eco del dramma uman	the echo of human drama,
il fragile strumento	the fragile instrument,
vassallo della man . . .	the lowly hand-maiden . . .
Mite, gioconda, atroce,	Timid, joyous, terrible,
Mi chiamo Fedeltà;	I'm called Faithfulness.
Un soffio è la mia voce,	My voice is just a whisper,
che al novo dì morrà.	which, with the new day, will die.

—FRANCESCO CILEA,
ADRIANA LECOUVREUR

larms sound. Like they always do. The emergency team descends. Like they always do. They bag me until, once again, I can be intubated and moved to the ICU. The doctors and nurses work like my life depends on it. It does. My lungs won't synch with the respirator though, and the excess carbon dioxide is slowly raising my blood's acidity to dangerous levels.

Late one night, Dr. Budev insists on driving Mom to the hotel. She hasn't left my bedside in several days. They walk to the car in silence.

Sliding into the leather seat, Mom breathes in deeply. Marie and she have been through so much together. She's family.

Driving down Euclid Avenue, Marie speaks first—

"Annette, how are you taking all of this?"

"Oh, well, it's a lot of work. But once we have lungs, Charity will be perfect again."

They stop at a red light. Dr. Budev turns to look at Mom. "Annette, Charity is extremely sick. I think you need to understand that, sometime soon, we'll need to talk about what she would want. About how she would want to go."

Mom looks back at Dr. Budev, sighing. "I know, Marie. I know how close she is. But with the kids here, with everything that has happened, I have to be positive. There has to be someone in that room who still believes that she'll get better."

Dr. Budev nods gravely. "Annette—we can wake her up. You can gather the family—get everyone here at the same time. They can say whatever they would like to her. You can all be together."

"They don't want to say anything to her." Mom shakes her head. "Not until after the transplant."

"I just want to give you whatever you need for this all to be as peaceful as possible," Dr. Budev says, pulling into the hotel parking lot.

"Marie," Mom responds, matter-of-factly, "here's what I need from you: I need you to call every source for lungs that you have. Do you ever call them?"

"Not really," she confesses. "It doesn't exactly work like that."

"Call them. Beg them to let you have the first set of lungs that might work for her."

Dr. Budev takes a deep breath. "Annette, I promise you—I'll do everything I can."

They say good night and Mom starts to walk toward the hotel's dingy lobby, past a group of men smoking outside. It's not until Mom is inside the elevator that she realizes Dr. Budev had been asking her to say goodbye. Mom leaves before the elevator doors close and comes back to the hospital room. She pulls two spindly chairs up next to my bed and sets in for the night.

The next day, two pulmonologists walk by the hospital room and Mom stands up from her seat. "Hello, Doctors." She waves at them as they pass. "How are you?"

They acknowledge her with nods. "How are you?" murmurs the first, more rhetorically than not.

"Well, we're just hoping to get lungs for Charity," Mom chirps optimistically.

"Yeah. You don't want that right now," mumbles the second.

"Excuse me?" Mom stops them. "Why would you say that?"

"Um. You just don't want her to get lungs right *now*. Nobody's going to touch her except for McCurry, and he's out of town," the other explains haltingly.

"I don't understand . . ." she says, pressing for clarification.

"Well, we don't usually transplant patients as . . . ill as she is. The only person who *might* is McCurry," continues the doctor.

"Well, Doctor," Mom says, "she's just like your daughters, except her lungs don't work. As soon as you find the right lungs, she'll be as good as new."

Flashing Mom pitying glances, they say goodbye and move on.

Later that afternoon, a red light blinks on Mom's phone. It's a voicemail from Irene, a dear friend who happens to be an acclaimed doctor herself.

> *Annette, I was so happy to get your call. You and the kids are in my thoughts. Hearing blood gas numbers like that for someone who's alive . . . I'm amazed they're going to do surgery. It must be an incredible surgeon because that just doesn't happen. I mean, those numbers are past any reasonable expectation of life. But I just wanted to send my love. Talk to you later.*

Mom looks at me. My stomach is distended like the victim of a horrible famine. I have tubes going in and out of every opening in my body with a couple more piled on top for good measure. I'm pathetic. Burying her face in her hands, she tries to figure out what she's supposed to do. Logically, she knows that the doctors are right. There is a leering neon arrow pointing to the inevitability of my death. But when she prays—when I receive blessings and when she reads her scriptures—she knows there's still hope. Still patience. Still life. As she sits there, trying to decide if she's been wrong to keep pushing, a steady voice comes back to her over and over again. *She'll live*, it whispers deep inside of her.

But the blood gas just keeps going up.

The next day, Yoni and most of my brothers are at the hospital. When the surgeon comes in, everyone hopes for good news.

A number of other patients on the floor have already received transplants—patients with the same blood type as mine. They're all hoping the doctor carries the news we've been hoping for.

"Annette," he says, "can I speak with you privately?" They walk into the bay next to mine—Dr. Budev, Yoni, and my brothers standing a few feet away. "You should understand that your daughter's time has come, Annette. Letting her go peacefully is a service—to Charity and the family. This is a brutal intervention. It probably won't work and it is a terrible way to die. People who try to keep their loved ones alive past their time aren't doing them a service. They're just being selfish. You are not a selfish woman, Annette, and you should seriously consider gathering the family together and saying goodbye," he repeats, this time more emphatically.

Mom had come back from the hotel early the night before, making it three nights since she's rested through the night. It takes her sleep-deprived mind a moment to distill the doctor's words into meaning.

Slowly, she steps toward him and begins. "Doctor, I know death. I've seen my son die, and when it was his time, I let my husband go. If I thought it was my daughter's time to go, I would let her go in peace. But, Doctor"—she says, with an intensity that grows with each word—"I *am* going to make you fight to keep her alive. I will make you break every last rib in her body to get that final breath out of her. Because it is not her time yet, and I will *not* let her go in peace."

Bristling at the directive, he replies, "Then she's going on ECMO. It doesn't happen bedside. I'm taking her into the OR for surgery if her blood gas doesn't drop to eighty by the next time we check." He stalks off, upset by the experience.

Mom sits down in silence, her three sons and Yoni looking

on in a sort of terror-filled awe. Ten minutes later, the surgeon comes back.

"Eighty-five," he says. "If her blood gas doesn't drop to eighty-five, I'm putting her on ECMO. Immediately." He orders medication through the IV to paralyze my body in hopes my breathing will synch with the respirator and leaves the room. Everyone is silent. My blood gas has been over a hundred for days.

Kafka couldn't imagine a more nightmarish scene. There's nothing for Mom to do but sit at my bedside and pray. She doesn't even fully understand exactly what the doctor's order entails, but she knows she doesn't want someone who believes her daughter's case is hopeless performing a dangerous surgery.

Matt, the respiratory therapist, carefully adjusts my airflow, goading it to match the rhythm of my body. My nurse, Davida, comes over to help him. Over the next hours, they work with Mom and Yoni with all the precision of a professional athletic team. Slowly, the blood gas numbers begin to fall. But the surgeon will be back any minute. He's been gone for hours. Mom bows her head to pray.

In the middle of her silent pleading, someone walks into the room. It's the surgeon. A lump forms in her throat. Why couldn't he have given them another hour? They're so close. Drawing another blood sample, he sends it down to the lab. It seems to take hours for it to return. When it finally does, my blood gas is down to eighty-four.

Over the next days, my blood gas numbers continue to fall until they settle in the low seventies. They're still about three times what they should be, but it's an enormous improvement.

Late one afternoon, Dr. McCurry comes to visit.

"Annette," he says, "we've gotta get her on ECMO."

"Really?" asks Mom, surprised at his directness.

"Yes," he reiterates. "It's the only way we can keep her alive until we get lungs."

"When do you think we should do it?" asks Mom.

"Right away," he says without hesitation.

"Really?" she asks again, expecting some sort of ultimatum like she'd received before.

"Yes," he says with no equivocation.

"Will you do it?" It's her final question.

"Certainly. I'll use an Avalon on her. I'll do it tomorrow. But then you'll have to get her out of bed. She has to be stronger for the transplant."

Mom calls Yoni to discuss the ECMO with him as soon as Dr. McCurry leaves the room. Both of them agree to defer judgment to the all-star surgeon.

First thing the next morning, Mom walks me into the elevator and I go in to have a hose-sized catheter inserted into my chest. When I get back, Dr. McCurry prescribes exercise. "Wake her up—get her walking again. She needs to be strong if she's going to have this transplant."

Not long after, I wake up.

Soon, I notice my little sisters, Mercina and Glorianna, by my bedside. *But they're supposed to be in school. They should be focusing on their schoolwork. Maybe they're visiting for a holiday?* Mercina has always had a knack for lip reading. I click my tongue in her direction and she sits down next to my bed.

"I love you! But why aren't you guys in school," I ask, sincerely concerned about their academic futures.

"Because we want to be here!" She pauses for a moment.

"Don't worry—we took the semester off, so it's not like we're neglecting anything important. Shiloh's back from his mission in Japan and Zenny's here too. We couldn't let you and Mom go through this alone again."

Overwhelmed by emotion, I realize that, once again, my youngest sisters and brothers have become caretakers for my mother and me. They make sure Mom eats. They stagger eight-hour shifts with two of them constantly in the room so Mom is comfortable enough to go sleep in an actual bed. Yoni drives in late Thursday night and stays over the weekend. I have my own, extremely competent transplant team rooting for me, pushing me, and helping me however they can.

Our schedule seems impervious to change. Every morning at 3:00 a.m., a man with long brown hair saunters in with a large machine. Turning on the light, he announces, "X-raaay." Placing a cold, hard board behind my back, he puts a lead apron over my lap. After snapping two films, he leaves. At 5:00 a.m., the phlebotomist comes to take blood. At 6:00, the nurse gives me my medications and at 6:30, the new nurse arrives to go over notes with the night nurse. At 7:00 a.m., the doctors usually come in on rounds. From then on, every half hour, someone comes to check on me until midnight, when I have a few short hours to try to sleep before it all starts again.

All I want to do is walk, but everyone except Mom seems opposed to the idea. After a few days, the combination of drugs and sleep deprivation is literally driving me crazy. The scenery begins to change.

"What's happening now," asks Mom by my bedside, deeply amused.

"I know it's not real," I mouth, "but you all look like giant house cats, standing on two legs. It's quite disconcerting."

Another day, I think my nurse April, who has hair like Rapunzel, has taken me to her house and put my bed in a dark playroom, piled high with toys. With each new place I visit, my eyes grow wide with wondrous terror.

My in-patient adventures don't really matter until they start to affect my medical care. For days, I think I'm in the children's ward of the hospital. In my mind, nurses place ugly bracelets on each of us. When I try to take mine off, a real fountain of blood erupts from my wrist. I've managed to rip out an arterial line. I look up to see Shiloh clasping my wrist, covered in blood, and looking as startled as I feel. Another day, I imagine a pudding cake has spilled all over me. I become totally preoccupied with the thick red Avalon catheter in my chest, imagining the blood is actually fruit filling that has messed up my pretend party gown.

"Charity," shouts Mom as my brothers hold me down. "Do you see those tubes?"

As she says it, the imaginary cake filling coalesces into two red tubes. I nod my head yes.

"Do you know what is in those tubes?" she continues.

I shake my head no.

"Charity, every drop of blood in your body is going through those tubes. If you take them out, you will die. Quickly. You need to stop this right now. The doctors don't want to transplant you as is. They won't be *able* to if you're dead. Do you understand me?"

As she speaks, the cake, candy, pudding, and kitchen counter where I thought I'd been sitting disappear. I'm back in my hospital bed, my brothers pinning my arms to my sides. It's surreal and uncomfortable.

A doctor walks into the room. "What's going on here?" he demands.

"Oh, nothing," assures my mother, cheerily. She's concerned that my mental state, combined with my extremely precarious medical situation, will be enough to dissuade the doctor on call from transplantation. Dr. Budev has left town for a previous commitment and Mom feels like there are transplants happening all around me. People with the same blood type as me. People of a similar size. She wonders why I'm still waiting. She knows the doctors have to believe that, within the context of my extremely precarious medical condition, I'm as well as I can possibly be if I'm ever going to get lungs.

When I'm not lost in hallucinations, I'm sadly aware of my situation. I've been on ECMO for weeks. Usually it's a stretch to use it for a few days—a week or two, at most. But I'm fast approaching the month mark. Each hour brings an increasing sense of hopelessness.

The despair dissipates slightly whenever the mail comes. Packages from my sisters and cousins, cards from friends, relatives, and acquaintances, notes from fans, and pictures from kids brighten my dismal room and warm my dampened spirits. On one of my more lucid days, Mercina brings over a package. With her help, I detach the card from the box. It's from Sonia, the smiling woman from TEDMED. The card tells a Japanese legend of the thousand cranes. Whoever receives them would be granted one wish. I open the box to find it overflowing with string after string of colorful, folded birds folded by Sonia and her colleagues. We hang them all over the room.

A few nights later, I go to bed after my midnight check-in. I see the blood going out of my body through the ECMO tubes. I'm physically and emotionally exhausted. My evening prayer is more of a conversation with God. *I'll feel tremendous guilt if I die,* I explain. *Everyone else here seems to be getting their transplants.*

My family has done so much to keep me alive, but as days turn into weeks and months, Dear Lord, I just don't see how I am going to get out of this hospital alive. I am so weak and so ill, I just don't see how it will be possible.

I ask for nothing, I just want to talk. I don't feel like I can share these feelings with my siblings or with Mom. They've been working so hard for my survival—I'd hate for them to feel guilty about it. I know God will hear me, but he won't take my morbid realization as a surrender to death. God is the only one I can count on to really understand what I mean.

Maybe my body can continue for another day or two or three, but I doubt I'll make it out of this hospital alive. I fall asleep, hoping that, whatever my future holds, my family can finally have some peace.

It's dark outside when Mom shakes me awake.

"Charity," she urges, "Marie is on the phone. Charity, they have lungs for you! They have a match! They have a match!"

I look back and forth at the people around me. "Is this a dream?" I mouth, curious if my imagination has, once again, taken over.

"No," Mom assures me, kissing my forehead. "This is very real. You have lungs! We finally have lungs!"

It feels unreal. My grandma Nancy and Auntie Margot are in town. Yoni flies to Cleveland in time to see me into surgery. Kimber, Levi, Corban, and Liberty are en route from DC. I hang up with Dr. Budev as Dr. McCurry goes to prep for my surgery. So many people I love are here to celebrate. Silently, I press grateful tears from my eyes. Mom is crying too. I can tell her tears have fear in them along with joy. The first transplant was so hard, the path to recovery so long. Nightmares have been playing out in plain daylight for months now. How can we sustain this for another three months?

As nurses roll my gurney toward the surgical theater, a voice deep within me confirms, *everything will be fine*. Flanked by Yoni and Mom, I squeeze their hands and pass the assurance along to them. "We've done this once. We'll do it again. I love you."

Inhale. Exhale.

I've always thought of my life as an opera. It's only now, lying flat on my back on a metal slab, that I realize no opera could hope to capture the messy, grotesque, gorgeous truth of life. Still, as the anesthesiologist tells me to count backward from one hundred, I remember a rule common to both: *breathe first*. Everything else follows. Around me, the operating room slowly fades to black.

THE ENCORE

Taking a deep breath, I exhale into a small, clear plastic tube. The spirometer's fan lets out the same whir it has every day for the past three and a half years. I repeat the process three times and wait for the digital screen to beam out the same numbers it always does. It's been a wonderful three years. Yoni and his cousin have started a burgeoning educational technology company and he's returned to his pre-groomzilla self—as thoughtful, optimistic, and incorrigible as he's ever been. The album I recorded with Joela and her husband Richard reached #1 on *Billboard*'s classical charts. Yoni and I never took a real honeymoon—I was in the hospital for three months following our wedding—but in the spring of 2015 we went on our first vacation together, hiking in the Southern Andes. I've been performing all over the country and, in June, I began to write my memoir. The process has been more emotionally draining than I anticipated; for some reason, I hadn't expected that reliving the most traumatic events of my life would be so challenging. But, hardships aside, I'm doing all the things I only dreamed of doing a few short years ago. Best of all, I'm alive. And my life right now is closer to normal than it's ever been. For that, I am grateful.

The digital screen finally flashes my numbers. They're low. I'm not sick. I don't have a cold or temperature. *It must be a glitch.* Again, I go through the exercise, blowing into the machine one, two, three times. Once again, the numbers are low. Placing my spirometer in its case, I finish packing for our trip. As Yoni takes the bags down to the car, I scribble an email to Dr. Budev. The good news: I'm already scheduled to see her on my way back from a wedding in Ohio.

We drop by Mimo's apartment to pick up Mom. There's a six-hour drive ahead of us, but on the other side, we'll find Hope.

Two years ago, I received a Facebook message from Danielle, a nurse's assistant and friend from my second transplant. Since I left the clinic, she's become a missionary. Occasionally, she would write to tell me about developments in her ministry or give me more general updates about her life. She was living out one of my fondest dreams, and I was always eager to hear about her service.

The evening she sent the note, Danielle's prayer group had joined with a neighboring congregation. Early into the meeting, a young woman named Esperanza got up to speak—explaining that she'd received a letter from one of the people saved by her mother's organ donation. She wanted to open it with friends. As she read the note, it became clear to Danielle that I was its author.

Huddled around a glowing smartphone, Danielle facilitated Esperanza's virtual introduction and mine. We've since become close friends. Our lives, like our names, complete a common narrative arc. Fluent in English and Spanish, Esperanza's dream is to have a bilingual musical ministry. My voice is big and powerful; hers, exquisite in its soft soulfulness. We have different dreams, but we both want to do good with the voices we've been given.

It's a perfect day for a drive. The sun is shining, it's not too hot or too cold. Appalachia's ancient hills roll by in shades of emerald and gold. Armed with a bevy of podcasts, Yoni steers us toward our destination. Ira Glass's monotonous lilt lulls me to sleep as the warm sun reflects off of my lap. I jolt awake. "Don't fall asleep!" I shout unnecessarily, grabbing Yoni's arm. He laughs as we pass underneath one of my very favorite highway signs: OHIO AND WEST.

Passing Cleveland, we make our way toward Canton, Ohio, stopping for church along the way. After services, we head to the campus where the wedding will take place. The hall at Monroe College has a standing-room-only crowd. It seems no one has been left out of the joyous celebration. Danielle—one of the bridesmaids—walks down the aisle before the bride. Slim and petite, Esperanza's gently curled black hair drapes over her shoulders, leading to an A-line gown. She's a picture-perfect bride, with the groom to match. My waterproof mascara never had a chance. But at least my panda eyes have company—the room is awash in tears. I'm not the only person here whose life has been, in one way or another, saved by this beautiful duo.

White lights twinkle inside the barn where the reception is being held, and we get to know some of Esperanza's mentors and friends. She knows it's unlikely I'll have my own children and has seated us with a couple who have adopted their children from Haiti. It's a magical night and a perfect wedding. Not because of the fairy-tale venue or the gorgeous dress, but because of the loving-kindness that overflows from every aspect of the evening. We still have a long drive ahead of us. Once the cake is cut, we kiss the bride and groom and head toward the exit.

As we walk down the road, the sounds of celebration fade, replaced by a symphony of crickets and the babbling of a stream.

The wheat field ahead is cloaked in darkness but, every few moments, a gentle breeze awakens a milky way of fireflies. The bugs twinkle away in the cool black of the summer night, setting their own tiny world aglow for a few moments at a time. It's been ten years since I studied with Éva. I've fallen in love, I've gotten very sick, and I've worked more than I ever knew was possible. But there are still opera companies that refuse me auditions, roles I haven't sung, and experiences I lack that I've always assumed were prerequisites to artistic greatness. I no longer fear their absence, though. While I know Éva believed in my talent, I've come to realize that her promise was about so much more than scales, arpeggios, and lyrical singing.

Ten years after I first embarked on my great medical saga, I no longer feel the stage fright I used to get before doctor's appointments. I no longer fear rejection. Walking beside the woman who gave me life and the man who taught me to love as we celebrate the young woman who gifted me breath, I feel complete. Even the greatest divas die. But like a timeless melody, true greatness never does. The greatest music, thoughts, innovations, equations, and scientific breakthroughs move from one person to the next, traveling to far-off places—different continents and bodies. They are revised and amplified, deconstructed and stripped down until their very existence seems to be irretrievable. Only from that precipice—that abandonment of self for love of something more—can lasting greatness ascend.

As I gaze smiling into the prairie galaxy stretching out ahead of me, I don't realize that this moment will end and, with it, my long season of calm, of joy, and accomplishment. As we walk, the drugs that protect my lungs from rejection are simultaneously eating away at my body's natural defenses against cancerous sun rays. My vulnerable porcelain complexion has already been invaded by soon-to-be-visible clumps of spindle squamous cells. They'll breed at astonishing rates and migrate from my forehead all the way to the parotid gland near my jaw. Over the course of weeks, I'll watch helplessly in the mirror as my visage is mutated by grape- and softball-sized tumors. The next months will bring more surgeries. Chemo. Radiation. A year from now, my beautiful, beloved face will have been forever changed—irreparably marred for the sake of saving my very life. The agony of a slow and incomplete recovery will ask much more of me—my faith and my resolve—than I ever could imagine being able to give. Perhaps hardest of all, the removal of a cancer-infested nerve in my cheek will leave me unable to ever really smile again.

But none of that matters right now. Right now, I'm playing a bit role in something truly great. Somehow, I know this is a moment to be still. A moment to feel awe and to bask in the greatest wonder of all: the love that binds us together and gives us reason to live. The love that offers each of us a small measure of immortality. The love that continually testifies—whether or not we're wise enough to listen—that we've been Great all along.

CURTAIN CALL

I t would take volumes to adequately acknowledge every person who made not just this memoir but also my continued existence on this planet a reality. So, for the sake of brevity, please keep up the applause for this highly abridged list of accolades. Thank you very much.

Rakesh Satyal, between music, writing, and so many other things, I couldn't have imagined someone better suited to understand this complex story. Thank you. Sarah Branham, when you believed in this project so doggedly, you made me believe in it too. Thank you for signing an unproven author, for the time you spent on the manuscript with me, and for being a fierce advocate on my and the book's behalf. Judith Curr and Peter Borland, thank you for your vision. Paul Olsewski, Albert Tang, and the entire Atria and Simon & Schuster family, thank you for accommodating my many challenges and bringing me into your literary family. To Isolde Sauer and your team, thank you for your attention to detail. Loan Le, Anne Badman, and Haley, thank you for keeping things from falling through the many cracks that exist in the publishing world. Elisa Rivlin, thank you for your excellent judgment.

Glorianna Tillemann-Dick, this book would probably still be unpublished if you hadn't come to its rescue. Who would have thought my baby sister would be such a gifted editor, friend, and literary architect? I always knew you were one of the more brilliant people I'd ever met. What I didn't realize was how I would come to depend on you to find my voice on the page. There were late nights, long months, and fights (nasty and ill timed, of course), but you have taken my literary mess of human experience and helped me create something of true beauty.

Sloan Harris, you should be some dreamy and benevolent character in a book. Like my dear mother, you know that excellence demands time, effort, and the fear of God. You demanded nothing less than my best; you knew when I could give more, and you inspired my most literary self, my greatest writing, and, occasionally, my ire. Thank you for giving your best to me and all of your protégés. Truly, your best is *the* best in the business. For that and a host of other things, I thank you.

A. J. Jacobs, thank you for your help. You're the dictionary definition of a mensch. Joel Warner, thank you for your encouragement during this punishing journey. Michael Lewis, I would have never believed that an author I fan-girled over would have been so instrumental to me signing my own book deal. Thank you for getting me started down this perilous road of memoir. Dr. Greg and JaLynn Prince, thank you for being among the very first to encourage my writing, for putting a roof over my head, and for the hours you spent interviewing me—preserving my story should I not have made it through my second transplant. Janet Walters and Katie King, thank you for your patience, your encouragement, and for being my very first editors many years ago.

Karen Clifton Kappler, I didn't practice like I should have, but it didn't stop you from being a compassionate teacher who made a difference in my life and starting me on my road to music. Amina Harris, bless you. Bless you so much. You set the stage for so much happiness—a magical interlude in a beautiful but challenging life. Thank you so much for your kindness. Bruno

Rigacci, Pietro Rigacci, and Ulla, thank you for making me a part of your musical life and your world in Italy. I hope to join you again sometime soon. Gidon and Suniva Graetz, thank you for changing my life for the better, for opening doors to your home, your hearts, and a life for me in Italy. There were few times happier and more carefree than those I spent in Fiesole.

Éva Ándor, without you, I doubt I would have ever stayed on the path to music. You and Gabriella Gyöker's belief in me made me believe in myself and my talent. Éva Márton, to study with one of my musical heroes, to work with you and be mentored by you, taught me more about artistry than almost anything. Rita Patane, thank you for teaching me a technique. I never understood what a real technique was until I sang with you. I miss you and I hope you are so well. Cathy Kasch, you are a wonderful teacher and thank you for helping to shape my gifts. David Michael Heath, thank you for helping me find my voice again. Deb Birnbaum, thank you for helping me find my breath.

Joan Dornemann, you're one of a kind, and I am so grateful to count you a mentor and friend. Erzsébet Kocsis, thank you for taking time to teach me and mentor me. I imagine Zoltán still making amazing music somewhere in the universe. Joela Jones, as musicians and partners, your and Richard Weiss's friendship has been a balm to my soul, your faith bolstered me through dark nights, and your musicianship inspires me. Stephanie Rhodes, Dr. Nan Shannon, Zsuzsanna Hynoncyi, Ella and Noam Sheriff, Erzsébet Hegyi, András Batta, Julia Paszty, Susan Weiss, Steve Rainbolt, Ernie Ligon, Karen Salient, Amy Beth Kirsten, William Johnson, Mignon Dunn, Marlena Malas, Gerald Martin Moore, Mark Robson, William Woodruff, Lawrence Edelson, Joachim Schamberger, Bob Cowart, Hemdi Kfir, Eileen Cornett, Phyllis Bryn-Julson, MaryAnn Squassabia, Marc Oswald, Lisa Hopkins

Seegmiller, Joseph Olson, Moisés Kaufman, David Binder, Michael Friedman, Barb Wollen . . . there are a dozen more of you whom I love and thank for all your encouragement, your wisdom, your time, and your guidance over the years.

Emily Roskowski, my St. K(C)atherines—Katie Lyon Dayton and the Lyon family, Kathy Ruekberg, Katie Fredriskson, and Cathy Bleck—Ruth Eldredge Thomas, Pingkan Zaremba, Susan and the Casteras-Schnapper family, Mohammed Al-matrafi, Christina Kim Homer, Mary Salmon, Jen Gonzalez, Elder Jeffrey R. Holland, Lori Laitman and Bruce Rosenblum, Csilla Nagy-Prunier, Marina, Lavi, and Nicoletta Karam, Christina Germani Killian-Benigno, Ann Robert, Shannon Michelson Duplisea and family, the Palmers, Bert and Carol Walker, Marty and Ali Bell, Danielle and Michael Gross, Daisy Soros, Ginny Kooyman, Jjana, Char and Niels Valentiner, and Nancy and David Rivard; Krista Linford, Tarannum Jaleel, Sui Lang Panoke, Darren Howell and MaryJoy Ballantyne, Nancy and Robert Ricks, Elindra Garvin, Tawanna Lassey, Elaine Qualter, Sonja Sweek, Jovy Cone, Stephanie Soper, Wanda White, Haylie Swenson, Tanya Spackman, and my sisters and brothers in the Capitol Hill Ward and Relief Society; Norris and Carol Mills, Jenny S. Preece, and my congregations in Baltimore, Budapest, and Florence; Jeannette Estruth, Craig Webster, Damian Stammer, Elyse Pitock, and Nancy Livingston, I'm crunching you all together because you're the vertebrae in my friend backbone. You hold me up when I can't do it myself. You bolster me when I need it most. I know that if you're all still my friends, I won't fall. You won't let me. You'll help me fly again. How fortunate I am to have all of you.

Christine, Ben, and the whole Sandoval family, Elizabeth Vigil, Celeste Gallegos Applegarth, Ginger Jones, and my old

D-2 crowd, thank you for the cards, prayers, and love through this whole drama. Thank you to the Cohen crowd, my North Denver crowd, to Fr. Michael J. Sheeran and my friends and mentors from Regis University and the broader Colorado community for the encouragement and support. Lauri, Ted, Dan and the broader Leslie brood, my family in triumph and tragedy, you are my exemplars and dear friends. To my transplant sisters and all my PHriends, each day you inspire me to push on. To Melitta Weber-Hunter, I miss you but thank you for your generosity of spirit. Your wisdom got me through my second transplant.

Nate Mook, and David and Sylvia Steiner, thank you for your kindness, friendship, and support. Esther Coopersmith, thank you for being there from the start. Mike Bates, thank you for marrying an amazing person (Christine, you're wonderful), for seeing something in me and jump-starting my career when I worried there was nothing to salvage. Marc Hodosh, thank you for trusting Mike Bates, for believing in me, for offering me wisdom, advice, and friendship. You're a wonderful man and I'm grateful to know you. Sonia Rhodes, gosh, I am happy I ran into you that day in the ladies' room. You were leaning in before it was a thing. As a colleague, friend, and example, I thank you and your team of angels from the very bottom of my engorged heart. Michael Hawley, Nina You, David Bolinsky, and Patty Harris, I am so grateful for the wonder-makers of the world like you.

Dennis and Elizabeth Kucinich, thank you for coming with me to those first Cleveland appointments. You sat there with me and Mom all day just so we wouldn't feel alone. We love you. Todd and Yadira Patkin, your friendship and generosity over the years have been a source of both inspiration and peace. Thank you for your love, wisdom, and kindness, and for finding happiness. Dawn Arnall, you've always rendered such selfless service and loving friendship when I was in greatest need of it. Todd Albrecht and Joe Keller, thank you for marrying Claudia and Emily, respectively. What beautiful families you two have built on faith and service. Thank you for rendering so much of that service to me and to so many others.

Thank you to the families of my surgeons, doctors, nurses, techs, and administrators. It must take herculean love to help these women and men care for the least among us. You sacrifice family dinners, recitals, sports games, milestones, and, sometimes, a personal life with your loved ones and allow them to care for patients like me. To the grandparents, parents, siblings, friends, spouses, and children who support this call to care and to give life, thank you.

Dr. Christopher Lang, I had a lot to say about you, but time after time your sections were cut out of the book. Sometimes the most important heroes go unsung. While your role in the book wasn't a central feature, you've been center stage in facilitating and preserving my life for more than a decade now. You and your wife and family are examples of purpose-driven lives and of the best Ohio, Kaiser Permanente, Colorado, and America have to offer. Sarah O'Leary, Faye, and the whole team—thank you for helping sort through the bureaucratic nightmare that is my life. Libbie Griffin and Joan, I am so grateful you have one another and that I have you. Thank you for your friendship and dedicated service over these many, many years. Kaiser Permanente, I'm sorry I've cost you so much money. Thank you for taking care of me anyway. I'm so grateful to have health insurance that ensures my *health care*. Thank you to everyone who's helped instead of being a roadblock. My blood labs at Kaiser in Wheatridge, Denver, Capitol Hill (Abeba, Kenny, Kim, and Keith), and the Cleveland Clinic—thank you for never missing a prick and for making those morning blood draws less traumatic. Jeff and Anita in Cleveland, thank you for always taking such good care of me. Thank you, radiology team—Lydia and all of my techs, nurses, doctors, secretaries. Thank you to the emergency clinic and the docs there who have nursed me to health or helped me in my darkest hours. Dr. Mayo-Olano, Dr. Naftanel, Dr. Meltzer, Dr. Mesfin, Dr. Martinez, Dr. Lee, and Dr. Vongkovit, your skill, patience, and assistance have been central to my life continuing. Thank you for always making time and making sure the job gets done and gets done well. Dr. Paul Hasoon, Dr. Atul Mehta, Dr. Louis Christopher Benjamin, Dr. Andrea Moriera Gonzalez, Dr. David Badesh, Dr. Irene Lang in Vienna, Dr. Ashish Maskey, Dr. Hunter Champion, and Dr. Susan Mills (I believe that is your name. You were the first person to diagnose my PH), Dr. Eileen Hsich, Dr. Chapman, Dr. Mohanka, Dr. Dan, Dr. Adeli, Dr. Kaiser, Dr. Bourdakis, Dr. Robin Patel, Dr. Tathagat "Tiger" Narula, Dr. Joe Kabazza, Dr. Rafid Fadul, Dr. Olufemi Akindape, Dr. Christine Koval, Dr. Michael Machuzak, Dr. Gohar Dar, Dr. Gosta Petersson, Dr. Tom Gildea, Dr. Randall Lane, Dr. Maryam Valapour. . . . There are far more of you than I could hope to list. Thank you all for taking care of me, for helping to keep me alive or helping to bring me back from the dead. More recently, I want to thank Drs. Burkey, Adelstein, Prendes, Koyfmann, and Vidimos, and your respective teams. Ming Tang Xu, you are a wonder and a gift. Thank you for using your talents to help me and so many others.

My respiratory therapists in the Crile building, ReSCU and ICU, thank you. Matt—a light in the midst of so much darkness—when you came into my room, I knew everything would be OK. Thank you for helping me breathe when no one else could. Marko, Margaret, and Bill, you were my dream team. My music man Gerry, Russ, Chelsea, Kathy, Kim, and David Wheeler: Thank you so much.

To my teams in J5-5, J8-3, and ReSCU, I was so drugged out that I've forgotten a lot of names. But I know that you saved me so many times. You were my friends, my rescuers, and my family during a very dark time. You made me feel safe and secure. As soon as I was rolled into ReSCU, I remember this tall, handsome black guy with the awesome band tat around his bicep. He was this Iraq vet who'd served a few tours—the definition of hard core. But that man was as kind and gentle as a mother with a newborn. That's how you all were. You were tough as nails, while treating your patients with nothing except respect and compassion. Lidia and your team on J8-3: Lady, you run a tight ship! Allison, Andrea, Antoinette, April, Ashley, Barb, Bill, Bisi, Brandee, Brittany, Bruce, Carol, Cassie, Claudia, Chivelia, Christina, Cindy, Colleen, Craig, Dana, Danielle, Davida, Dean, Desiree, Elisa, Evalina, Fred, Greg, Katie, Katie, Katie, Katherine, Kay, Kristen, Kirstin, Christine, Christian, Gary, Hannah, Heather, Hia-Chun, Ilona, Janet, Jay, Joe, Judith, Laura, Laura, Lauren, Leonard, Mirabelle, Mary, Marleen, Melanie, Meghan, Matt, Michelle, Marc, Molly, Myrna, Nick, Peaches, Ronnie, Sandy, Sarah, Sarah T., Shannon, Tracey, Cheryl, Valeria, Vaughn, Zoe, and my guy team of nurses—I don't remember all of your names, but thank you for taking such good care of me.

In my attempts to contact my caretakers for this project, I found out that one of my favorite nurses, Ryan D. Williams, died a year after my first transplant. To his family and friends—Ryan's kind, dedicated service was an inspiration. He used his physical strength and kind spirit to make my life easier. His patients loved him as much as his colleagues. During a very insecure time, he always made me feel safe. I am so grateful to have known him.

Judge Nancy McDonough—you tough, wonderful lady, I am so grateful to know you! John Kosko and Helen, thank you for being right there with us through this. Jane and John Jr., you are super troupers. Lynn Clutter, I think about you so often. Thank you for being our neighbor and friend through so much of this. Huda, thank you for being my sister in the hospital. I love you dearly. Dana, Piper, I hope you're both doing so much better!

Dr. Kalpana Trivedi—you're the best dentist in the DC area. Alex, Angie, Cathy, Keith, Keylynn, Livia, Laura, Nora, and Summer—also Tracie from Johns Hopkins. Thank you for helping to keep me alive for all of these years.

Dr. Robyn Barst left this world in 2013 after a valiant life before and after cancer. Today, there are twenty-nine drugs approved for the treatment of pulmonary arterial hypertension. She is an example of how one life can push forward change that makes the world measurably better. To Nomi, Lindsey, and Dr. Samuel Barst, thank you for sharing her with us and for allowing me to use her letter.

Dr. Marie Budev, thank you for being a role model, a dear friend, and a truly exceptional doctor. Drs. Ken McCurry, Reda Girgis, Robin Avery, and James Yun—you are four of the finest people I have ever known. You are gifts to science and humanity. Dr. Toby and Anita Cosgrove: thank you for running an incredible organization and for making me feel like a part of the Cleveland Clinic and broader Cleveland family. You've assembled one of the most remarkable teams in the world, and I feel so blessed to have benefited from both the care you oversee and your personal kindness. Jeanne Murphy, you are an angel of mercy. Angela Kiska, Andrea Pacetti, Scott Heasley, Dave Braun, and the Cleveland Clinic's media office, thank you for all of the time you have devoted to helping me.

To Carol and Josh Gat, thank you for graciously housing us so many times and for having a great crew like Tanya, Michael, Maya, Tarkan, and the grandkids. Maya Gat and the Branching Minds Team, you've built an amazing product, and I'm grateful to be connected to something that is making education better. Marsha,

Eldad, Shelly, Daniella, and Noah—thank you for making me a part of the family. Last year was quite a ride (can we promise to never ever try that ride again?), but somehow we survived.

Grandma Nancy, thank you for your independence, your zest for life, and for making such wonderful people with Granddad Howard! Justin, Helen, Orion, and Haven, I am so proud of all the good you bring into the world. Margot, having you in my life is like still having the best parts of my father with a softer, Margot touch. Your kindness, thoughtfulness, and willingness to be there when people (oftentimes me) need it most have been a source of strength, love, and stability in my crazy life. You and Uncle Bill give me and Yoni examples of how to live meaningful lives and share joy. We love you.

Katrina, Dick, Chelsea, Keato, Shebby, Chante, Kizzy, Atticus, and Sunday: thank you for the love, the cards, the packages, and the support, even as we thought the end was so fast approaching. SO excited for all the new babies!

Mimo, your writing entertains me and your quests for understanding inspire me. Thank you for bringing us to a faith that binds us together even after death and for helping connect us to a past from which we learn so much. Mary Bush—there is a reason you are the most trusted woman in Washington, and I am so grateful you're part of my family.

To my family related by breath more than blood—my every moment is an extension of the life you share with me. I don't know who prolonged my life for two years so I could receive a better match. To the family of my donor, "thank you" will never be enough, but I hope that in some way this book can serve as a testament to the goodness that life held. I hope to meet you someday. Esperanza and Luan—this year you bring yet another life into the world, but Esperanza, you already brought a life back from the dead. You give me so much confidence in the hope all of our futures hold. I know your faith, love, and extraordinary gifts will continue to bless many lives. Eden and Odin—I couldn't have completed this book without meeting you and I'm so grateful that you're a part of my life now. I can't wait to see what you'll accomplish in your futures. Karen and Kevin Gorby couldn't be a more perfect match for the two of you, and I love you all.

Dulcia, thank you for being my friend. Thank you for caring for me, singing to me, and so often making me feel loved. Tomicah, thank you for setting such a high mark. Your success, hard work, and example paved the way for every successful sibling that followed. You and Sarah have built such a beautiful family, and I can't wait to see how Eli, Thomas, Lincoln, Miriam, and Isaiah continue to follow in your footsteps. Kimber, thank you for your love and encouragement. Your capacity for vicarious joy has taught me about myself and how to be a better person. Esther, Phineus, and Willa make me much more content about not having my own children. On that note, unless you and David distract me with another baby soon, I might have to get some of my own.

Corban, thank you for helping me negotiate some of the most challenging parts of this book, for coming to see me with Tiny Timber and Narae when I needed it most, and for being someone every one of us can always count on. I am so fortunate to have you. We all are. You're the son and the brother Dad always knew you would be. Narae's and your capacity for forgiveness and love are an inspiration to me. Liberty, you're a gorgeous writer and person: you have a knack for catchy names and beautiful framing (aka this book cover). Thank you for bringing both Premal and Rahm into our lives. You're a beautiful mother, and I love you and your family so very much. Shiloh Benson, you knew I needed someone who loved me and didn't care about the book—you only cared about making me feel valued, included, and entertained.

You brought me doughnuts and told me stories about the world outside of my ever-expanding Word document. Thank you for your genius, your humor, and friendship. You're deeply gifted and one of my very favorite people.

Mercina, when I came home after cancer surgery on my face to find every one of my mirrors covered in comics, I broke down into a soppy mess. You understand the details that make a person, an event, an organization feel cared for, myself included. Your combination of beauty, insight, and competence is rare. Honestly, it doesn't seem fair. Thank you for sharing your gifts with our whole family. Zen, when I was in the hospital waiting for the second transplant, few people could make me feel as safe and protected as you did. You'd sit by my side and talk with me in a way that made me feel you understood—that you cared. I know my challenges have taken more of a toll on your life than they've taken on anyone other than me. But I am so proud of all of the good decisions you make and all of the good you have yet to do.

To my brother Levi—you were the one who told me it was time to write a book, and I knew you were right. But after two lung transplants and cancer, writing a memoir like this is certainly one of the most awful things I've ever endured. Thank you. Thank you for sitting with me for hours and editing my proposal, for guiding me through the process, for offering your advice when I needed it, for wrangling the siblings to help, for believing in me, for loving me and reassuring me through the torment and isolation of writing, for being a true friend, and the best kind of brother to me. You've always encouraged me and seen my potential, cheering me on and helping me up when I fall down. For all of our differences, you manage to see my gifts. When others saw me as an entirely new species of human, you saw a partner in adventure. Some things don't change. I love you dearly.

Noni, you are a truly wonderful sister. You always knew it wasn't your angelic appearance that made you remarkable; it was your intellect, creativity, goodness, and soul. Your patience, empathy, and capacity to refrain from judgment make me want to be a better person. Your skill as a wordsmith has made me a better writer. I hope Mongolia is an exquisite adventure. I miss you dearly and eagerly await your return.

My dearest husband, when you gave me that card during our first Christmas that said we make a great team, I found it disappointingly unromantic. We were so in love. Was that the best you could do? After nearly a decade, I see you were right: We are a great team. And there's no one who I'd rather have by my side during this terrifying, incredible, infuriating, beautiful, joyous life. You make my happiness brighter, my peace more tranquil, my challenges lighter, my sorrows bearable. You even make me feel beautiful when I look like a monster. You combine all the messy, hard, complicated ingredients of my life into something deliciously exciting. You're my Vitamix dreamboat. I am so grateful that we'll have an eternity together. (To the reader: If you find someone who makes chemo and radiation feel more like an unpleasant but restful vacation, don't ever let them go. Ever.)

Dearest Mommy, the gift of life is more than any of us deserve. But if *nobody* can ever repay their mother, I must merit an entirely new debt classification. You not only gave me my life, you gave me yours. And your life is something uncommon and incredibly fine. You devoted yourself to me and my beloved brothers and sisters (thanks for them too, by the way). Then you saved my life not once, not twice, but countless times. Both Heaven and I know you'll probably save it a few more times yet. Momo, you are my harshest critic, my greatest hero, and my beloved friend, teacher, caretaker, and cheerleader. How you do it all will never cease to baffle and amaze me. You've built your weaknesses into strengths time and again and you are my most important exemplar. Didi was right in thinking that nobody could ever deserve you, but we're all lucky to have gotten you anyway. Thank you for your goodness, your faith, and your complete devotion. Thank you for never giving up on me and for never giving into the chorus of opposition you faced at so many junctures in your life. You are the strongest person I will ever know. I love you.

Dad, we miss you. Sometimes, I can hardly forgive you for not being here to see all the wonder you planted. The harvest is beautiful: wonderful people, interesting thoughts, communities from around the globe and in your own home. North Denver, quinoa, stevia, home schooling, urban living—if only you could live everything that's happening on this big ball of blue and green since your dramatic departure. You and Mom were always about thirty years ahead of your time. Even your book about this sprawling, faithful, liberal family came a couple decades too soon. But you were a dream planter, and now we're the ones reaping your vision. Impractical as it may have seemed, the life you and Mom built together gave us all a foundation of eternal love, sacrifice, togetherness, and understanding. Thank you for never letting the untried scare you away from trying. We miss you so much, Dad. Thank you for giving us so many wonderful people. I have a feeling that, for all your differences on earth, you and Didi—Lincoln, too—are planting even more beauty in the great beyond. And now, Grandpa Howard is right there in the fields with you too. Thanks for looking out for all of us even though you're so far away. We still need it. We love you.

ABOUT THE AUTHOR

Charity Tillemann-Dick is a soprano and top-selling *Billboard* classical artist. She studied music at the Peabody Institute at Johns Hopkins University and the Franz Liszt Academy of Music in Budapest, Hungary, where she was a Fulbright scholar. Raised in Denver, Colorado, with eleven brothers and sisters, she currently resides with her husband in Washington, DC, and Denver.